GALACTICA

A Treatise on *Death, Dying* and the *Afterlife*

Out-of-Body Travel and *Mysticism*

By Marilynn Hughes

Order this book online at www.trafford.com
or email orders@trafford.com

Most Trafford titles are also available at major online book retailers.

Print information available on the last page.

ISBN: 978-1-4120-0856-3 (sc)
ISBN: 978-1-5536-9931-6 (e)

Trafford rev. 06/16/2023

www.trafford.com

North America & international
toll-free: 844-688-6899 (USA & Canada)
fax: 812 355 4082

DEDICATION

I dedicate this book to my courageous friend, Karleen, who having passed from this world to the next during the writing of this work, had the humility to share her journey after death with me.
Further, I dedicate this work to Arta and Helen Uzebacheff, great-great grand-parents of my children, and Joseph Uzebacheff (their son and great grandfather to my children) whose lives inspired me. May their lives remind all of us who stand now, that many have fallen before us who sacrificed everything for a dream which would never be theirs, but would be given to those who were to come.
And we are they.

Photo by Merlyn Photography, Tucson, AZ.

Karleen

Also Available by the Same Author:

The Mysteries of the Redemption
A Treatise on Out-of-Body Travel and Mysticism

The Former Angel! – A Children's Tale

To contact the author or to inquire about the CD containing performances of the 32 songs in this book, please e-mail:

MarilynnHughes@aol.com or go to www.outofbodytravel.org

CONTENTS

GALACTICA

A Treatise on **Death, Dying** *and the* **Afterlife**

Introduction	5
Chapter One	7
Chapter Two	21
Chapter Three	41
Chapter Four	53
Chapter Five	65
Chapter Six	73
Chapter Seven	83
Chapter Eight	95
Chapter Nine	103
Chapter Ten	116
Chapter Eleven	128
Chapter Twelve	135
Chapter Thirteen	148

PAINTINGS - Starting on Page 153
HYMNS – Starting on Page 155
ANCESTORS – Starting on Page 173
PROPHETS – Starting on Page 184
BIBLIOGRAPHY – Starting on Page 188

INTRODUCTION:

GALACTICA

A Treatise on **Death, Dying** *and the* **Afterlife**

Afloat above the waves of eternal bliss, I had just finished the arduous task of completing 'The Mysteries of the Redemption.' Reveling in the finality, not only of writing the book but also of the journey itself, my soul began flying towards a city of light within the outermost reaches of space.

Calmly floating towards this city, I saw upon one of the golden streets a small bookstore. An instinctual knowing led me to enter within this holy abode and begin to browse around the sacred texts exhibited before my eyes, finding myself drawn to an area which discussed extra-terrestrial intelligences. Inward promptings thrust my gaze to a shelf just behind me and towards my left wherein a large royal blue book was exhibited. Energy drawing me in, I picked it up without pausing to gaze at its cover.

Within its pages, an array of spiritual understandings were expressed and began to form in the ether above me as tiny vortexes, flitting and dancing off of the page. Mesmerized, I watched as hundreds of heavenly objects appeared in holographic form in front of me and just above the pages; planets, moons, suns, stars and galaxies, nebulae, black holes, vortexes and heavenly mists.

Within the pages of this book lay a unique knowledge of God. Flying before me in holographic form, the sacred wisdom of the Earth merged, and was eclipsed, by an as yet unknown sacred wisdom of the Universe. It was as if all I'd traveled to date was a mere nothing in regards to that which I had yet to go. Continuing to watch as the tiny galaxies spun, merged and breathed . . . an energy filled my soul. Unity exists between the Earth and these other galaxies, things we didn't yet know, and I was fascinated, dumbfounded, excited, mesmerized and elated!

In an instant, I realized that this book was my own, and it was the next one I was to write. Turning the large text back to its cover, the royal blue came out at me as an energy filling me with my new task. In one word, the title blazed forth from the cover, filling me with an understanding of my mission. 'GALACTICA,' it read. As the holograms began to re-enter the book in a rush of energy, I quietly placed it back on the shelf.

"Where will my new book begin?" I asked, as rushing energies were filling my head like a torrential river flooding its banks. Catching an ecstatic wave of energy, I was immediately transported towards the blackness of space. With the rushing stars cascading by my soul, I flew at the speed of light towards an unknown heavenly destination. Within my sight were nebulae, galaxies, stars, planets, suns . . . and all were resonating a holy spectral vision to my soul. Heavenly music was playing, the music of the spheres, which resonated from all of the heavenly bodies; a sacred music filled with voices which sang in a language I did not understand.

To my left, a vortex of swirling blue stars which formed into a mist performed its heavenly chorus for my soul, as I turned to notice up ahead yet another beautiful vortex of bluish light. Shooting past them, I found my eyes resting on an orb of stupendous beauty which overwhelmed my soul to tears at its magnificence.

A large, shiny, glowing, purple sphere laid ahead, its unusually slow movement calculated like that of a planet; but its texture and appearance was unusual and I couldn't help but wonder if this were actually a planet . . . or maybe . . . a space station? I waited, listening to the continuing echo of the music of the spheres. My breath was filled with light as it came to and fro between my spirit and this heavenly abode. In ecstasy, it was as if I was no longer even human, but somehow had become part of a much larger scheme of life. It all filled me with the blessedness which I knew to be possessed by this orb which appeared before me.

And suddenly, as quickly as I'd been taken to this wondrous place amongst the stars, my soul shot like lightning back to my Earthly body, returning me to humanness and all the limits that come with it.

But yet, I was changed. It would all begin here, at this moment. I would wait on the angelic hosts to guide me to this yet undiscovered country knowing full well that everything I'd known up until this point was as nothing. I would wait . . . in awe of my God.

CHAPTER ONE

Beyond my grasp, beyond my sight, lay the images of what I beheld. All I could now surmise was that I had arrived at an entirely ancient destination. This beautiful place held wisps of memory and knowledge from a time gone by.

My soul remembered a time of peace and harmony in Atlantis, when all things were working together for the one, but that had changed over time. A grand uprising had occurred when several people in political positions of power had taken over the country. Greedy and power-hungry, they demanded to be worshipped as gods; similar to the ancient Roman practice wherein the emperor was considered a god. A counsel of six, all wishing to be gods, ruled the empire.

In order to enforce this practice, martial law had been instituted and people were punished overtly and with great severity for small infractions of the law. Remembering these things as the beginning of the end for Atlantis, my soul was gazing upon a beautiful temple which represented a time before, a time of peace.

Alit with a glittering essence, the Atlantean night sky appeared as if gold dust had been thrown in the air. Having arrived via the time tunnel to this grand destination, the ceremony was about to begin, but I didn't rush to enter this magnificent silver and gold temple cascading high into the night sky. Rounded domes and triangular pillars sent a message to all who came here that this was a very sacred and holy place. Walking with a man I recognized as my spouse, I noticed that I was wearing flowing veils of sea blue over my equally sea blue bodice gown. Another triumphantly beautiful element of this temple was that the night sky was exposed, there was no roof. Holding an equally grand quality, the floors were born only of the Earth.

Entering the tabernacle left my soul in a state of wonder and awe as I looked upon a purely symbolic rendering of all the races of men. Every race of humankind upon the planet Earth was represented here in various edifices, murals, statues and architecture.

As the ceremony began, I joined a group of women, similarly dressed, who were gathered in a circle to start with the customary water dance. Representing the synchronicity of life, there was another element to it which is hard to describe or fully understand. This water dance represented the sea, and somehow this oceanic rendering was important to the Atlantean people, perhaps because they were a continent surrounded by waters, and it provided them with sustenance. But aside this oceanic nuance laid a very powerful representation of unity, and the intensive understanding of the fragile elements which held life in place. Required to be in basic synchronicity, these elements remained necessary in order for all life to flourish and continue. Somehow, this knowledge that they expressed through the water dance had come from another place and another time, of which I could not yet surmise, but it was profoundly important to the Atlantean people to never forget the synchronicity of life, because they held a very serious understanding that it was the key to their survival and continuation as a people.

As the water dance came to a close, a master of ceremonies emerged wearing simple white robes, a symbol of his position in this rite. All the people were now standing in a circular fashion inside the temple facing the center where these ceremonies had begun. Taken aback and even frightened as he released a huge black bull into the center of the temple, it was held in check by twelve men with ropes attached to the bull's neck. Raging all over the temple grounds as many of us leapt in fright, we did not leave our circular position and we waited for the men to bring the bull into the center as they formed yet another circle outside of the water dancers. Instinctually, I began to remember things about the meaning of all that began to transpire before me.

As the men held the bull, they began a series of moves which were designed to 'break' the bull, much like modern day ranchers will 'break' a wild horse, domesticating him for humanity's use. The ceremony depicted the dissipation of negative energies, karmic purification, which was represented by the wild bull. Very skilled and artistic in this process, it was ceremonial in design, and as they continued, the bull slowly became placid and peaceful, a symbol of purification. As the bull's wildly negative energies calmed and became peace, the crowd held a deathly quiet, as a form of respect for this holy process. Silently, the bull was led out of the temple to a hushed crowd.

Stunned by what I'd just seen, my soul tried to remember what these things meant, as I'd only recovered a few memories of the tremendous meaning of this ceremony. But before I could ponder deeper, a large flying object which looked somewhat like a kite was released into the sky. Upon its center was the image of the bull, and inherently I understood that this release of the kite was a symbol of the final remnants of karma dissipating as the soul began to look to the heavens and away from Earthly concerns.

Floating up to the ceiling of the temple, a huge rush of silver and gold dust was released into the air, cascading throughout the temple upon the people present. The beauty of this moment cannot be described as the night sky was lit with the stars from on high and this light reflected the millions of gold and silver particles now floating in the air.

My spouse turned to me and without explanation took gold dust which he had within his pocket and began to spread it all over my body. Instinctually, I took the dust and did the same for him. In this moment, something grand happened and changed all that I was experiencing, as if we had somehow permeated into another dimension and I was continuing this experience from a *spiritual* plane, leaving the *physical* memory of this Atlantis beyond, but remaining in a spiritual overlap.

Beginning to fly above the crowds, many of those present were not consciously astral in this element, and thus, were unable to fly. As we continued to dance in the sky, a voice began to speak loudly from above the temple and higher into the celestial heavens. With this voice, we descended back to the ground, and listened.

Speaking of the many different planetary races that had lived upon our planet Earth; he related the time of arrival of each of these races which had coincided with a great cataclysm upon their native world. Calmly, he spoke of the Pleiadians, some of whom had come to Earth at a time of great danger to their galaxy. "These Pleiadians," he had said, "began the ill-fated Atlantean race which was to perish under similar circumstances. Others remained behind and had been successful in rebuilding the Pleiades, which had eventually evolved into a spiritual world, rather than a physical one."

Forming in the center of the temple, the gold dust flew high into the night sky forming into an image of a dove. Inherently, I understood this to be the symbol of the Holy Spirit, of which these Atlantean people were very much attuned. But it also represented the transformation of mankind into a higher spiritual reality.

As the dust was forming, I gathered a gold chain which lay aside my feet on the ground and placed it around the neck of my spouse. Removing the black one which he had been wearing, this represented the transformation from darkness to light. Smiling with gratitude, he repeated this process, placing a gold chain around my neck as I discarded the previous one and we began to fly.

Soaring towards the exit, we reached our hands out to others inside the temple who were unable to fly, carrying them along with us. The grand dove inside the temple was about to explode in light and everyone was running frantically towards the exit to get out before this occurred.

As the dove exploded, gold dust fell all throughout the temple covering the ground and all who lay within its walls. But the backwind from the explosion of gold dust began to reveal something very fascinating, something that had been placed there for my eyes to see. Turning to look, my spouse and the others began leaving the temple in droves while I flew around the temple floor to observe what the gold dust was revealing as it blew away from the ground. Artifacts appeared everywhere of many extra-terrestrial intelligence's who had come to seed this Earth, lightly dusted books, pictures and maps from differing star systems were all revealed.

As I saw these things, my soul began to receive an energetic influx of knowledge regarding the many migrations from different star systems to seed our world. Coming about due to great calamities, many of those worlds had actually survived the catastrophic times. At the time of migration, these worlds had suffered destruction for a great deal of time, some due to nature, and others to the actions of mortals. Again, the Pleiadians were mentioned as being among the systems which had been partially destroyed, and they had come when a turnaround of their situation didn't seem possible. The story was much the same for all the extra-terrestrials represented here, without exception.

Returning inside the temple to retrieve me, my spouse took my hand, again flying us towards the exit. Turning to witness the dove in the sky which had reappeared, it again exploded in another cloud of gold dust which began showering the temple from the sky. Finally dissipating, the dove was no longer visible.

A rushing torrent of energy retrieved my soul, grasping me quickly away from the man whose hand I held, and sending my spirit through the tunnels of time to return

to my Earthly abode.
****

Appearing truly spectacular as he lay before me upon the back drop of the stars, the cosmic master's essence was astonishing. Feeling very familiar in this visionary state, my waking self held no memory of him. Amidst this spectral monastery which floated in the heavens, my soul had been gathered together with many others in need of instruction. Our cosmic teacher of truth was not one to mince words, and was known for his bluntness. Another aspect which made him unique was that he had a somewhat 'physical' approach to solving spiritual issues. Celestial and galactic knowledge permeated every pore of this being of light, and no words came from his mouth unless they were deeply meaningful and filled with power.

All who had come were in need of a cosmic adjustment of some kind to remedy an energetic dysfunction in their waking physical life. The cosmic master's task was to quickly alter the pathways of dysfunction and turn the directional indicators of the soul towards a more galactic perspective. Doing this in a very unusual way, the master approached each individual, identified their area of difficulty, and quickly altered their energies through sheer brute force. I don't mean this metaphorically. Many of the alterations came about through 'physical' injury. Very serious and direct, the master knew that, of necessity, changes were required immediately, and thus, techniques which would bring about immediate alteration from the spiritual to the physical vehicle were employed.

Particular illnesses or injuries had the ability to significantly alter a person's energy more quickly than other gentler means, and thus, these aspects were used to alter elements of energetic misunderstanding from the spiritual to the physical octave.

Turning to me, the master was serious and direct and within one second I knew what method he was about to employ. Cringing, I knew that he was about to 'break my back,' but this breaking was only to occur in the spiritual realm, not the physical. Although it would be painful, I would feel it primarily in this spiritual state.

In the Earthly quest for knowledge, our souls are often taken from one extreme to another, for the sole purpose of eventually achieving a place of balance. Because I had begun my journey with very few boundaries, I had necessity to travel from a state of laxity to an opposite extreme of rigidity. It was the cosmic master's judgment that my soul had become too rigid, and that this alteration would necessitate a new energetic influx inculcating freedom within the boundaries of morality. 'Breaking my back,' would bring that needed flexibility into my soul.

Done in an instant as a searing pain went through my back, the greatest pain lasted only a moment before a higher aspect of my husband, Andy, appeared to begin assisting me with the remainder of the adjustment. Going through a series of exercises in expressive emotion, Andy's higher aspect guided me through this initially controlled and uncomfortable situation to a peaceful surrender to the divine influx of love. After this, we entered into a long melting embrace which opened my two heart chakras, the one directly in the center of the chest, and other which lies just outside it and directly in front, which altered my ability to give and receive love.

Within a few moments, my soul had been drastically changed energetically. Pleased with the changes, the master moved on to the next soul. As I stared at this grand being in awe, my spirit was pulled away to another destination.

Placating myself that my back would be as good as new before I knew it, I found myself soaring through space at a grand speed. My destination was a very unusual one as I observed a woman who was diligently working at her desk which hovered in the stars. As she was calculating the mathematical implications of the second coming of Christ, I'd been sent to offer her energetic protection from those who wished to steal her calculations and use them for ill effects. Although I would be want to explain the larger meaning of this woman and her work, I inherently knew that she carried great importance and significance with the Lord, as her duty was sacred and it was vital that she be left alone to complete it. Creating an energetic wall of protection around her, I watched with concern for her safety and well-being.

Looking up to me, she shared with me the master number of the Messiah, making it very clear that I was not to record or share this number, and that it would be taken from my memory within days of returning from this journey. In a momentary flash, she made me to know that the Earthly perception of Jesus is much too narrow, making specific mention of the denominational views which doctrinally offered vicarious evolution through the majesty of Christ, rather than the true nature of evolution in the individual spiritual path, transformational change effected by a recognition of the *ideal* within Christ.

As she turned again to her mathematical calculations, I quickly observed that the field of protection I'd created for her was intact and my soul began jetting towards Earth at the speed of light. My back remained sore for about two days.
****

Standing at the doorway to the celestial temple, he appeared in the garb of a man from India. Around his head was a tightly wrapped turban, and upon his bodice the garb of 19th century India. Two other masters resided in this heavenly abode, but I was not to see them as of yet.

Waiting outside the door, the master's were deciding upon whether or not they would allow me entry. Hesitating because of my lack of knowledge and true mastery, they regarded me as a novice. Although there was no way of getting around that, they agreed to allow me to enter because, for some reason unbeknownst to them or myself, the Lord had allowed my spirit to fly to this destination of which I had no knowledge. As they argued amongst themselves, they seemed to agree that I would not have been allowed to find them, if not for the permission of the Most High.

Slowly entering their abode in the stars, I was surprised to notice that in the entryway, there were some very old, dusty statues representing humanity's various vices. These statues seemed out of place in such a celestial sphere, but the masters began to telepathically transport information into my soul, as I observed and looked closely at each one, walking slowly down the entryway. As I came upon each one, I picked it up, and was filled with an inexplicable energetic knowledge. Each statue represented a different karmic impulse which held souls back from reaching the ascension. Contorted according to their vice, their impurities were manifest in symbolic renderings upon the statues. One element which held true with all of these statues was that they were all in motion, agitation and almost a sense of impenetrable fear. No peace or serenity radiated from them, as they were distorted and grotesque, in both observation and feeling. When you touched them, a certain inexplicable distasteful abhorrence filled you of these karmic abnormalities, this lack of unity with God.

As I passed from the entryway into the interior corridor of the masters, I noticed that another female pupil had already arrived and was waiting patiently for me to sit down with her before the masters. Intensity filled her eyes, and I sensed her grandeur as a soul. Knowing that I must seem like a little worm to these spectacular servants of the Lord, I observed that the turbaned master was playful as he came towards me.

Expressing to me that I'd had trouble in my many lifetimes dealing with pain, he placed his hands on my lower back as the other two masters followed suit. Unprepared for this step, I almost jumped back as I began to feel the intense heat and pressure flow into my back and up into the rest of my body. Retarding that instinct, I knew that I was here as an uninvited guest, so I surrendered to this process. Beginning to fade, the heat and pressure could no longer be felt although they continued to touch me. Continuing to send energies through me, I no longer felt the pain.

Looking toward the woman who had been totally silent and peaceful, I was surprised to see her cringing. Before I could ascertain why, the turbaned master had approached me from behind and cut one of my fingers. My first reaction was of pain, but the turbaned master looked deeply into my eyes, saying very quietly, "I feel no pain, I feel no pain." Conveying to me in energy, I saw that he wished for me to focus on my existence *within* God, rather than *outside* of Him. Waving his hands in the air from above to below in a motion to direct me to calm myself, the pain disappeared. After many moments had passed while he stared at me with an intensity I would be unable to duplicate, he proceeded to heal the wound with light from his hand.

Thinking the surprises might be over; I gently followed him when he took my hand to guide me to a small garden path inside the celestial abode. As we were walking, a bumble bee stung me on my foot. Surprisingly, I felt no pain whatsoever, and the stinger was actually unable to penetrate. With this, the turbaned master smiled and looked to the others with a glance implying, "I told you she must've been sent here by God." Intention apparent in his thoughts, he was pleased that they were able to make such progress with a novice. Relieved, the masters gathered around me and began transmitting understanding regarding what they had just done.

Preparing me to repulse the attacks of the enemy, Satan, who often sends hordes of bees, wasps, and spiders to infect a soul aspiring to reach God, I couldn't help but wonder if this knowledge also had something to do with the many saints throughout history who became impenetrable; unaffected by fire, poisons, swords or one of many other horrendous forms of torture.

Seeming pleased with my quick study in this area, they again mentioned my many lifetimes wherein I had trouble with pain. One of the other master's approached me and in a manner somewhat scolding, spoke to me of the lifetime I'd had as a conqueror which had been revealed to me long ago. As I'd been a horrible specimen of humanity, I felt ashamed, and responded like a defensive idiot getting into his face. "I know! I know about that lifetime!" Laughing hysterically, I realized that they were 'playing' with me, and I'd played right into their hands. Embarrassed, I became immediately less serious.

Returning to assist me through several more pain-associated rituals to assist me in repelling pain and the attacks of the enemy, the turbaned master taught me well. When time came for me to leave, I quietly asked them for help. "Will you help me to focus my remembrance of my journey here so that I can write about it in full detail?" Agreeing very wholeheartedly to assist me, the master touched my third eye above my forehead as my soul returned to my body in a euphoric state.

Returning to me several hours later, the turbaned master took me on a splendid journey beneath the ocean. A spectacular yellowish aura appeared around him as soon as we were submerged beneath the sea. As I was unable to take my eyes off of him, he pointed directly behind me so as to indicate that I should look over there.

Turning, my eyes met such a magnificent sight! Spiritual cities of light appeared beneath the sea, there must've been at least five within our current view. Shining in glorious heavenly light and containing the entire spectrum of color, it was as if this heavenly light were being brought into the city through a prism creating a rainbow effect. Saying nothing, he pushed my spirit up towards the surface as the erroneous hum of the spirit wind returned my spirit back to form.
****

Stunned by the brightness of this immensely holy being, I found myself humbled when I realized who it was. Therese Neumann, the Catholic stigmatist (one who mysteriously bore the wounds of Christ) from Germany who lived in the mid-twentieth century, was looking upon my countenance with a glowing eminence which overwhelmed me. An aura of light shone around her form which seemed to go on forever. Only her smile could surpass the radiance of her mere presence. Glowing at me with love, she conveyed to me that my soul was not in a good place because I'd begun reading some books by a particular author. "Do not follow the New Age or other false paths," she said, "the time is coming for you to become Catholic." Surprised by this pronouncement, I shouted to her as she began to fade from view. "Does that mean that reincarnation is untrue?" She smiled as if to convey that this was not relevant, and that I simply must obey the holy command. Nodding back to her, I watched her disappear from my view, taking the ominous light with her.
****

Running aimlessly through a starry realm, my spirit came upon a circling stairwell hovering gently in the heavens, covered with an indescribable ornamentation. Feeling myself immensely drawn to where this might lead, I soared towards it and up.

Two large, carved, wooden, brown doors waited for me at the peak, and without hesitation, I rushed to open them and see what lay inside.

Sitting in the lotus position, a small and very skinny man with long, curly brown hair was meditating. Opening his eyes slowly with utter calm, he looked up at me. "I am Chooshu," he said, as I immediately knew that he was one of the masters. Before I could ascertain the purpose of this visit, he made it clear that my time was almost up. "Please return when you can, so that I can teach you how to meditate to Feng-shui." Interestingly, I'd used many of my own ideas similar to Feng-Shui in my own home for years, and had received heavenly guidance about the placement of certain holy objects, pictures, statues, etc., so this idea of meditating to Feng-Shui did not seem odd or unusual. Rather, it seemed like the natural extension of creating an environment meant to enhance certain spiritual qualities and states.

Without knowing what was happening, my spirit instinctually zipped out of the room traveling quickly down the stairwell to a newly manifested classroom which resided at the foot of the stairs. Going inside, it became as any other Earthly schoolroom, completely enclosed with chairs, a blackboard, and a teacher.

Upon my arrival, the classroom was darkened as the teacher prepared to show us a movie entitled, 'Purgatory.' Many students were here to watch this interesting motion picture but as the movie began we were all swept into the film. No longer in the classroom, we were now living within the scenes of the movie.

In an interesting turn of events, this movie which was supposed to be about 'Purgatory,' seemed much more like 'Armageddon.' Becoming very confusing, we experienced some horrible event in the future which appeared to a part of some distant diabolical war. (This occurred about one and a half years before the fall of the World Trade Center) In reality, we were experiencing the war between good and evil within our own souls, and within the world around us. Although I didn't yet realize it, the Lord was showing me that the Earth is a purgatory realm.

Aircraft were landing in airports without permission, while armed snipers exited planes and other war vehicles, wandering through towns and cities murdering and pillaging everybody in sight. Everybody was running for their lives, trying to remain hidden from these demonic snipers carrying machine guns. Trying to stop the killing, the United States had a difficult job because they were not employing the usual means of war; armies confronting one another on a battlefield. Rather, they were targeting people in their normal place of business and their homes.

Amidst the chaos, those of us who were members of the class on 'Purgatory' were trying to protect ourselves and others. Despite this, many of those in the classroom were killed. Eventually, however, the forces of the United States were able to overcome the terrorists, but not until much bloodshed had already occurred.

As this tremendously disturbing scene began to end, the students and I re-entered the classroom as if we had been watching a movie all along. All were in shell-shock from the horrendous experience, and many hadn't survived in the movie, but were immediately restored to life in the classroom.

Awaiting some bold pronouncement from this teacher regarding the hell we had just witnessed, we got no such thing. Pulling out a book entitled, 'Purgatory,' the teacher looked at us with expectancy as if we should somehow understand. All very confused, the image of what we had seen seemed more like 'Armageddon' than 'Purgatory.'

In the Catholic tradition, 'Purgatory' is one of the places one can go to after death. Heaven, Hell and Purgatory are the three possibilities. Those who are evil go to Hell, those who are wholly good go to Heaven, but those who are not bad enough to go to Hell, yet not good enough to go to Heaven, go to Purgatory. Purgatory is a place of purification where a soul cleanses itself of sin in order to become pure enough to enter into Heaven. In medieval times, people feared Purgatory because it was depicted as a realm very much like Hell complete with burning fire. A soul underwent tremendous pain in its purification, but the saving grace was that Purgatory wasn't eternal, your salvation was assured.

In modern times, Purgatory is often depicted as a place where the soul's torment is primarily experienced in the absence of God. For a soul who loves the Lord, this absence is extremely painful, but seemingly appropriate, because the soul willingly turned away from God when committing sin during life.

Because this experience was a foreshadowing of a true historical event to come, I didn't realize its full import until after this occurrence. There is a war going on in some part of the world, almost all the time. Most of these wars are true Armageddon's, battles between good and evil. What if these wars, and other smaller battles which occur in individual lives, *are* one of the mechanisms of 'Purgatory?' In the Old Testament, there are many wars which are intended as a cleansing of the sinfulness of the people.

In my travels to the hell realms, I'd been shown on several occasions that many souls were given the option of reincarnation before entering hell. In the 'Pistis Sophia,' a Gnostic text, it says that souls who have committed certain sins are sent to Hell to undergo specific punishments meted out according to their sin. But when they have undergone this punishment, they are then placed in a body with certain features; physical, mental or spiritual, which correspond to their previous bad acts, and returned to the Earth. With this in mind, you can see how Earth operates as a 'Purgatory' realm, a place of purgation (Not unlike the Moon, which was revealed in 'The Mysteries of the Redemption' as a 'Chaos' realm.).

If various heavenly bodies may encompass diverse realms, and my previous writings primarily considered the journey of those of us confined to the Earth, imagine how many more realms may be found encompassed in planets, stars, galaxies etc.

Looking upon the face of the teacher, he revealed nothing more. As our eyes met, my soul began to disappear to this classroom in the stars.
****

Awakened, my soul found itself standing amidst a grand forest. All around me were the benefits of the wild, the trees cascading high above me in this almost iridescent and yet somewhat waveform world. Beginning to prance along the wilderness path, I looked around to find the purpose of my arrival in this spiritual world.

Wavering through the forest sheath, I began to see the vague outline of a form ahead of me. As he began to materialize, it revealed a Native American man dressed in buckskin riding a white horse. Back facing me, he was riding slowly along the path. Following this immensely mystical mirage, I began to run towards him, but then began to soar so that I might catch up.

Stopping before the side of a red rock cliff, he turned to look at me for only a millisecond, as his image and that of the horse began to fade. Beginning to make out what lay before him on the path, it was a doorway. Although there was no visible outline of an entry, the stone rock wall led high into the sky.

Looking up, a woman dressed all in white appeared at my side. Shimmering in the wind, she began to speak words of passage which she bade me not to repeat to any Earthly soul. (As usual, they were also then taken from my memory within a few days of the experience.) Highly evolved and very calm, she took my hand and a small screen appeared in the rock face of the mountain wherein our faces were now visible.

Without words, the woman conveyed to me that I was being examined for signs of readiness by those of the elect who resided within these walls. Suddenly, the lines which would indicate a door appeared and opened before us in the rocks. Two stools quietly lay within, and she guided me to join her in sitting upon them. As we did, the doors closed around us and we transmitted to another dimension.

Words cannot express the bliss I felt upon arriving in this majestic kingdom and being granted the privilege of seeing my long lost friend, St. Harmony Crystal Fire, the white-winged horse who had traveled to so many distant places with me, and who had guided me into many doorways and realms of knowledge. It'd been a very long time since I'd seen my beautiful white-winged horse, and I was brought to tears upon visioning his beauty.

Arriving through a similar multi-dimensional gateway, St. Harmony Crystal Fire passed through a machine which was somewhat like an x-ray. You could see the skeletal structure of the horse and his wings as he passed through, but in order to be allowed entry here, you had to have certain auric markers indicating that you were sufficiently evolved. St. Harmony Crystal Fire passed with flying colors.

Previously unnoticed by myself, there appeared at St. Harmony Crystal Fire's side a woman who was apparently responsible for bringing him here. Summoned to go with them for some sort of preparation, the woman who had led me here left with them while I was to remain behind.

Time passed before I was telepathically airlifted, without any verbal warning, to St. Harmony Crystal Fire's side. Seeing before me two states of energy, they were demonstrated to me in a way which my limited understanding did not comprehend. Because of this, I was led through a series of lights which were designed to bring your vibration higher, so as to gently guide you to an understanding of these two lights which were apparently very important. As these little lights were understood, they would then merge within your spirit and become a part of you. My case was a difficult one, however, as I was having trouble comprehending the energetic meaning of these lights. Thus, my own lights were not igniting properly, which posed a problem for the patient guardians who had brought me here this evening.

Approaching me, a man dressed in white appeared in the essence of peace and serenity. Guided by a higher voice which belonged to a woman, I could not see her. Everyone present, however, was aware of the telepathic impetus which was received from her by this man. Because the other method had not worked (that of showing me the lights and attempting to integrate their knowing within me), he was attempting to transfer the knowledge of these lights telepathically. Eventually, this would lead to my spiritual link-up with St. Harmony Crystal Fire.

As this process bore fruit, I saw before me the first light. Lighting up as a holy rage, I immediately understood it to be an inferior understanding. 'Holy Rage' was an excessively angry response to the sins of others or the world. The second light was a calm and calculated energy which acted for the sole purpose of evolution. Recognizing misdeeds or sins as such, it held within it a proper recognition of the place of sin in the development of souls. Entering into this knowing, the second light lit up and entered my spirit.

As soon as this was accomplished, my soul began to waver in and out of energy, as I watched the final link-up with St. Harmony Crystal Fire achieve itself. A line of energy which looked very much like a laser beam, formed from my heart to his. Beginning to be drawn away, there was little I could do about it.

Conveying telepathically as I began to disappear, the guardians thought, 'You must release the purpose of holy rage, which is an extreme you've traveled to in balancing your understanding. Embrace calculated evolutionary energy as the proper balance in the understanding of deeds, your own and others, perpetuated upon the planet Earth.' Completing this process according to their instruction, St. Harmony Crystal Fire and I melted into one another, as we both disappeared.
****

Unaware of how our souls had made this grand journey, Andy and I continued soaring towards the star room where the pilots of many spacecraft from various civilizations throughout the Universe were gathered to visit with one another. Humans, as well as, extra-terrestrials were gathered, but despite this very interesting spectacle before me, I couldn't take my eyes off a huge runway which lay in the other direction.

Noticing our Earthly space vessel, it had just undergone extensive repairs. Perhaps we had ridden this vehicle sub-consciously? Set to go at the entry to the runway, I grabbed Andy's hand, and we began running towards it. Entering this very small saucer-shaped vessel, it ran itself, starting its ignition and soaring down the runway at voluminous speed.

Words cannot express the wonder and awe experienced in our ascent to the stars. Before us lay the unadulterated Universe, and the stars sped by us like snowflakes on the windshield of a car. Heavenly bodies could be seen from great distances, their colors brilliant and defined. Galaxies in the distance held every possible hue of white, purple and blue, while the sun and stars emanated orange, red and white. Surprised, I looked in a direction I hadn't yet peered through to notice that the Earth was in our view. At a good altitude above it, something was beginning to go wrong with our vessel. Noticing a star-station in the near-distance, it was our best hope of assistance. As the craft was obviously failing, my eyes fell to what appeared to be a rotating pastel mist of color. If we could get the ship into and underneath this mist, the star station would pull us into its orbit, and eventually down into the bough. Maneuvering the craft towards this star station, we were able to accomplish this feat easily.

Pulling in, the craft was controlled by a force within this grand space airport, leading us to a safe landing. Exiting the ship, I noticed a group of people very obviously from the 19th century being led on a tour. Remaining sub-conscious for this journey, the extra-terrestrials were seeding them with knowledge to hopefully assist them in their current time-frame below on the Earth.

Offering Andy and I the opportunity to take a short journey on one of their crafts which were distinctively more advanced than our own, we accepted their kind gesture and soared through the take-off pod at a speed which cannot be expressed. After experiencing the take-off, however, the ship returned of its own accord to the star-station wherein we were led into a re-materialization chamber to prepare for our return to our Earthly bodies. As would be expected, we became sub-conscious, only to return to Earth, relishing the opportunity we'd been given to leave behind our Earthly craft for a moment, and experience the heavenly vehicle of the stars. For a moment, we had become Galactic!
****

Awaking in sleep, I found my soul had entered into an all-white room where a table had been placed. At the other end of the room by the table was a large, magnificent painting of Jesus wearing the robes of white and red, His Sacred Heart emanating from it brilliantly. Having approached the table, I noticed that there were several old wrinkled photographs lying next to this painting on the table. Immediately picking them up, they were pictures of Therese Neumann and her family. Because her life as a stigmatist had been filled with criticism and controversy, the Lord wished to convey to me that she was a legitimate messenger of Christ. There would be no doubt as to the authenticity of the message I'd received at her hand, as this was no deception of the enemy. "Thank you, Jesus." I prayerfully said, bowing to the picture which now became animate.

Without words, Jesus conveyed to me that I must embrace my reclusive lifestyle as He had chosen me to be a contemplative in order to fulfill His will through my writing. Further, I was to raise my children, in His eyes an exalted role. Reaching my hand to touch His, my spirit became invisible to the room.
****

About six months pregnant with my third child, who would be Jacob, I'd been ordered to bed rest. A serious undiagnosed condition remained beneath the surface, however, one which would not be discovered for another two years. But when it would be discovered, it would affect my life in a huge way.

Falling off into a deep, ecstatic, transcendental state, my soul was hovering amongst the stars. Honoring my soul in this brilliant and peaceful place with the presence of my two daughters, Melissa and Mary, we hovered together for hours absorbing the celestial impetus given us by the Lord. Being able to watch my two jewels made this heavenly experience all the more joyful, and I thanked the Lord for his kindness.

****

Taking my soul on a hellish journey, the disgusting ogre had arrived with permission from the Lord to make an effort to tempt me to despair. Because I'd been so sick throughout my pregnancy, I'd already been struggling with depression, and Satan felt that he knew just what might take me over the edge.

Reaching his hand to me, I refused to take it, looking at him as though he were delirious. "I will go with you, because it has been ordered by the Lord. But I shall at no point touch you," I said. Acting insulted, the devil began falling as if he were traveling through an endless pit. Without any conscious participation on my part, I fell in line with him as we entered into the deepest caverns of the Earth.

Arriving at two pits of fire, the horrific stench was only outdone by the moans heard in the darkness. Deeply touched, I remained unmoved in my countenance refusing to look upon the face of the ogre; but inwardly, I mourned and lamented the existence of this hell realm, and beyond this, the terrifying reality that some souls actually condemned themselves to such a place.

Everything was as dark as the deepest of caverns, the soil and pith sloppy and gooey, like mud beneath your feet. Filled with the energy of evil, these were the pits of fire.

Looking to Satan, he was waiting expectantly for a reply, or even better, a horrified reaction to his kingdom. Looking at him emotionless, I said, "The Lord does not wish us to despair, but rather, to focus on heavenly things . . . hope." Looking deeply disappointed, he didn't move, but his face showed no more sarcasm. Continuing, I quietly replied, "And that is exactly what I intend to do." Immediately, I disappeared.

Aboard a huge circular craft, several hundred sub-conscious astral souls were soaring through the heavens to bear witness to some of the wonders of God. Immediately, I noticed that we were all wearing inflatable socks upon our feet and lower legs to battle the cold of outer space. Holding a book in their hands, a group of human looking spiritual beings showed it to us, communicating that this was to be given to the extra-terrestrials at the space station, which was apparently our destination. Sacred and holy, I couldn't help but open my naive mouth, querying their disapproving faces. "Why haven't you also brought them ancient sacred texts?" Immediately I understood that they had brought some of the ancient sacred texts to them. Looking at me as if it should be obvious, they said, "As pertains to the galactic heavens, some of the ancient sacred texts upon the Earth are out of date. Although some things, such as the Bible and other holy scriptures, remain timeless and relevant wherever they may be, there are others which are obsolete in our realms, although highly relevant to those of you remaining on the Earth." Embarrassed, I could *feel* the highly evolved nature of these galactic beings who far surpassed any intelligence I'd ever seen.

Unfortunately, they didn't expand on this because the time had come to look upon our destination. Following their instructions, I looked out of the window in our craft. To our right, was a magnificent space station, much larger than the one I'd seen recently. But what absolutely confounded me in a state of wonder and bliss was my witness to a most profound debacle of heavenly beauty filled with knowledge of great galactic significance. Surrounding the space station were huge magnificent paintings with gold frames, encircling the city with their holy protection and filling us travelers with the wisdom that they had been placed upon the sky to impart. As these paintings hovered in the heavens, they seemed to be attached only to the heavenly landscape. Stars cascaded around them as if they were somehow alive, and indeed, in an inexplicable way they were.

Enraptured by the brilliant artistic renderings of Jesus Christ, Mother Mary, the Twelve Disciples, St. John the Baptist and a panoramic display of the Life of Christ, they had been placed in chronological order and completely surrounded the space station. Profound but simple was their message, Jesus Christ was just as significant to the galactic heavens as He had been to the planet Earth and His life on Earth was a great galactic and Universal moment! Seeding us to one day become a part of this much larger, universal, grand and galactic union, this amazing redemptive journey had been etched upon the stars with a patient knowing. Someday, the tribes of the Earth would awaken, and grasp the knowledge of the spheres . . . that of Galactica!

CHAPTER TWO

Roaring blew in from overhead as a pulsing energy heralded the vessels in the night sky. Although the spaceships are silent in the physical environment, they are distinctively loud in the realm of the spirit, and their rhythm moves deeply within your molecular structure. Now in my spiritual body, I hovered over to the window to look at the first vessels to arrive. A flat base with an enlarged dome at the top, a pulsating red light came from several points along the seam between the two parts of the ship. Several more were to follow, a rectangular ship which was huge and seemed to fill the sky, as well as, a whole host of Pleiadian vessels. Having seen the Pleiadian ships many times, they were very familiar. A rounded upper part glowed in purple upon a flattened metallic center plate which beheld another rounded lower metallic piece.

Before I could ascertain my situation, a large white globe of light came from the Pleiadian vessels, approached my spirit and entered my head; not once, but several times with each onslaught of ships. As it entered, a tremendous pulsation could be felt within my head. As this continued for quite some time, I found myself becoming exhausted by the continual onslaughts of energy, although there was exhilaration, as well.

Preparing to leave, a bright light came from below one of the Pleiadian ships as two very small creatures descended from the vessel. No more than two feet high, they were wearing the brown robe's of an Earthly monk. Standing on two legs, their skin was sheer and off-white. Several wrinkles formed around their mouths, and their eyes were very large and brownish-black.

Finding them to be very cute, I almost regarded them like little pets, but in order to quell any such arrogance, they conveyed that my time had come to learn from them. Meanwhile, I must be alone to receive them because other people would be unable to tolerate their energy. Before I could respond, they were sucked back into the ship, and the entire battalion of ships sped off into the night.
****

Within the depths of the night, they came towards me like a swarm of bees, angered at the spiritual changes which were being wrought within my soul. Five ugly reptilian demons had come after me followed by a huge vortex of black energy which carried with it the most horrendous humming sound. Individual molecules of evil could be seen within the cloudy vortex. Feeling immediately overwhelmed, I called out to Mary, Mother of God, to assist me in this battle in which I was obviously outnumbered.

Appearing in the heavens before me, she wore a five pointed crown on her head and was covered in a swirling robe of blue. Awestruck by her beauty, I didn't immediately notice that the demons with their energized black vortex of evil had immediately disappeared as soon as she had come. When the moment had passed, I was filled with amazement at how quickly she had vanquished them.

Whenever I've been in trouble, it is the members of the royal lineage of souls upon whom I call for assistance; Jesus, Mary, Buddha, Zarathustra, Avalokiteswara, etc. Perhaps this is a lesson in *true* significance, rather than that which is vainly perceived through worldly eyes.

****

Long black mane blowing in the wind, the master Babaji was soaring through the stars. 'Babaji' is a well known master from India, and quite familiar to those who've read the books of Paramahansa Yogananda. Very, very old (several hundreds of years), he is said to be able to travel between realms, appearing at one moment as a physical being, appearing in another as a spiritual essence at will, manifesting in and out of realities.

Although I saw him soaring, I was unable to keep up with him and stopped to catch my breath. Not my physical breath, mind you, but a breath it is, despite its immateriality. Hovering in the heavens, I noticed that a tiny three-foot high witch had appeared in the sky in front of me. Attempting to dissuade me from finding the great master, she said, "I have much to teach you of sorcery." Laughing at her suggestion, I replied, "Sorcery is a practice which violates eternal law, and don't you think that the green pointy hat and straw-like hair is a bit obvious?" Frowning at this, she disappeared, as a disgusting gull demon appeared. Gulls are the demons of destructive sexual energy who appear as humans with bat-like wings and such. Often, but not always, their hair is greased back. As would be expected of such a demon, he began to make sexual gestures towards me, as I pushed him aside, declining his offer of vice.

As Babaji was now long gone, I began flying in search of him or someone who could lead me to him. As the stars passed by my vision like snow on a windshield, I finally noticed up ahead a golden temple. Approaching the huge gold/marble door, it bore a sign which read, 'Temple to the Masters.' I was elated!

Knocking upon the door, I was not given entrance. Disappointed, I recognized my unworthiness, but was happy that I was allowed to look upon a set of pictures. About thirty masters resided in this temple, and they were shown in their entire splendor. Babaji was not among them, and I noticed that these masters were different than the others I'd already encountered. Bearing an adventurous quality to them, they seemed to be energized in a truly unique manner. Unlike the masters, saints and prophets of the Earth, whose holiness was calm, serene and effulgent, these were powerful stewards of creative energies, almost reminiscent of the Assisi Marauders (who rode white-winged horses with whom I'd encountered long ago.). Active and highly energized, these masters seemed to be involved in energetic action, while the other equally holy ones seemed to be more involved in 'being' with God.

Humbled and in awe, I quietly left this golden marble temple without entering, and continued my quest for Babaji.

****

Drumming filled my psyche as I sat around a circle of Buddhist monks. Several types of drums were in the center of their circle, all of which were being played by several monks who sat around them. As the beating filled my head, an intermittent energy of detachment began to wave through my soul. Continuing for quite some time, the monks conveyed that I must come to a place of detachment in regards to the way others viewed my soul. Falling outside of myself, it became a true surrender. Spiritual development requires a continually evolving process of discipline which comes about through continual evaluation. Such evaluations serve the purpose of recognizing the preferable from the less preferable; good and evil. In those whose philosophy is 'anything goes,' such discretion and discipline is viewed as contrary to freedom. Despite this view, the disciplined mind is fully cognizant that true freedom only comes about within the confines of moral certitude. In essence, it should not surprise me that my blunt words might make some people upset, but it remained irrelevant to my purpose.

As the drums continued to beat a rhythmic energy of detachment into my spirit, the monks sat calm and serene.
****

Traveling with my vision removed, the spiritual world was taking me through the aeons to a very holy place. As my vision was restored, I struggled to regain consciousness in the realm I now occupied. An image of holiness and splendor arrayed in such simplicity lay before me, that of Indira Gandhi, the wife of Mahatma Gandhi. Dressed in an exquisite, but very simple, immaculately white wedding gown, her holiness could never be expressed. Stunned, humbled and moved, a voice spoke, "Gandhi was a saint, not just to the Hindu and Indian people, but to God. The people of the world must know this, especially those in the Christian world who do not believe that a Hindu man could not only go to heaven, but be a *true saint* in the eyes of the Lord." Having known some Christians to say such things, wouldn't it be interesting if they were given a moment to compare their own status in the eyes of God, with such a man as this? Perhaps they would be greatly humbled and deeply troubled by their lack of insight.

Indira was just as holy as her husband, and in some respects, she was even more so due to her silent but powerful influence during life in supporting her husband. She was his strength, courage and stronghold. Literally glowing with light, Gandhi suddenly appeared next to her. Very friendly and hospitable, he was anxious to talk to me. Other sub-conscious astral souls were in the room who did not recognize the obvious level of his saintliness. Disappointed by this, I pointed it out to them because they were completely unaware of the great honor which had been bestowed upon them. Indira and Mahatma Gandhi had lowered themselves from their usual place within the high heavens to deign to speak to a lowly worm such as myself.

Gandhi walked quietly over to me in the same humble manner he bore in life, wearing traditional Indian garb and adorned with a smile which could only speak of the eternal happiness which had been bestowed upon him and his wife for their courageous and holy efforts to save a people through non-violence. Showing me the similarities between the Catholic and the Hindu religion, his purpose was to discard the differences and begin a peaceful discussion with the hopeful conclusion of achieving understanding and unity between peoples. Pointing out that both the Hindu and Catholic religions honor an incarnation of God and a divine mother, he also noted a similarity between the mantras of the Hindus, and novenas of the Catholics. Both honored many symbols, pictures, images and statues of the holy divinities and/or saints, and each religion had an extensive theology of demons. Pointing out the different spelling, the Hindu spelling would be 'daemons.' Finally, Catholics pray to saints for intercession, while Hindu's pray to demi-gods for intercession, which is just another word for saints.

In order to express this unity in a more meaningful way, the entire gathering of people, who had now become completely enamored of this saintly simple man, performed several Hindu mantras together following this holy ejaculation with several Catholic prayers. As we prayed the Hindu mantras, Gandhi made appear Hindu icons and pictures, and when we began the Catholic prayers, he changed the pictures and icons to those of the Catholics. Engaged by the holiness of the moment, I was taken by surprise when I began to fade from this realm.

Waving good-bye to these two amazing souls, I couldn't help but shed a tear as my final breath took me away. Awaking, I had no words, but chose to remain silent for a very long time in honor of this amazingly holy visitation.

****

Before the delivery of my third child, Jacob, the Lord Jesus appeared personally, showing me the status of a soul who was apparently about to encounter an early death. Despite having a family who needed to be cared for, I was shown that this soul had earned a place in hell because of his extreme atheism and hatred for God. Screaming in the fires of the abyss, I cringed at the fate he was about to endure which the Lord had bade me to witness. Asking me to offer up the pains of my labor as a sacrificial penance for this soul, the Lord said that if I were to do this for him, he would be given another opportunity to continue to live, and thus, possibly change his wicked ways. Agreeing to do so with great fervency, this chastisement was indeed lifted and this soul was given another chance at life. Only time would tell how he might use it, however, and whether or not he would save himself from this hellish fate.

Continuing to journey into the status of various souls, I was bidden to observe a pitifully sad situation wherein a soul, who had been given great spiritual opportunities to advance by the Lord, was allowing herself to be taken down the road of perdition by a boyfriend. Succumbing to temptation, she had yielded all that she knew to be true in order to be with a man who was obviously following the wide road to perdition. Having chosen the status of 'death,' which had been emblazoned upon her chest, her body was decomposing. Experimenting with her decomposition, her boyfriend repeatedly said, "She needs to go to hell, she needs to go to hell . . ." Very concerned, I made it clear to him that he was now responsible for the state of her soul and that he would pay dearly for this in hell. Unconcerned, he couldn't care less but because of the many bad choices she had made up to this point in bringing her soul to such a pitiful reality, there was little I could do but wait and hope that she would stop this horrid reality before it became solidified and final on the ground.

Giving me an opportunity to warn this soul in her physical waking world, she eventually broke free of this defilement, and became one with her eternal destiny.

As a sharp contrast to the former experience, I was shown a soul who bore within her a twenty-foot high, blue-green, rounded and fat demon of sloth. Literally taking the breath right out of you, it was smothering in its incessant wants and 'needs.' Unrelated to work ethic, this sloth demon had appeared from laziness in regards to spiritual development.

Giving me an opportunity to warn this soul in her physical waking world, it inspired within her a torrential flood of transformative energy which resulted in the expungement of the demon and a grand deepening of her spiritual life.

Finally, the Lord Jesus allowed me to experience a demonic battle wherein I'd called to Him for help and none had come. Feeling this absence, Jesus wanted me to understand the isolation of those who live consciously sinful lives (hardened, repetitious, actual sin); those who seek repentance in words but not deeds. Because they belong to Satan, he may torment them at will, and they may not always receive swift help. Differing from the type of temptation or torment meant to *try* a soul, Satan must have permission to reach one who already belongs to God, and the purpose is expiatory, to build a crown of strength.

Returning to form, I immediately went into labor as Jacob was born.

****

Covered in blood, the muddy path seemed ominous as I looked ahead to see where my spiritual guardians might be taking my soul. A gathering of satanic worshipers loomed ahead. "Oh, geez!" I thought, as the Lord made it clear that I *must* go. The angel aside me quietly and very calmly said, "The Lord asks for your presence." Not replying, it seemed that they were awfully calm about sending me to such a horrific place.

As soon as I'd arrived, I took notice of a throne in the center of all the activities with a small statue of Satan sitting upon it. The people were wandering around in a state of dazed confusion; many of them had joined together in smaller groupings to 'do their own thing.' (Their own things were violent, sadistic, sexually deviant, etc.) Ceremonies had yet to begin as I wandered around observing, remaining as incognito as possible. Because these were demon-filled Satanists, many knew immediately that I was a Christian and filled with the Holy Spirit.

Running towards me with fists upraised, an entire band of them began coming after me to take me out. As they did this, I yelled out various truths about Jesus Christ, and began calling out His name, over and over, "Jesus, Jesus, Jesus, Jesus . . ." Continuing with His many titles, I said, "King of Kings, Jesus is the Lamb, Jesus is the Messiah, Jesus is the Savior. You are following a false king, for Jesus is God." Beginning to speak words from the gospel of John required in the discerning of spirits, I was inspired! "Jesus came down from heaven and became flesh; He is the Son of God. Jesus rose from the dead and ascended into heaven. Jesus is the King."

As I spoke these words to them, there were three reactions. The really violent and vicious ones would get angry and want desperately to rip me to pieces, but they couldn't because I was protected. Others that were not as rooted in evil would just walk away because they knew they couldn't do anything. Those that were lukewarm in their satanic leanings, thus borderline and open to the possibility of conversion, would start crying openly and uncontrollably; which embarrassed them to no end. Waving for me to go away so that they could stop this embarrassing display, I stayed and spoke more about Jesus. Having no control over this process, the Lord had literally taken a hold of them as they were 'convicted in the spirit.' I felt sorry for them, for evil knows no joy.

After a good long while, about fifty of the approximately two-hundred participants had been taken to this state of conviction and I was hoping I might be able to leave. But when I least expected it, one of the truly nasty Satanists grabbed me from behind and sat me down in a chair, blocking my view of what was going on to the right of me. In a moment, he moved away to reveal that I was sitting next to the throne I'd seen earlier, but it was now occupied by Satan himself. Looking like a caricature of a big time wrestler with gray colored skin, the texture of sand, the bulging muscles in his chest were overtly large, exaggerated and frankly somewhat frightening. Proportionately large, his head was separated into two bulging sections like a large brain with horns coming out of it. Having no hair, his image held two large black eyes.

Laughing hysterically in his own unique evil way, the ogre didn't waste any time in letting me know his purpose. According to him, I was going to die in my sleep tonight because I'd been chosen as the sacrifice for this particular satanic black mass. Surprised by his pronouncement, I quickly regained my composure and began to laugh right back at him.

"I'm not going to be the sacrifice tonight," I said, "I know that you have to have permission from God to bother me, but I also know that you *don't* have permission to do *that*." My knowledge of this had come from the book of Job, in the Old Testament of the Holy Bible. Frowning, I continued, "And besides, Jesus is the King of Kings, and you're the king of nothing." Roaring with anger, I began to recite the Apostles Creed, "I believe in God, the Father Almighty," as I said this, he moved a few inches away from me, his roar becoming more of a growl, "Creator of heaven and Earth; and in Jesus Christ, His only Son, our Lord;" his facial expression became one of doubt and confusion, "who was conceived by the Holy Spirit, born of the Virgin Mary, suffered under Pontius Pilate, was crucified, died and was buried. He descended into Hell; the third day He arose again from the dead; He ascended into heaven, and sits at the right hand of God, the Father Almighty." Flinging himself out of his chair, he waved me off and ran away, but so as not to appear bashful, I shouted after him, "I believe in His holy church!"

As I said this, several of his wards became invisible, planning to assault me without my awareness. But before they could touch me, the Holy Spirit filled me and took me away. Before I could awake, however, the Holy Spirit began repeating something over and over to me. "Check your house for a gas leak, check your house for a gas leak . . ." When I did awaken, I had the power company check our home for a leak and sure enough, we had one. Satan had been serious about his plans to take me out, but the Lord would not allow him to do so . . . because he didn't have permission.

The following night, a swarm of wasps came towards me as I was drifting off to sleep. Hitting me directly in the heart, I immediately felt like I was having a heart attack or stroke. Entering into deep prayer as I struggled to breathe - chest pain and pressure searing, tingling and electrical sensations traveling throughout my body - I remembered the words of the masters. "I feel no pain, I feel no pain." Centering on my place within God, I gradually began to feel better.

Although the Lord had not allowed the viper to take my life, I had suffered a grievous injury ordained by God which would not be revealed for another year and a half, a trial which was now brimming within my body and soul . . .
****

Walking along an old dusty road, a large convention center loomed ahead. Announcing that a New Age convention was in progress, a large banner was displayed near the doorway. Going towards this building, I began running as I planned to go inside and see what might be happening. When I came near, however, an invisible force resisted my attempts. No matter how hard I might try, I couldn't go in due to an immense force-field which had been placed upon my path.

Suddenly in the sky above me, something began to form. In bright yellow-white light, the aura of a starry emerald phantasm came from the heights of heaven. Waiting to see what it might become, I was humbled and a bit ashamed when the image became clear. The cross of our Lord Jesus Christ hung in the sky at least a mile long and a half mile wide. Instantly, I knew that I was not to 'enter' into anything New Age again. Profoundly intense, this was not a friendly reminder, but a stern reprimand. Bowing to the Lord's wishes and looking down in embarrassment, I began to disintegrate.
****

As my soul was being mercilessly assaulted by a large group of demonic entities, I was calling out to Jesus for help in this precarious situation. Something very unusual occurred, however, in that Jesus did not come Himself, but rather sent to my aid a Franciscan monk. Immediately vacating the dark spirits, he turned without delay to chastise me.

I was clearly forgiven for that which he was about to discuss, but my sins were serious and had energized karmic retribution. Looking upon his face, I knew that I was about to really get it, and I adjusted my energies to an appropriately serious stance.

Earlier in my journey, before I had rewritten and completed the books involved in 'The Mysteries of the Redemption' and 'Galactica,' I had published two books under the New Age genre. Having allowed them to be dispersed too soon, I had neglected to obtain the complete picture, and expressed two very serious untruths. Despite the Lord's understanding of our delusional status, we remain accountable for that which we do and say. Every jot and tittle of the law shall be fulfilled.

Speaking of how many of my previous books had actually been sold; the monk mentioned that somewhere between 10-20,000 people had bought them. By publishing standards, this number was pathetic, but by number of souls misled, it was significant.

When I'd written the books, I'd been completely sincere in believing that what was within them was true, although I'd expressed *opinions* in regards to things which had not yet been revealed to me, which were judgmental and absolutely incorrect. A common problem among those of us awakened to the spiritual realms, I'd given myself to comment on that which had not yet been revealed, simply because of the nature of that which had. Making assumptions about a broader truth based on my limited understanding of a series of mystical experiences, I made the broad leap that they contained within them *all* knowledge. A good example of this same arrogance came to me when I read a very short booklet written by a young man who'd had a near-death experience as a child. Explaining what he had seen, he began to mock those who had made mention of the cherubs, because he'd only seen angels of adult stature in his one experience. As a result, he believed that cherubs simply did not exist. It is unwise to create your own theology of all that is, based on one or a few mystical experiences. God's kingdom is much too vast. To do so is small-minded and lacking in humility.

Although they were not based on my experience, but rather my false conclusions extending beyond them, I had deduced two things which were untrue. 1) There is no hell, Satan or demons, and 2) because we create our own reality; those who are sick can heal themselves. (Please be assured that all such falsehoods were removed long ago, under divine direction. Neither of these versions will ever be in print again.)

Essential understanding lies in this. In both cases, I'd made assumptions based on what I'd seen, ignoring that which I had not yet seen. Because the Lord *begins* the mystical journey of the novice by taking him into the heavenly realms, I assumed there must not be hellish realms. Because I'd been shown the basic mechanism of reality creation through thought, I assumed that *all* reality was thought based and conscious. Because I hadn't yet seen the deeper movings of the mechanics of existence (something I should have assumed that I did not yet know), I hadn't realized that such things were a working of intricate levels of existence, thought playing only a partial role. The will of God and the laws of nature are intricately involved with such things, stupid, stupid, stupid . . .

Having commanded me to get my earliest books taken out of print years before this current experience, the Lord Jesus had been kind and forgiving of my error, because it was to serve a greater purpose. As I had taken them out of print years before, the Lord shared that I'd been allowed to publish them as part of a karmic path which would lay the foundation for my later eternal work. Having now spent years rewriting the books from the standpoint of knowledge, the Lord laid everything out for me like a map.

In following my karmic impetus which had stemmed from vainglory and greed, I'd pursued publication of my books (at that time) because it appeared (on the ground) like the correct thing to do. An eternal program requires the will of God to reveal such matters.

Steady, sure, just and swift, my soul received karmic retribution. For the first untruth perpetuated through my hand, the Lord gave permission for the dark side to continually tempt my soul. For the second, the Lord gave permission for my body to experience the ravages of a disease whose prime manifestation had yet to be diagnosed.

(Although I had been diagnosed with Lupus by this time, another deeply foreboding diagnosis was yet to come.)

Feeling ridiculously stupid, the monk had made things abundantly clear, but I couldn't help but notice his disgust with what I had done. Disgusted with myself, as well, I noticed that his energy changed as he observed my true contrition.

Becoming abundantly merciful, he took my hand, and we walked towards a meditation cell. "I'm going to pray for you," he quietly said, as he bid me to know that another awaited who would also assist.

Arriving in the cell, my soul could not believe the beauty the Lord in his infinite compassion had prepared for me. Pope John Paul II was waiting for us, incredible warmth upon his face for such a sinner. White robes gleaming with holiness, there was a three-foot high, shining, gilded, golden crown emanating from the top of his head. The holiness of this man was abundantly clear. Above it, ethereal aspects of the crown radiated into the molecular structure of the air in a manner which lit up the whole room. Falling to my knees, I lowered my head in shame, as he placed his hands upon me and said, "I love you."

Tears flowed from my eyes as he took the hand of the monk, beginning to pray that the Lord would forgive me and lift this just retribution from my soul. Beginning to disappear, I shouted out my thanks for their blunt chastisement. As they smiled with deep compassion, I disappeared.

****

As I was reading the following passage from a vision beheld by the most saintly Padre Pio, a most amazing consolation was given me by the Lord:

"My soul was suddenly carried away by a force stronger than itself into a very large room illuminated by a very bright light. On a high throne studded with jewels was seated a lady of rare beauty. This was the most holy Virgin who held in her arms the Child of majestic mien, his face more resplendent and luminous than the sun. All around them was a great multitude of very beautiful Angels. At the end of this large room there were two small beds, in each of which was a person who, to judge by appearances, must have been in great suffering. One of them was suffering so much as to seem on the point of bidding farewell to this life. Before the throne on which the Virgin was seated there was another person, completely absorbed in contemplation, who was the personification of happiness. The Child came down from the Virgin's arms, and followed by his Mother and the Angels approached the person wrapt in prayer. He threw his arms around that person, clasped her to his breast, kissed her an infinite number of times and bestowed on her innumerable other caresses. The Virgin and the Angels did likewise. Then he went towards the beds of the two sick persons. To one of these, who was sitting up in bed, the Child addressed just a few words of comfort, rather coldly and unceremoniously. At the other sick person who lay at full length in the bed and had greater need of comfort, he did not deign even to glance, and as if he hated even to punish her, he ordered the Angels to beat her. These did not hesitate to carry out his orders. They approached the sick person, one of them took her by the hand and the

others began to punch and kick and slap her. This scene seemed very cruel. But what a strange and wonderful thing! The poor creature did not complain, but in a very weak voice exclaimed: 'O most gracious Jesus, have mercy on me while the time for mercy still lasts. Do not condemn me, most sweet Jesus, when you come to judge me, for I should not be able to love you anymore. O most compassionate Jesus, if your severe justice intends to condemn me, I appeal to your most loving mercy.' The Child turned to me and said, 'Learn how one should love.' I understood nothing. This sight made me tremble like a reed exposed to a violent wind, for I expected this soul to be rejected by Jesus. But alas, how different from the reality is the sensual man's estimation of spiritual things! Wretched me! For many years I have attended the school of suffering without learning anything. May the infinite mercy of our God be eternally blessed for his great goodness and patience in bearing with me! But to banish all fear from my heart the Lord willed to show me also the souls of these three persons. How beautiful are the souls in whom the heavenly Spouse reigns! If all were to be shown this beauty, we should certainly not see so many of our foolish brethren hastening to where God is not to be found. All three of these angelic creatures were in God's grace; all were adorned with merits, though not in equal measure, for the third was more fully adorned by merit than the second and the second more than the first. Since I could not understand why the Lord treated in such different ways these dear spouses of his, he was pleased to come to the aid of this wretched creature and by a clear and explicit interior locution he began to say to me: 'The first was a soul still weak and in need of caresses, otherwise she would have turned her back on him; the second soul was less weak and to keep her in his service she still needed some little sign or affection; the third was a beloved spouse of his, because, in spite of the way he afflicted her, she remained constant in her service and faithful in love.'

Padre Pio of Pietrelcina - Letters, Volume 1, Letter 139, Page 436, (Christianity, Catholic, Words of Padre Pio)

As I read this vision of Padre Pio, I allowed myself to consider that maybe this sort of thing was happening to me. After all, I started out my spiritual life receiving many consolations in the form of visions and holy dreams, but now was very often left to battle the wretch on my own, not to mention that I'd been suffering great illness. But I didn't want to be presumptuous, so I began to let that thought go, when suddenly . . . a light from heaven came down and surrounded my whole body.

Immediately wrapped in a state of ecstatic bliss, all around me began to glow with light, even down to the last particles. Molecular light was filling the air around me as a spectacular shower of white glowing dust fell from the heavens to the floor of my bedroom. Literally *feeling* the Holy Spirit come into me like a torrential flood of energy, I immediately became aware of the presence of the Lord Jesus at my side. 'I wish for you to read this as a consolation to your own soul,' He said. Reassurance that my sufferings were not an indication of God's wrath, but rather, an indication of God's confidence in my loyalty to Him, despite the active purgation being experienced in my body, was undeniable.

Knowing without *any doubt* that the Lord was happy with me, He still loved me, despite the just consequences of my former sins. In that moment, I realized that it was through *these very consequences* that my soul was becoming sanctified. Perhaps this is one of the ways God heals us, as suffering with grace brings its own reward. Knowing the sincerity of my contrition, the Lord conveyed that my sins had been blotted out, but purgation was under way.

Surrounded by this heavenly light for about ten minutes, I cannot even describe the eternal ecstasy which I experienced within that time. In this totally conscious, physical waking state, the presence of Jesus was so comforting and clear, and the light had manifested to my physical vision. The Lord had not left me to muddle in the quagmire of past sins, but rather, was preparing me to receive of heaven! Having grown up in the Lord, it was time for me to *stand tall* for the Lord, irregardless of heavenly consolations I did or did not receive.

Receiving a similar ecstatic consolation two weeks later while watching the holy mass on television, the priest had spoken about those who were unable to attend mass (due to personal illness, taking care of babies, or attending to the sick). Saying that Jesus was with us in our suffering, I immediately felt peace and saw as heavenly hosts appeared visibly in multitudes around the room. The Lord conveyed that He not only *approved* of my absence from the holy altar, but *preferred* it, because it was a sacrifice. Given for the benefit of my children or on behalf of souls when I was sick, the heavenly lights descended from heaven, and I was *completely filled* with the presence of the Lord. "I prefer sacrifice and surrender," Jesus said, "to the strict adherence of rule."

As the lights began to lift in the room, St. Patrick appeared (Patron saint of Ireland), hovering in the air above the floor. Nodding quietly in approval of my sacrifice, he disappeared as the entire heavenly host vanished.

****

Sleeping peacefully on my bed, I reached my hand over to grasp Andy's, assuming he was still there. Sometimes I don't realize it when he's already left for work, and this was one of those moments. Feeling a hand on the bed, I placed my hand within it, but I couldn't have been more wrong in assuming it was my husband's.

No sooner had I done this than the ogre had hurled my spirit into the air, throwing me around the room. Obviously, Satan had laid a trap for me, and I'd fallen right into it. Because of what had happened the previous day with the Lord, however, I became very courageous and bold.

Once he stopped throwing me all over the room, I regained my composure and began to look around to spot the haggard fool. Looking in the direction of where his energy had been, I noticed that he was invisible at this time, which frankly, was a great relief. He's so ugly! Instinctually, I knew that he was planning to materialize in front of me at any moment, so I shouted at him. "You idiot!" I screamed loudly, "Don't you know that you could've been up in heaven with Jesus! God made you such a beautiful and powerful angel and you are such a fool!" Angered by my statement, a sense of his imminent materialization was forthcoming. "Oh, please don't do that! You're so ugly and so gross! It's so sad what you've become. Please don't ruin my day my making me look upon your disgusting countenance."

Energetic quiet overtook the room, as it appeared that he might be embarrassed. Surprising me, it probably shouldn't have, because after all, Satan *is* the Lord of vanity and all deadly sins. Within a moment, his energy had completely dissipated. Calmly, I went back to sleep.

****

Having exited my body early this morning, I was floating around the house just checking on things, energetically speaking. It's always good to do this if you have the ability to travel 'in the spirit,' because there are often unwelcome guests lurking in your home which need to be extricated, for which there is no other way to identify.

Off in the living room, I noticed what appeared to be the spiritual aspect of my husband, Andy, coming towards me with the obvious intention of some sort of intimate embrace. Intrigued, it seemed to me that it was probably past the hour in which Andy had left for work, and this was not likely to be his soul, so I boldly walked forward and confronted the spiritual being.

"Are you an aspect of Andy's soul," I asked, "are you coming to me as a servant of Jesus?" Instantly, he replied. "Heck, no! I don't even *know* Jesus." His reply indicated an unconscious service of the dark one, so I asked, "Would you like me to tell you about Jesus . . . so perhaps you may no longer serve Satan?" "Huh!" he shouted, "I don't serve Satan!" Calmly, I replied, "Indeed, although you may be unaware of it, only Satan could send you to me in the form of my husband seeking embrace. This is not the work of virtue and morality which would come from on high."

Very confused, he didn't say anymore, but looked at me as if he would like to know more. Beginning a conversation about Jesus, I told him all about the redemption as he listened. When I had finished, he touched my hand in a show of deeply contemplative gratitude, and disintegrated slowly into space.

Perhaps some 'lost' souls are flying around the cosmos unconsciously serving Satan because they don't know the Lord and have not developed proper discernment to distinguish between virtue and vice. Because of this, they become easy prey to the designs of the dark one in doing his deeds, being completely unaware of what they have actually agreed to do.

****

My soul was honored to observe the last days of St. Paul; his life, death and a small part of what seemed to be his journey into heaven . . . and a resurrection. Beginning my journey this eve, I was allowed to inhabit the body of St. Paul in a way which permitted me to experience the history of this man as if I were living it myself. Inhabiting the body of another disciple of Jesus in a similar fashion, my husband, Andy, was with me. St. Paul was speaking quite verbosely regarding the resurrection of Christ, condemning the actions of His executioners with extreme flame and fury. A plot was being hatched behind St. Paul's back to poison him to death, but St. Paul seemed to have a foreknowledge of their affairs. Telling those gathered that he, too, would die and be resurrected; he was speaking of the resurrection of the spirit.

Following St. Paul after his death, somebody had poisoned both him and his disciple (whom Andy was traveling through) on the day of his death. Following their spirits beyond death, we came upon an interesting gateway which seemed to be a borderland into heaven. As the two had died they reawakened on a beach. Next to the beach, was a huge wall of water bearing onto the sands at least one thousand feet high. Filled with oceanic life, this wavy mirage was a self-contained body, as though it wasn't really water, but perhaps an energy field waving to and fro like an ocean. Knowing he would be transported to heaven as soon as he stepped in, St. Paul did not step. Rather, his soul was resurrected automatically into the spheres, as was the soul of the other disciple.

Andy and I reappeared in the physical world, sitting naked upon each other's lap. A sign of purity, it was now the 20th century.

Because there was a great deal more to this experience which is totally inexplicable, I have left it unsaid.

Flown around the world to witness a marvel of the present age, Pope John Paul II stood atop every mountain and high point of the world waving to the people. Holy eminence a sight to behold, I flew above him in the realm of the blue-green ethers as my soul was somehow receiving of the sacred embers which came from his hands to the people of the world.
****

After several months of chronic pain and various infections, I found myself in a ballpark wearing the robe of a monk. Head pounding with a migraine, my neck was sore, and I was coming down with another high fever. Andy was sitting on the bleachers a few feet in front of me, while I was standing in the wings trying not to make my discomfort obvious. One of the ballplayers left the field, coming directly towards me. "You poor thing," he said, "always trying to smile, even though the pain never goes away." Emanating great compassion, my soul was immediately transported to a very glorious place.

Amongst the celestial heavens, stars cascaded around the metaphysical convent as a very old woman came towards me wearing a nun's habit. Blue-green skies shimmering, her long gray hair and deep blue eyes held compassion in this magnificent cathedral which claimed the stars as its walls and the cosmos as its altar.

Coming towards me, she reached out her hand to mine as I eagerly grasped it. Tears filled my eyes. "Why are you crying?" she asked very sweetly. Not knowing quite what to say, my embarrassment eluded the fact that I was just ecstatically happy to remember her. "I'm home," I said quietly, accepting the momentary reunion as a gift in reward for perseverance.
****

In the darkness of the night, her image appeared before my soul. Ten feet high and framed in gold, the Blessed Virgin Mary wore a sky blue robe over the inlaid white one below. Stars appeared all about her garments, and cherubim were singing and playing musical instruments, mostly harps and trumpets. Below her was an emblem which read, 'Our Lady of the Rosary.'

Unable to remove my ecstatic and fixed gaze from her beauty, she withdrew with this simple message of the importance of this magnificent Catholic prayer. Thunderstruck, I breathed for the first time since her appearance, and drifted back to sleep.

****

Called into service, my soul entered the sub-conscious dreaming of a rock musician. Having no idea who he was, I was immediately made aware that his music was inspired by Satan and it carried a mesmerizing quality which lured unsuspecting crowds of people into his web. Angered that I was being called in to interfere with his loyal and devout ward, Satan appeared to thwart my attempts at saving his soul.

Throwing my soul around the room, he actually lifted my body up off of the bed as he prepared to throw me against the wall. Before he could, I called to Jesus for help and was delivered from this brutal attack before it could reach fruition.

Amidst the sub-conscious dreaming, I followed the rock musician through many epochs of his life. Observing the demonic content of his soul, I noticed that he was given to demonic rages, sometimes going so far as to allow his eyes to roll back into his head. When he performed for crowds, he appeared as a very normal, attractive man, mesmerizing many young people into the lure of the dark side unconsciously.

Following him, I continually prayed to Jesus to free this tormented soul from bondage. Speaking to him, I spoke to him of Christ's love for him. After several hours, I noticed that his soul had begun wrestling with the demons within him. Shouting loudly towards him, I told him that he must *fight* Satan and force him out.

Fighting continued for quite some time and I was unsure who was to win this battle, but once it was over, it was complete. Hurled outside and raging, the demons were screeching as his body became calm, serene and peaceful. Guiding him gently, he spoke the words indicating his acceptance of Jesus into his life, thanking me for giving them.

As a crowd awaited his next show, he quietly explained the changes which had taken place within him and his conversion to Christ. Immediately, three quarters of the crowd just left because his mesmerizing quality was no longer present. Despite this, he remained calm and accepting. Knowing that discarding the demon and embracing the truth would require sacrifice, he was now willing to make it.

****

Dragging me through the mud of my past sins, a demon had tried to bring me to despair. Mother superior appeared with a priest, expunging the demon. Retaining focus of past sins disallows forward movement.

Accompanying me to my home, the priest performed a mass in my living room, consecrating the Eucharist and placing it in a tabernacle upon the altar, making complete the transformation of our home into a monastery.

****

Ominous in its import, the celestial sphere was overrun by beautiful music which made it more difficult to concentrate. Floating in heavenly spheres, we were surrounded by the stars. Though a barrier clearly existed around us, the walls of the space were invisible. The celestial vision of the heavens was so earth-shatteringly stunning; it was excruciatingly painful knowing that I could not stay here forever.

Inside of our heads, an instructor showed us what appeared to be a cyclone of energy, which looked like a small tornado whirling within our brain at great speed. Pointing into deep space and guiding our eyes back down to the Earth below, the instructor now allowed us to watch as incredible laser beams of light appeared, originating from heaven and continuing all throughout the vast expanse of space to the Earth below. Amazingly, we were told that these were the lines of the Holy Spirit flowing from heaven to Earth!

Placed into a sitting and meditative position, we were directed to lean back our upper body in an attempt to have these cyclones within our heads meet with the line of the Holy Spirit. The alignment had to be just perfect for the intended effect to occur and this was very difficult, but we were told that when that alignment hit synchronicity, we would be swept away immediately. As they said this, they had snapped their fingers to indicate the quickness of the alteration.

Trying many times before I could make this link, it didn't come easily. Finally hitting the alignment perfectly, my soul was instantly transported to another location.

No bliss can ever hope to attain that which was now my own. Riding on the back of a gigantic being, approximately forty feet tall, I was leaning upon his neck and shoulders looking directly into his face which happened to be larger than my spiritual body. Small in comparison to him, I was like a little mouse sitting upon a person's shoulder.

Looking into his eyes, I felt a serene wisdom which surpassed everything. Blank and tan, his eyes were the color of his skin while we were traveling the Earth, uniquely fashioned to bring focus for his specific mission for the Lord. Falling gently below his ears, his somewhat curly and flowing hair was of a blondish-brown color. But as we shot off into space, his features took on a violet and white color, reflecting the colors of the galactic heavens.

Before I had a chance to realize what had happened to me, I'd entered into the power of this individual, feeling an incredible thrust of heavenly propulsion. In some ways, it was as though I were riding on the back of a rocket . . . as St. Michael the Archangel was taking me for a ride.

Patrolling the Earth looking for loose demons, I noticed that he was going after those which were not specifically attached to souls. Those demons which were already inside of people were left alone for this particular journey, as those who were lucidly looking for prey were immediately annihilated. St. Michael literally snapped these demons up in his two forefingers, pinching their neck and tossing them aside, as they fell back to the pit.

Along the way St. Michael found several dogs that were possessed by demons and had become extremely violent. Pinching the neck with one fell sweep of his two fingers, the demons were extricated and annulled. No words exist for the tremendous immensity of the energy pulse which I was honored to behold while riding upon his back. Circling the Earth several times, I was in a total state of ecstasy.

During our ride, we came upon several people who were misusing eternal power received unlawfully; souls in positions of worldly power who had used non-eternal means to achieve their ends. Snapping his fingers, several of these people simply dropped dead in their tracks.

Finally, St. Michael was done patrolling the Earth for now and conveyed to me that he had a secret to tell me and it was something very important for me to know about myself. Motioning that he was going to make an 'etheric' phone call to someone on Earth who also needed to know, he allowed me to eavesdrop on the conversation. Sending an eternal impetus through the ether, the soul of the person answered the call of the spirit asking who might be on the line. "St. Michael," he said, "You know, the Archangel." Not believing him, he hung up. St. Michael looked at me with a calm disappointment, conveying nothing more regarding the secret. Stunned that somebody had hung up on St. Michael, I was sad for this soul who had just denied an eternal option given to him on the ground.

In my estimation, as many as nine out of ten eternal options are refused, perhaps more. I've known souls to deny two or more eternal options with soul-mates because they are too dense to recognize them (the same applying to their life work). Ego's get in the way most of the time. Most of us wish to believe we are fine the way we are, and thus, we don't wish to make the changes in ourselves which all eternal options require. Because of this, the Lord's intentions are blocked in mortal realms, and the whims of the dark side win again.

Without any warning, my soul was swiftly hurled upon the light beam of the Holy Spirit returned to my body below.
****

In a desert like oasis, something amazing and spectacular emerged. Standing upon the edge of a beautiful sand dune, a large gathering of heavenly hosts appeared before my eyes. Appearing in human form, their bodies were composed of white light. Heading the most sacred ensemble was Jesus Christ; at his side St. Michael the Archangel. Standing humbly behind them, the Blessed Virgin Mary stood before a gathering of a literal torrent of saints. Angels surrounded the holy ensemble, as they all stared at me with intensity. No words or thoughts were emitted as they stood amongst the desert sage and tumbleweeds.

Because this experience seemed so conscious, I became confused and began to look for a camera in my purse. 'With the level of brightness these hosts are emitting,' I thought, 'they will most assuredly show up on film.' Walking towards my Lord Jesus and St. Michael, I snapped a picture of them as they instantly vanished along with the entire host.
****

Walking along a deserted valley road, I looked up towards a large orb in the sky.

Huge, it was about eight times the size of the Earth's moon and lit up the entire atmosphere. Broad daylight, this orb was clearly visible at midday upon the backdrop of a light blue sky. Wonder and brilliance filled my soul, as I wandered closer, first walking, and then beginning to run towards it. "I should go there!" I thought.
****

Given to return to a haunted mansion which I frequented regularly for years, I'd gone there to loose many of the lost souls who had been trapped there by their own delusional thinking. Located in an 18th century setting, this group of mansions was ornate and lush. A ballroom with them had always been the most densely populated place upon the property. In fact, it was so filled with lost and dark spirits, that I was really quite terrified of it for quite some time. Each time I returned to retrieve souls, I felt intimidated by the sheer number of lost souls and dark spirits confined to these walls.

Over the years, I've gone through this mansion so many times I couldn't possibly count them. Processing some of the energies with each visit, I had never really noticed much of a change. Despite this, I met and talked with many souls who were not yet ready to leave, but might be in the near future. Giving them information on how to extricate themselves, my business would be accomplished and I would go.

Stunned by what I saw upon entering this familiar haunted place, I immediately noticed that there was a huge decline in the haunted energies within the house. What used to feel like perhaps several hundred lost souls and dark spirits, had diminished to perhaps a handful. Terror did not even strike me as it had done so many times in the past.

Many times over the years, I'd questioned the true and deeper meaning of this mansion, and wondered if it represented my own karmic issues in some sense. That theory was put to rest as an angel appeared and whispered into my ear. "This place has nothing to do with you," she said, "I come to proclaim the deliverance of the captives! The Lord wishes for you to see the fruits of your many labors." A place which had literally been teeming with darkness was now almost completely liberated! My work had not been in vain. Unworthy and quite honored to see how the Lord had deigned to use me, I thanked the angel for allowing me to understand this enigma. On my knees, I was in tears thanking my God.

As I did so, she faded from my view, and I disappeared to the remaining wards of this haunted place, reappearing in a darkened building filled with Christian worshippers.

Waiting in a darkened hallway, two men were carrying a large silver pot. Asking them what they were doing, they said, "This pot is filled with the life-giving water which comes down from heaven and never ends." Begging them to pour this water over my own wretched soul, I fell to the ground as the Holy Spirit filled me with an intrinsic roar.
****

Praying on my knees in the astral state, a huge torrent of energy swept me off of my feet and into the cosmos. St. Michael came this time as a huge shadowy figure, almost like a thundercloud, but in the definite form of a man. Appearing as he does in popular statues, he wore a shortened metallic skirting adorned with body armor, as his huge wings protruded explosively from his back. Sometimes he appears as a shadowy bolt of energy, and sometimes he comes in pure living color. Magnificent size not diminished; there was something unusual about this visit. Just as huge, a female stood beside St. Michael. Flowing straight brown hair caressed her shoulders, and she wore a glimmering white robe down to her feet. Energetically, she was just as powerful as St. Michael and left me in ominous awe as I understood that she was a member of his league of angels.

Placing me upon his shoulder as he'd done in the past, St. Michael was very stern with me this evening. Wishing to discuss my visions with a particular individual who was supposed to be well-versed in spiritual direction, St. Michael and I were flying all over the world at a speed indescribable as he showed me an image of this person in the heavens. "Do not discuss this with him," St. Michael said in an energetically powerful way, "you listen to *me*!" Conveying that this person would give me false guidance regarding the mystical realms, St. Michael allowed me to see that he could jeopardize my divine mission.

Swooping down towards a building below, I saw a demon who was trying to interfere with this eternal directive. St. Michael flew by, and the demon was struck dead. (I was unsure if this striking dead was a literal rendering, or if they were struck dead in energy, annihilated in their ability to render destructive force towards the work of the Lord.) As quickly as he had swept me up, St. Michael returned me to my place of prayer on the floor of my bedroom and was gone.
****

Continuing the influx of eternal energies which had been heralded by St. Michael, my body began in an ordinary vibrational state and was separated from form. Intensive energies began to overtake my body, as an invisible angel beside me took hold of my soul and thrust me towards heaven. Soaring past the Earth into the universal spheres, I rode an eternal wave conducted by the angel below.

As my soul gathered celestial energy, it was immediately thrust downwards to the Earth below, but as I emptied myself of these sonic pulsations, I was again thrust into the heavens to repeat this process. Continuing into the night, with each ascent into the heavens, came a descent back to Earth to bring the energies down. While soaring towards the heavens, I instinctually shouted, "Lord Jesus Christ, Son of God, Have Mercy on Me, a Sinner."

Remembering the importance of discerning the spirits, I turned to the angelic guardian. "In the Name of the Lord Jesus Christ," I asked, "I demand that you reveal your identity to me." Appearing as a very beautiful creature of brilliance, I finished, "Are you here to serve the light?" Swept in a thunderous energy as he spoke, he replied, "Yes."

Although I knew that he was male, he had no features like hair or eyes that were visible. Wearing no apparent clothing, he seemed to be anatomically sexless, although his essence was very clearly that of a man. Lighted and iridescent, brilliance shone outwards from his very distinctive form. This was no nebulous creature, his form was well-defined, although clearly made of light and in a splendid array of colors; pale violet, blue and white. Upon the backdrop of the stars and the heavens, this magnificent angel shone with a splendor which can only be termed stunning.

Confident in his identity, I shouted to the heavens. "Lord Jesus Christ, shall we take a journey with these eternal energies across the mountain pass, and distribute them to all who must be energized?" Shooting like lightning towards the pass, the spirit world had made my soul aware of a pocket of darkness which needed seeding in the light.

But as I came to the edge of the location in question, there was an energetic barrier clearly present which had been placed there by Satan to mark his territory. Reinforced by souls on the ground unaware of their alliance with the ogre, I shouted, "Lord Jesus Christ, Son of God . . . Archangel Michael, Destroyer of Demons, allow us to pass through this demonic gateway." St. Michael's thunderous presence became abundantly clear as we were allowed to pass through. Coming upon the people in this area, some of them had been filled with green sludge.

As there was no more I could do, St. Michael simply said, "NO!" as he quickly changed my direction. Able to bring the light in, we were unable to seed it as of yet. This eternal program was de-energized by mortals on the ground. Free will is a powerful thing.

Passing through the demonic boundary, St. Michael left me with the angel who'd come before, as we continued the process of bringing heavenly fruits into the Earthly mortal realm. Flying through the heavens together this time, a bold thought entered my mind and I conveyed it to my compatriot. "Perchance," I thought meekly, "I could go to the throne room of God?" Offering no reaction to my bold request, the angel thought, "Don't ask me, ask God." Gathering my boldness to make my grand proclamation, I shouted to the heavens, "Lord Jesus Christ, Son of God, may I come to the throne room of heaven?!" Shooting immediately through the universal beauty of space, I was given to see many tremendously awesome things.

As we'd traveled a great distance in a very short amount of time, I saw ahead a very brilliant city of light. Our souls were edging closer to this magnificent place, and on the periphery of this city of light you could see light trails leading from the outskirts of this heavenly mirage to within its sacred walls. Coming close enough to see details, I noticed that there were children playing who had distinctively human features, but yet, were surrounded by auras which made it clear that they were not physical beings. Light beings were walking down a side road near the children, as well as, other adults who looked more like the children, with physical features but distinctive auras. Happiness, serenity and bliss emanated from the city, and I felt honored to view it from such a close proximity.

As I expected, however, the Lord did not deem me suitable or worthy to go to the place I'd requested. Instead, because of my boldness which the Lord had apparently enjoyed, He'd allowed me to come to this periphery of what appeared to be heaven, and he gave leave to my angelic host to take me on a most spectacular journey through the galactic heavens.

A celestial tour ensued wherein I gave witness to visually and energetically stunning solar systems, galaxies, stars, planets, orbs, black holes, nebulae, etc. Entranced by this panorama, I shouted a sigh of thanks to the Lord of hosts, whose presence was with me, inside me, around me, and one with me as I soared through this newfound, magnificent world . . . this world was Galactica.

CHAPTER THREE

Entering unaware of what lay before me, the production was in full force. A group of actors had been preparing for a grand production about the life of an Irish psychic from long ago. Many of the women were arrayed in various veiled outfits, while others were dressed as belly-dancers. Immediately, I was approached by the producer of this grand gala, who grabbed me excitedly, exclaiming that he had saved the title role for me! Not quite sure what was happening, he shoved a picture in my face of the psychic he wished me to portray. Although the man was clearly not evil or dark, I noticed a wild hairdo and that a great dramaticism had been played out within his life. Unfortunately, this dramaticism had leaked into the portrayal of his psychic gifts, as well.

Looking up at this anxious man who assumed I'd be honored to partake of this role, I quietly said, "I'm so sorry to disappoint you, but I don't feel that I can play this part." Looking confused, he waited for me to explain. "I have a very deep and innate feeling that St. Patrick would have whipped this guy's bootie," I said.

St. Patrick, the Catholic Patron Saint of Ireland, had been taken by the Irish as a slave while a young boy, but as he worked in isolation tending to the sheep, he began to undergo grand spiritual changes which were noticed by many. As a result, he became known as the holy youth, because of the virtuous life he lived.

Many had become aware of his mystical experiences which were leading him ever closer to his Lord, Jesus Christ. Beginning to have visions, he was led by them to escape back to his native England. Despite this escape, shortly after he returned from Ireland, he had a vision which told him that he would someday go back to convert the Irish to Christianity, and that someday he'd be the Bishop of Ireland.

Years passed by in a monastery before this opportunity came, but when it did, he jumped on the chance to fulfill the vision of his youth. All these years, he had practiced great austerity, penance, obedience and virtue and had led a very holy life. When he returned to Ireland, the Druids were the primary religious body in the country, and among other things, they practiced human sacrifice, divination, prophecy and the use of magical or mystical powers.

Miracles of amazing stature are reported in regards to St. Patrick, who overturned the rule of the Druids in a very short time. Among the legends, it is said that St. Patrick became immaterial when his former slave owner tried to kill him with a sword, and the sword passed right through his body. The Druid High Priests attempted to poison him, and he was unaffected. When the Druids challenged him to a trial by fire, which was their ultimate test of whose God was supreme; they demanded that he send one of his followers because they believed that St. Patrick was practicing some form of high magic. St. Patrick's follower came out unscathed, wearing the mantle of Patrick upon his shoulders. The Druid and his belongings never came out.

Although suffering a great deal from many persecutions, some from his own church, he never wavered in his great faith and commitment to God. Despite the fact that he was Bishop, he never ceased participating in the difficult daily chores which he could have easily given to others, like building shelters, feeding livestock, or gathering water or food.

Standing before me confused and lost, the man who was to run this production was completely clueless. He didn't know the difference between a saint and a psychic! So I began to convey to him some of the elements of importance. "A psychic," I shared, "is someone who has received a spiritual gift. That is all. Being psychic does not denote that someone is leading a virtuous or holy life, because the gift itself is not related to any merit on their part. We cannot even be sure with such cases wherein the spiritual gift is coming, as it could be coming from either side, God or Satan. 'You may judge them by their fruits,' as Jesus said. Manifesting in a life ever deepening in virtue and holiness, and in the lives of those they aid with their gift, a similar response, another fruit would be modesty and humility in their appearance, as opposed to, excessive displays of vanity to make them stand apart. They would not be guiding people to riches, sex or fame, but rather to simplicity, purity and selflessness."

"A saint may display many spiritual gifts, but they are not a saint because of these spiritual gifts. Living a life of heroic virtue is what defines a saint, although it may also be said that it is likely that such saints receive so many spiritual gifts because they use them for the sanctification of souls. The Lord Jesus said in the parable of the talents that He would give more talents to those who used the first talent He had given to them faithfully. A great energetic chasm exists between saints and psychics, which cannot be understood through mere words. I can't for the life of me understand why there are those who seem to perceive that having a spiritual gift, in and of itself, denotes holiness. It doesn't denote evil, either; but it is a talent, a gift, which can be used for good or ill."

Having made my point as best as I could for the moment, I shook the man's hand and thanked him for his kindness in offering me the part. "I'm gonna stick with the saints." I said, as I disappeared.
****

Beyond the barrier which lay in front of me was a place which filled me with fear. The Lord called it 'the bowery,' and His internal voice directed me to invoke the protection of the Blessed Virgin Mary before entering by saying one 'Hail Mary.' As I did, I became invisible, in the sense that I was protected from danger, although the people in this place were able to see me.

Coming into the bowery, I was to see what was perhaps the poorest and most violent, criminal infested and dangerous part of the city. Former tall buildings lay in ruins before me, partly torn down with windows and doors missing in most places. Rotting on the inside, the buildings were infiltrated by an unusually gross mold.

Passed out or high on drugs, most of the people who lived in this place were just mere shells of the beautiful creation the Lord had intended them to be. Their surroundings could easily be called 'Hell on Earth' without any fear of exaggeration.

Bodies broken down from drug and alcohol abuse, hunger, poverty and insanity, the people reached out to me asking me to tell their story so that those who had forgotten about them might try to help. But amidst this horrible display of degradation, I felt totally helpless, and I didn't know what to do.

Speaking in my ear, the voice of Jesus Christ whispered, "Pancreas of Flowers, pancreas of flowers, pancreas of flowers . . ." Repeating this many times, over and over, my spirit began ascending.

Filling me with understanding, I had an internal visual already in place. Bizarre as it may sound, the pancreas produces insulin in the body. Without insulin, the body is ravaged and slowly destroyed by diabetes. Many diabetics eventually have limbs removed, piece by piece, because of the ravages of the disease, and it is impossible to number all of the body systems which are slowly destroyed; the eyes, heart, kidneys, limbs, etc.

Similarly, the people in the bowery were ravaged by hunger, illness and drug abuse, but their poverty was as beautiful as a garden of flowers to Our Lord. As He spoke the words in my ears, I could feel His tremendous and unending love for these poor, forgotten people.

My soul returned to my home.

****

Joining a group of souls praying the rosary, we were being led into a chapel by a group of older ladies. Beautiful and ornate, the church was filled with paintings and images of angels which were surrounding Jesus Christ and His Mother Mary and was appropriately called, 'Our Lady of the Angels.' Stone pillars framed the entrance to this wondrous abode.

Inside the chapel, I looked intently at pictures and mementos of a great bishop, as I suddenly noticed his spirit standing in front of me. Peacefully, the bishop had a simple message to impart to me. "If you are praising the Lord with other Catholics," he said, "feel free to go ahead and pray the rosary together, but if there are Protestants in the group, it is not necessary to convert them. Focus on your mutual love for Jesus and praise Him in a way which is comfortable for both." As our group had been praying the Rosary, we immediately changed our prayers as a group of Protestant souls arrived, joining together in a mutual expression of love and unity for God. He disappeared.

After a short period of time, there were several hundred souls praising the Lord in a unity of spirit, irregardless of their dogmatic or doctrinal differences.

In an interesting dichotomy, my soul was led a fortnight later to another Christian church. Inside the building, a woman's spirit was wandering around the vestibule seeking ways to 'bewitch' the holy tabernacle. Within my soul, I was given immediately to know that this woman, who had once followed a path towards God, had strayed by following witchcraft, and thus, partaking in a pact with the devil.

Another older woman was sitting quietly at a desk when a sudden and odiferous presence made itself known to her. Before she had a moment to ascertain what was happening, she fell to the floor having a full-blown heart attack. Quickly, several more angelic hosts arrived to tend to this poor woman's needs as I was summoned to follow the witch throughout the church and abort any satanic missions she would attempt. Entering into the church library, the witch was trying to place a bewitched book upon the shelves. Grabbing it from her, she then fled to the nursery wherein she attempted to place bewitched baby blankets. Continually going in and out of demonic control, this woman's spirit was almost completely possessed. She would seem normal one moment, and then her face would contort horribly as the demons inside of her would regain control.

Beginning to perform an exorcism, I noticed that her possession was not yet complete, and that she was not totally convinced of her decision to serve the ogre. Becoming disoriented, going back and forth from herself to demonic entities, I told her that I sensed great confusion on her part. "You are divided!" I shouted, "Satan does not want a servant who is divided!" Pausing a moment, the Holy Spirit came upon me and impressed me with a message for this poor lost soul. "Jesus wants *you*. Yes, Jesus does." Matter of fact and very calm, her face contorted for a moment to that of Satan, before he left her body for good and my task was complete.

Waking to the presence of a small being laying next to me on the bed, I first believed it to be that of my second eldest daughter, Mary. Coming over to hug her, I quickly noticed that it was an imp. Chastising the foul creature, I ordered it to leave my home under the authority of Jesus Christ as it scurried off into the night.
****

Hovering amongst the clear blue sky above ancient Egypt, the Dalai Lama appeared to give me instruction. "You need to look for the invisible upon that which is visible," he quietly stated. As my eyes were directly looking upon the side of an ancient pyramid, an image began to slowly appear from invisibility. Upon one side of the rock face was a large eye, just as I'd seen during my journey through the mysteries. "Come," the Dalai Lama replied, "I will take you somewhere where I can show you how to do this." In an instant, he had taken me to a huge wilderness wherein I became sub-conscious for the remainder of the journey.

On a subsequent night, a very saintly nun appeared to me saying, "You need to sit still and meditate on the life of Our Lord; His passion and death."
****

Appearing to me as a human, the commander of this unearthly vessel was a man with a powerful presence. Taking me through a series of epochs in the life of our planet, I was horrified to witness century after century of brutality, hardship and war. Exploring the ages of tyranny in our world, he took me through time to witness world wars, national wars, guerilla operations, and multitudes of prisoner of war and refugee camps all over the world throughout every possible time zone.

As we had crossed through the relevant time periods, he showed me a total of three anti-popes, men who wore the garb of the Bishop of Rome and to the naked eye appeared to be holy men. But the extra-terrestrial commander allowed me to witness their energies which were dark and foul.

All throughout our journey, as I witnessed the sad and desperate state of affairs of a humanity which had clearly been lost throughout many epochs of time, there was a tiny strand of humanity which remained and had been recaptured by various saints and holy people throughout the aeons. As I was given to see this miraculous happening, a sad and desolate melody played repetitively in the heavens around me lamenting the status of mankind. "Earthly remnants of love, Earthly remnants of love, Earthly remnants of love . . ." It went on into the night, filling my soul with a great dismay over the little love which remained active in our world, and a determination to do all that the Lord would deign to allow me, to restore that which had been lost.

Among similar lines, my spirit was then led to witness an enigma of all that had been shown to me. Before me stood a unique looking demon, who apparently was involved in much warring in our world. Clearly he was not limited to global catastrophe, because I was shown that he worked on individual souls to wreak havoc among families and/or communities, as well.

Manifesting as a very large man with large muscles like a body builder, he wore jet black pants while his chest remained bare. Upon his chest were a myriad of depressions which bore no particular form, but reminded me of the states within our country and their various shapes. Eight of them penetrated his chest, each representing a particular aspect of the vice of rage. Each represented one of the eight aspects of rage which could be ignited in this demon who was also surrounded by a very huge force of jet black energy. Every word which proceeded out of the mouth of this creature came at you like a torrent of rage, surrounded by a black vortexing cloud of endless demise.

In battling this horrendous creature, I found that de-energizing him was no easy task. Approaching him with the opposite virtue of the particular rage manifestation he would present, you had to simultaneously push upon the matching depression in his chest. Difficult to do, containing his rampant energies was very hard. Presenting quite a challenge to those of us upon this Earth, it was no wonder that the Earthly remnants of love were squandering for fertility and life. Each and every soul capable of being fertile for the growth of love must do so in order to energize a force large enough to counter this creature who has dominated the history of the Earth.

****

A horde of demons approached in the black and red cloud of dust which came in their wake. Hundreds of them appeared to me as a legion of dark reptilian creatures with bat wings coming towards me. The demons swarmed like vermin in the inner part of the cloud, and the outer part of the cloud was jet black with no boundary. As they came near and surrounded my soul with their stench, I could see and feel them all around me, but their attack felt like it was coming from the inside of my body. Clearly visible outside, they surrounded my body in vociferous smoke and odorous hues. Writhing, they came in waves of red as I felt internal symptoms from their assault.

Intrigued by this fact, I'd never experienced something quite like this. Although demonic attacks do affect you physically, what I'd experienced in the past were attacks which clearly delineated their way from the outside in. Although these demons were very clearly outside of me, their attack was coming from within, although they hadn't actually even touched my soul.

Standing before me in the form of a black tunnel filled with swarms of satanic hosts, I knew that I had to fight my way through them in order to prevail. Pushing with all my strength and might, I shouted out for the assistance of Jesus and St. Michael to help me wage war and break free from this demonic stronghold which wished to overcome me this night, and as I did, I began moving ever slowly through their ranks, pushing them aside. Screaming for help, I also shouted out physically, for my husband shook me awake, releasing me from the grip of the demons for this night.

After this battle had been waged, it very quickly became known to me why the demons had sent such a stronghold to stop and de-energize me the previous night. Attempting to de-energize my spirit because the Lord intended to use me in a planned effort to redeem a very lost soul, Satan wanted to keep it. Thus, I was targeted.

Arriving in an old hospital, I had no idea what had led me here until I heard some of the staff speaking of a haunting which had been occurring on the pediatric floor. Deciding to go investigate, I was very shocked at what I found. A young boy of about nine years old was haunting this floor and was *very clearly completely demonic*. As soon as he saw me, he came after me like a torrent of lightning. Appearing as a mixture of white and gray matter which had formed in the manner of his former body, the demon's medium-length white hair stood on end as if held by electricity. Coming towards me, this little child had the appearance of a madman.

Remaining calm, I grabbed a hold of his arm and began reciting over and over again the 'Hail Mary.' Sending him into a tizzy, he was now feeling dazed and confused enough that I was able to corner him and take a firmer hold of his soul. "Lord Jesus Christ, Son of God, have mercy on this lost soul." Repeatedly, my cries shot through the ether into the heavens, and as I did this, his soul began to be de-energized as demonic power left him. When it was finished, he became limp and powerless.

Knowing my job was finished, I handed him over to the angelic hosts awaiting the return of his soul. All were happy and joyous, for we all knew that Satan had put up a huge battle for this little one, because it gives him the greatest pleasure of all to steal the soul of an 'innocent;' innocent in the sense of his age, but not in any other regard. Although it was somewhat shocking to realize that even a small child can be completely demonic and aligned with darkness, it was very clear that they *can* and *do* choose such things, and it was important for me to know.
****

If only the human language could encompass what I've seen this night! My soul was taken over the threshold of death to witness many beautiful and rapturous things, almost none of which I have been allowed to retain in memory.

While enjoying the freedom of spirit, however, I asked Jesus, "Would it be possible for me to see something very holy? It doesn't matter to me what it might be, just as long as it's very holy."

Soaring towards space, approaching what appeared to be a 19th century schoolroom, it was steadily afloat amongst the stars as if it had been given immortal status. Landing inside, the schoolhouse was filled with happy children playing. Sitting down quietly, I was unsure of what to expect.

Before I was to be made aware of the purpose of this flight, a very attractive *appearing* man approached, attempting to entice me sexually. Apparently, he didn't want me to see this grand holy thing, and had come to detract my attention on something foul instead. Annoyed, I grabbed his hand and threw it towards him, away from myself. Holding a firm grasp, I shouted, "In the name of Our Lord Jesus Christ, I command you to leave!" At this command, he turned into a disgustingly grotesque gull demon, angry and writhing. Repeating my command, he lifted his grip, and at the third command, he thankfully disappeared.

Having passed through the throes of temptation, I looked again at the room which lay before me. An old man appeared in the room as an almost ghostly figure. Like an apparition, his human form was all in white. Wearing the coveralls of a man from the 19th century, he was almost completely bald. Many children were sitting down at their desks now which were neatly gathered at the sides of the room. Approaching the older man, I asked him politely if he knew where I might be. "Why, you are in the schoolhouse of St. Elizabeth Ann Seton," he said as he bid me to lie down on the floor.

Following his directive, he told me that the Lord was aware of my desire to know what it was like to die, and that he was going to allow me to experience it in part. Surprised by this revelation, he continued, "I'm going to allow you to experience a death somewhat like Mr. Seton," he said, referring to the saint's husband who had passed away after a short illness (This was prophetic in nature, although I didn't know it.). "Mr. Seton actually passed while his body was being ritually prepared for burial," the old man said, indicating that he was actually in a coma when he'd been pronounced dead.

As his words became an echo from another world, I began to see and feel my soul entering into a lightly blue-green misty place wherein I was slowly beginning to feel the closure of breath. Frightening me a little bit, I shouted to the old man, "I don't want to *really* die, you know!" As I said this, the state was immediately lifted and the old man had disappeared.

Annoyed at myself for making this comment which had indicated my fear of undergoing this experience, I knew I had to find the old man in order to try again. As I began running into a back room, I saw him behind a counter. "There you are," I said, "I'm sorry I messed things up, could we try again?" Without saying a word, I was immediately transfixed back into the state I'd been before.

Interestingly, there was a transition between life and death which was different than what I'd experienced in the astral state. Deathly aware of each system of my body shutting down, most primarily breath and heartbeat, I was still a bit afraid. As the body systems slowed to a stop, I felt a sense of concern over the difficulty one might encounter in adjusting to this different state of existence, sans body functions. Everything vibrated around me, as if I'd become aware of the molecular structure of ether and all spirit life.

Within a few moments, the old man slowly bid my soul return. In his hands, was a large chart. Showing me a graph of what he had done, there were several categories of experience involved in the bringing on of death categorized in the numbers one through six. Six, he explained, would indicate irreversible death, and he had taken me to a level four. "If someone had seen your body while this was going on," he said, "it's not likely they would have noticed these changes in your body. But if they looked closely, they would've noticed the respiration and heartbeat were significantly close to stopping." Interested in this chart, I shared with him how I'd experienced a small panic when my breathing and heart rate slowed. Nodding, he indicated that this was not uncommon, although this transition in true death took only a few moments. As a result, many souls didn't even notice it as they were dying because they'd passed through it so quickly.

As is *quite* usual, he began smiling as his spirit began to waver in and out of my view.
****

As my spirit was led through an inexplicable experience, I found myself in the service of two souls who had been born as males upon the Earth. Their destiny was to guide a group of about two hundred people to perform a very important work for God. Now that the two men had achieved adulthood, it was necessary for them to be united upon the Earth in order to energize this further task. Throughout the night, I wandered back and forth between these souls energizing lighted links which were being provided as a homing beacon to them.

Awaiting me to finish, a spectacular angelic guardian patiently hovered in the stars. Arrayed in magnificent light which shone outwards from her soul for several yards, this very old woman was a spiritual guardian to the two hundred remaining souls who would eventually be linked with the original two men. In order to bring this union about, the Lord bestowed upon my soul some very unusual spiritual gifts which I would be wont to describe and simply cannot. Somehow, through these gifts, I was able to take each of these two souls on a vast journey through a deep wilderness along the light trails of the energies which had been previously set up. After uniting the men in spirit, we followed a myriad of other trails set up by the angelic guardian which eventually led them to the two hundred remaining souls they were meant to guide in a work for the Lord. Making it possible to link all 202 souls, my inexplicable gift united them in purpose each requiring a myriad of light trails in order to energize fruition. Quietly smiling, the magnificent heavenly host met us, and the inexplicable spiritual gifts which had been given me were immediately energized.

Handing the two men over to her, an indescribably beautiful geometric form of brilliant light ignited lines from her to them, and then throughout the multitude. As soon as this specific purpose was completed, the inexplicable spiritual gifts were taken from me as the purpose for their manifestation had been fulfilled. At this moment, I was swiftly removed from the scene.

Now alit in the wonder of heaven, my soul looked upon a tremendous pathway which seemed to go on into infinity. Nearing ever closer, I noticed that this pathway began down below upon the Earth in the location of my current home. Flitting ever upwards towards the skies, it wavered and meandered, continuing up into the starry realms and the galactic mists beyond my current conception. In the distance, though well beyond view, my soul heard from the mouth of a heavenly host. "This path continues all the way to heaven." As I neared closely enough to vision the purpose of this mystic trail, I suddenly noticed that it was comprised of books.

Leading me to a particular position upon the trail high above the cloudy sky and permeating the galactic havens, I knew it to be resonant of my current status upon the path. Before me were beautiful books covered in exquisite artwork depicting the life of our Lord Jesus Christ, but the pathway was composed of the ancient sacred texts and writings of the prophets, mystics, saints and sages of all world religions; the various meanderings left to us in print by those among us who have moved onward to another higher reality. In the writings of the ancient sacred texts, we were given the opportunity to share the journey of those who had passed beyond the Earthly gates, and thus, be so honored as to receive of the wisdom of their flight. If only other souls knew the tremendous gift of these vital etchings left behind by the prophets, mystics, saints and sages, perhaps they would seek them out.

Looking heavenward at the continuing path of knowledge laid out for me to traverse and the books before me arrayed in beatific artistry of the image of Jesus Christ, I knew that He was the center of my journey, and as my eyes pierced forward, upwards toward the celestial city, my heart instinctually knew and felt the biblical words: "I am the Way, the Truth, and the Life. No one comes to the Father but by Me."
****

Having come into the room while I was sleeping, the demon lurked as my spirit sat up in bed beginning to separate from my body. Turning to Andy, he was sleeping and sub-conscious. Shouting at him, I said, "Andy, look!" Pointing in the direction of the ten-foot high, brown, reptilian looking demon with strange wing-like protrusions coming from behind his ears, I said, "Don't you see it?! Help me!" Andy was simply unconscious, and unable to respond.

While I'd been asking for help, the demon had taken a live electrical wire and placed it in my hands. Stuck to the chord, I was getting electrocuted and I struggled to release myself. But as soon as I detached from the chord, the demon reached for me and literally threw me across the room. Looking towards Andy, whose spirit was sitting up in bed in a sub-conscious astral state, I said, "Do you believe me now?!" Andy had no problem in recognizing the presence of demons; he'd had many encounters of his own. But he had no idea how violent these demons truly behaved towards me, although I spoke to him about such things, because it was not within his experience to be tormented at this level. As many people may believe things they haven't seen, their depth of understanding radically deepens once the experience becomes their own.

Nodding that he did believe me now, I noticed that his eyes were glassy, indicating that he was sub-consciously astral. Before I could surmise that I was on my own, the demon whipped up a huge wind of satanic energies which began blowing me all over the room. After this unpleasant encounter, he tried to force a very extravagant ring upon my finger.

Shoving it back in his face, I noticed that it was made with the most exquisite of emeralds, diamonds and other jewels of the Earth. But what horrified and stunned me, was that the ring was covered in blood.

Immediately, my soul knew without any tinge of doubt that the blood on this ring had come from aborted babies. An angelic host appeared above me for protection, funneling knowledge towards me regarding this particularly horrendous ring which the demon had tried to force upon me. A symbol of wealth, position and prestige, the extravagant ring was covered in blood, the symbol of the children who have died on the altar of the previous vices. Beyond the obvious profiteers of abortion, those medical practitioners who make their living performing abortions, there was a more discreet form of profiteering which cost these children their lives.

Because so many abortions had been performed for economic reasons - financial, educational status or position - many had sacrificed their children for whatever goals they had hoped to achieve as a result of terminating an ill-timed pregnancy. Some of these people had sacrificed the children in order to attain position or wealth which may not have been available to them if they'd kept their child. (Obviously, there are many reasons that women choose abortion and this is not meant as a blanket statement to cover them all, nor is it meant as a judgment upon them. Many women who have abortions experience severe regret, and their suffering as a result is immeasurable. But the healing from such things begins with recognition of the lies which begot it in the first place; our culture of death which states that children are a burden rather than a blessing, and that we may pick and choose such events in our lives as we please, even if we must destroy life to do so. This same world view is what fuels the ideas of Euthanasia, when a person no longer remains 'productive.')

In such cases, abortion has become a sin of greed, and the future 'success' of such individuals has been bought with blood. Looking to the angel, she sent a stroke of lightning towards this grotesque figure who was assaulting me. As it hit him, he and his gratuitous adornment of blood had disappeared.

Shaken, I reached towards the angel, who calmly took my hand and led me back into my body. Directing me to go to a church and sit before the Eucharistic Tabernacle, she said, "The Blessed Sacrament expels certain demons."

Along with this I was given to look upon a particular demon of deviant sexuality who *sometimes* inhabits those of a homosexual nature. But it was made equally clear that this demon does *not* possess *all* those who have the tendency, and that many souls who display homosexual tendencies are perfectly within the bounds of that which God wants them to be.
****

Staying the night in a motel, I was visited by about ten wandering spirits who wanted to speak to me. Coming into my room in the astral state, they said, "We're doing our 'Purgatory' by wandering the Earth as lost souls for a prescribed time period."

Unable to help themselves or others in any meaningful way, they were not allowed to share with me the sins for which they were paying. Agitated, they were in a state of definitive unrest.

"What can I do to help you?" I asked, as they began to fade and disappear, unable to ask for such help from me this night. Offering many prayers for these souls, I became much more cognizant of the need for patience in my daily life, and the opportunities for helping myself and others as I walk through this world.

As they disappeared, a book fell from the heavens onto my lap. Its title read, 'The Praxis of Suffering,' a prophecy of that which was coming (about my undiagnosed illness). Intrigued, I didn't know what the word 'praxis' meant, so I looked it up and found it to be a 'discipline.'

****

Hearing a summon from the Master, I immediately followed this beckon to see where it might lead. Traveling towards the stars, I found myself ascending a large mountain. Halfway to the top, I came upon a messenger who had come on behalf of the Lord, carrying a large binder full of instructions. "The Master is in need of you," he said, as he directed my attention to continue towards the summit of this snow-capped mountain.

Going with him, he took me to a large spiritual community which resided at the crest of this beatific peak. Marble temples had been erected in this magnificently sunny and bright realm, and I understood that the sky was lit with the light of God.

A gathering had assembled of about fifty people as I was led to take a seat next to a woman of whom I did not immediately recognize. Being the only newcomer, the others were natives to this place. Instructing the group from the front of the assembly, a beautiful lady appeared with long, slightly wavy, light brown hair which flowed halfway down her back. Speaking of living in harmony with one another, they began singing a song about how they all worked together to take care of the needs of each individual, and how all that they had was to be used for the community. The next song was about the fire which came down from heaven through the angels, to seed eternity upon the Earth.

When they'd finished singing, the woman openly introduced me to the group as a newcomer. Saying nothing, I noticed that when she mentioned that I'd come directly from the Earth, the lady beside me was upset and began to protest that I'd been allowed to come here at all. In a confrontational manner, she asked, "How many training sessions have you been to?" As I'd been to none, I didn't immediately respond, but the woman at the head replied, "Well, this is a humble soul who has learned through self-seeking and humility." Quiet remained in the room, as I became red with embarrassment. Beckoning me to come forward, I began to walk towards her. "Besides," she said, "the Master has need of her." Feeling a rush of tremendous awe and honor, I felt unworthy of this grand statement. 'How could I, a lowly, wretched human, be of any help to my Lord?' I thought.

Approaching the front of the assembly to join us was a young girl of about thirteen years of age. Reaching her hand to mine, she said her name was 'Lisao.' In awe, I recognized her as being one of the guardian angels of my second eldest daughter, Mary.

Asking Lisao with whom she would like to partner, without hesitation, she asked for me as I knew that I was to be a mother to her in some way, I was adopting her.

"There is to be a marriage today," the lady again spoke, "those who are to be married, please approach." Sitting directly in front of her, I instinctively stood up and a lone, tall, red-haired, skinny man had approached, now standing alone and staring at me. Whispering into the lady's ears, she openly replied to him, "Don't worry, she's stood up. But she's confused and doesn't fully know what is to take place." Taking my hand, the lady placed his in mine as I stood there, confused. Looking towards this man, I replied, "I have three kids, and apparently now, four, as I have adopted Lisao." Very quick to agree to adopt all of my children as his own, he seemed perturbed at my lack of understanding.

Despite this, the ceremony continued as I quietly pondered in my mind what could possibly be happening. It was also clear that this person was living on the other side, and not physically present upon the Earth. (Although I didn't know it at the time, I was meeting somebody who might become more important to me in my after-life. But because there were medical problems which remained undiagnosed, I didn't realize the potential momentousness of this revelation. In a short time, my status would be revealed and their import would become clearer.)

Lisao, this young man and I had wandered off together as the gathering concluded. Looking upon the sky which did not bear a sun but was aflame from the light of God, I hesitated to leave, but knew that I must. Releasing this young man's hand, I looked into his eyes which mirrored back to me an intensive longing on his part for me to remember who he was, something I sadly could not give him at this time. Meekly, I bid them both good-bye, releasing his hand to soar down the mountain.

As I began to soar, my spirit found itself waiting in a mountain temple with marble beams jutting high into the sky. Awaiting me was a young woman who appeared to be of royal descent. Looking as though she might have come from India, her long black hair was pulled back into a casual braid. A very simple golden band was formed around her head, and she wore an exquisite and colorful Indian garment, which was shimmering with pinks, purples and blues. In her hands was a golden gilded book which she immediately handed to me. Inside was the text of 'The Mysteries of the Redemption,' along with the imprint of a publisher. "I have a message for you from the Master," she said, as she pointed to the name of the publisher. Flipping through the golden gilded book to a page in the back, she handed it to me to read. 'Let Jesus take care of everything,' it said.

Looking up at this royal young lady before me, she closed the golden book, placing it in my hands for me to keep. Quietly, she turned and walked away, as the spirit wind took her essence into a molecular cyclone which then spun upwards towards heaven.

****

CHAPTER FOUR

Arriving without my foreknowledge, a spaceship had hovered over my house and landed in my backyard. Sub-conscious astral reporters had come to see what was happening and were inquiring with me regarding the unusual compression they had noticed in and around my house which would indicate an area of extensive psychic travel. Explaining to them that this compression had come about so that I may travel to other realms, I asked them if they might be interested in learning the deeper knowledge contained within the mysteries of the redemption. Ascertaining quickly that their interest lay only in a nebulous, intellectualized perception of psychic phenomena, rather than a true spiritual thrust which would include deep moral and ethical considerations and lengthy self-examination, I escorted them away and turned to greet my extra-terrestrial visitors who had remained unseen by these sub-conscious travelers during their short visit.

****

Given entry into this man's life only days before he was to die, I was astounded to witness the level of suffering from which he was about to be freed. Debilitating and fatal, his condition was shown to me in a graphic display as I looked upon his soul. In the symbolic image given me, I noticed that his spinal column traveled upwards from his tailbone to his neck . . . and then it continued down his left arm all the way to his hand. Unable to ascertain his exact disease, I knew it to be related to a spinal deformity.

For only a moment, the Lord allowed me to experience the pain this poor man was undergoing as his final death watch had begun. Unable to describe such pain in words, I can only say that it was deafening.

Having been taken care of by his mother all of his life, he was a grown man in his early twenties. Able to see her, although she was completely unaware of my presence, my purpose this eve was to die *with* this young man and bring him over the divide, assuring that his journey was completed properly.

As soon as his mother left for work that morning, his soul and body became transfixed in an unusual way, as if he were seeing into two worlds. It was at this time that he first became aware of my presence. Immediately as our eyes met, there was a confounding joyous love that we shared, as if we had perhaps known each other from before.

Allowing me a singular gift, the Lord permitted me to see beyond his very visible physical deformity, and peer within to witness his absolutely spectacular soul. Breathtakingly beautiful, I was able to see his overlapping spirit as it began its preparations to leave. Although his deformity was really quite difficult to look at physically, his soul was magnificently beautiful.

Knowing this beauty had come about through the experience of such a difficult life, he'd been trapped in a body which was both unappealing and non-functional.

Quite a trial for this soul, his spirit radiated empowered masculinity and strength. Although some people think that such afflictions are brought about by the way people think, lack of faith or karmic retribution, it was evidently clear that this was not at all true in this person's case. Clearly enunciated by the Lord, the purpose of this incarnation was for this very masculine, virile and powerful soul . . . to experience abject powerlessness and being despised by his fellow man. Karmic aspects were not relevant. Wow, what an amazing thing this was to see.

When a soul requires a certain experience to affect spiritual elements within their character, they have the experience irregardless of karma or other such matters. Learning absolute humility from this experience, this humility was all the more striking because I was witnessing it, side by side, with the true power and magnitude of his soul. Magnified by the attainment of the necessary virtue of humility, this power was actually strengthened from the experience of total helplessness, abjection and having to be cared for by others in every way.

No words can express the intense love I felt for this soul, as we spent these few days in timelessness (one night astral time) laughing and discussing his current life and my own. Our time together was made more special because there were many people, gratefully not including his mother, who were anxious for him to leave. Many considered him a burden and wished for him to hurry up and die. This was so sad, I cannot even express it. So many people think that when a person is obviously deformed, handicapped, chronically or terminally ill, or mentally challenged, that they are not aware of how others feel about having to care for them. But in this case, he was definitively aware and deeply troubled by the burden his existence placed on others.

When souls are near death, while their spirit is going back and forth from the physical body to their soul, they are often quite lucid and aware during the times in which they enter into the awareness of their spirit. Our time of death is a very important time, and most of us would like to have the opportunity for proper good-byes, Lord willing. Most of us would like to leave this world in peace, knowing our loved ones are at peace with us. It's painful to leave knowing resentment remains because of the manner in which you left this world.

After spending several days in timelessness together with this wondrous being, the Lord, through a great and merciful act, allowed me to experience his death alongside him as if I were also leaving the world. Feeling every pain right alongside him, I felt every system shut down. Amazed at the incredible amount of pain this man had lived with, I was grateful to have this window into the severity of the suffering of others. Experiencing this generated a great deal of compassion within me towards the sick. Although I'd had my own share of suffering in this life due to my disease, this was a totally different kind of suffering. Deformity is a cross in itself, but his condition caused constant extreme pain in the head, spine, back, and arms. Although my own suffering could be severe, it was usually transient, appearing in cycles, giving me breaks between severe bouts of pain. Giving a chance for regeneration between them, this is distinctly different from being worn down continually by severe pain that never leaves.

Feeling the body systems shutting down as the process of death continued, I again noticed that the most difficult adjustment for me was the cessation of breath, although I felt all of the systems shut down. It was as if there were a psychic bond between the soul and the various parts of the body, because you could definitely ascertain such things as the liver, the intestines, the pancreas, kidneys, etc., all shutting down. During this experience, they seemed to occur one by one, beginning with the cessation of breath, and then the heartbeat, followed by the remaining bodily organs and systems.

Entering eternity, I was surprised that this man had crossed over with his disability intact. Before I had a moment to contemplate this any further, we immediately began flying.

Mountainous and serene, we stood amidst a large desert valley in the center of a cathedral of peaks. A large, rectangular, crystal, transparent enclosure was graciously encased before us in the sand. Approximately twenty feet long and ten feet wide, the energy from this enclosure immediately pulled his soul inside, as he now appeared to be lying down within the confines of the crystal. Restoration the purpose, I watched as a beautiful light lit the heavens, surrounding him and myself as he fell into a deep sleep within the enclosure.

Although I had a great desire to wait here so that I might be present upon his waking, the arrival of a disc-shaped flying ship seemed to direct my attentions elsewhere. Four men exited the spaceship, wearing the clothing of common men. Knowing them to be angelic hosts, I found their humanness astonishing. Swift to let me know that I must now return to my body, my protestations were of no avail, as they firmly directed a wave of their hands towards my spirit. Within less than a second, I was gone.
****

Alit by the sun, the clouds were glorious as I arrived without foreknowledge of how I'd made my journey to this abode. Two priests were calmly awaiting my arrival, wearing the robes which are normally worn for the performance of the Mass. Today, they wore the color green. Hovering in the heavens, the priests directed my gaze in another direction wherein I immediately noticed a glorious stairway from the sky into deep space. Turning towards the steps, the priests handed me a stack of 8 X 11 cardboard markers which were to serve in some manner in the journey of which I was about to undertake.

A ritual process followed, as I instinctually threw the cardboard markers up the steps, tossing them into the heavens. It was absolutely vital that a correct synchronization between these markers and the steps occur before I could continue on my way. Coming together in the heavens, the markers synchronized into the first ten steps, as an angel appeared. "You've missed a few steps," she said. Gathering up and looking at the ten markers more carefully, I noticed that several appeared to be stuck together, so I prepared them properly and again flung them towards the heavens directly at this heavenly stairway which led into deep space. Counting, I gathered that I had now acquired twenty-one steps. Very patiently, the angel conveyed, "You have still missed some steps as there are a total of fifty four." Again, I gathered up and looked at the markers, focusing more intently on the hidden meaning that they might, as I flung them again towards the heavens along this galactic stairway. Watching in awe, they magically formed into a grandiose series of fifty-four steps into the heavens, beckoning me to follow. Imprinting themselves upon each of the etheric steps, they had become deeply imbedded a beautiful heavenly image of which I was not yet allowed to see. All I knew was that they followed a sequence of events.

Standing on each side of me, the priests had approached as if to protect me from the thrust which was about to overtake us as we prepared to enter upon this pathway into deep space. As they took my hands, one on each side, the images upon the steps became clear to me and I shuddered at the import of their meaning. Upon each of the fifty four almost invisible, etheric steps, were very distinct images showing the sequence of the holy mass. Jesus Christ appeared in robes of red and white, taking the place of the priest in the performance of the Latin rite, as His sacred heart blazed forth a reddish light which glowed in heavenly proportions. Each of the stages presented, brought about an energetic thrust within the souls of those who were open to them as they attended the mass.

Without a word, my spirit was immediately swept up into galactic space, as my soul followed the fifty-four steps of the Holy Mass undergoing a voluminous transformation as I traveled at the speed of light towards the stars. A rushing torrent of influential energies filled me with a solemn knowledge of this holy rite, and transformed my spirit as I followed its pathway.

Before I had the time to ascertain the meaning of this torrential flood of energy, my spirit came to a sudden standstill. Inside a very solemn and holy cave which held reminiscences of the sacred tomb of Christ, we were hovering in deep space. Because I had been swept up in a whirlwind of white energies, my spirit could not ascertain the path I had taken to enter this tomb. But as I stood here, I felt the coming together of each step of the journey. Each unique and individual image of Christ performing the fifty-four stages of the Latin rite of the mass at the sacred altar had been thrust into my soul.

Standing before me in an epiphany of light, the priests were preparing to finish this sacred ritual by consecrating the Eucharistic host into the body and blood of Jesus the Christ. Before I could ascertain any more, I noticed a holy visitor who had come to join us for this final procession of our faith. Standing beside the priests, placing his holy hands upon their shoulders, Padre Pio looked up to peer deeply into my eyes. Stunned by his entrance, I didn't know what to do or say. But before I could think, the spirits of the priests became ablaze with sparkly blue lights, permeating throughout their spiritual forms and encompassing the robes they wore. All around them, the sparkly blue lights were aglow as they began to speak the sacred words of consecration, which held within them great power now translated into my soul in a lightning-storm of power.

Huge power came from within the priests manifesting as a magnificent and large beam of blue light coming from their hands, entering directly into the sacred host which immediately came alive, bursting with blue energy and light. For a moment, I remembered long ago when I had been taken through the rites of the crucifixion and had been shown images of Christ during his passion. Interestingly, his body had been surrounded by beautiful blue energies, very similar to those which had now overtaken the Eucharistic host. Overcome with holy energy, the entire tomb was filled with an electric silence, the most notable being that of Padre Pio. My mind took note of the appropriateness of his presence, in that as a bearer of the stigmata (the sacred wounds of Christ); he had journeyed through his life as a living crucifixion. In this holy tomb, we had just experienced Christ's resurrection . . . and the most amazing thing about it was that every single soul upon the Earth could experience this magnificent moment any day of the year by attending the holy mass.

A flash of light occurred as our spirits were immediately transported into deep space, hovering amidst the stars. Padre Pio's back was turned to me, as he sat silently in a very still and meditative position. Feeling compelled to talk with the priests who had completed the mass, I was wondering if they had seen the magnificent energy and power which had come from them during the consecration. Because I'd not seen astonishment coming from their faces as all of this had occurred, I'd considered that maybe they'd experienced it in the mundane, the manner in which it is physically experienced on Earth. But gazing upon the back of Padre Pio, I had an inherent feeling that he might consider such a discussion disrespectful in regards to the holy moment of which we had just been allowed to partake.

Keeping my amazement to myself, I sat quietly in respectful obeisance to the Lord, and gazed upon the back of the holy man who was to grace my presence for only a moment more. In a flash, my spirit disappeared, returning to my familiar Earthly abode.
****

Becoming conscious in this horrendous place, I looked upon the disgusting pterodactyl-like creature, of which I knew to be a demon, ravaging a human victim. Pecking with his long beak into his flesh, he was tearing him apart with his claws and eating him. Doing this under the cover of night, the cowardly creature only performed his hideous function in total darkness.

Satanic high priests were overseeing the torture of the wards of this realm, who had appeared in the form of normal human men. Surrounding them were a host of snakes and two-headed serpents filled with deadly venom. One of the high priests approached me as I had lurched forward in an attempt to run away from this disgusting abode. Throwing me over a glass balcony, I was cut in the hip severely as I fell to the ground. Not moving, I realized quickly that my torture was to simply be present in this hellish place watching the torture of others. If I stayed put, the satanic priests did not approach me, at least at first. Many bodies lay all over the floors, appearing as if dead and there was a rack of bodies hanging as if on a closet rod on one wall. Also appearing to be dead, I inherently knew that they were suicides, although they were not your ordinary type. Unusual as it seemed, these were souls who had committed suicide believing that it would be an honor to do so for some evil purpose. (Of course, these did not include those who had committed suicide in order to prevent a torturous death at the hands of an enemy, or to prevent the revelation of knowledge that would harm others during a war.) Speculating on their motives, I wondered if they were the souls of satanic worshippers who had given themselves in sacrifice, not an unusual practice among Satanists. Another very odd circumstance that I witnessed was that after the demons were finished torturing the humans, they burned them to the finest ash. Everything burned, including their bones.

Before I could ascertain a means of escape, the high priests approached me. "You're not saved," one said, "and you are a fool to believe that the Lord could forgive your sins. You are totally dark and destined for hell." Although this frightened me, I said nothing, contemplating that their motive was probably that of despair. When I wouldn't speak, one of the more prestigious high priests grabbed me angrily and took me to a second floor area where there were no other humans present.

Covered with snakes and two-headed serpents, they were slithering around in hideous fashion. Throwing me to the ground, he had come towards me holding one of the two-headed serpents with which he had hoped to assault me viciously. Before he could, however, the serpent fell dead to the ground, infuriating and enraging the demonic host to no end. Thrashing the dead creature all around him, he banged it on walls and doors, raging at its impotence. Within moments, before I had thought to call for assistance, my soul was liberated from this hell but taken to witness another fascinating phenomenon regarding these wards upon the Earth.

As I watched totally unnoticed, the Lord bid me to observe the goings-on as several of these same high priests appeared as ordinary men walking upon our planet. Nobody could see me and this made it possible for me to observe some very interesting facts. In my inmost soul, the Lord bade me to distinguish between the regular people walking around this ordinary street corner on the Earth and those who were Christians. As you might expect, nobody could distinguish the high priests from others within the crowd, and they were regarded as regular ordinary people.

Very developed in spiritual power, the high priests were accomplished in their dark thrust. As a stark contrast, most of the Christians were not developed in this manner at all because they lived by faith. Because of this, they noticed nothing unusual about the high priests and were unable to discern their evil states. However, despite this difference in regards to spiritual power and attainment, the Christians, completely unknowingly, *tortured* the high priests simply through the power of their faith in the Lord!

Completely oblivious to the impact they had on these evil souls, the Christians approached them, speaking as if they would to anybody else. Unbeknownst to them, however, the energy of their faith would rebound on these evil wards because of the presence of the Holy Spirit within them. Allowed to listen to the energetic interplay, I noticed that whenever one of these dark souls was near a Christian, he was, in a sense, 'bowled' over.

Expressing his rage hearing the voice of the Holy Spirit, one shouted, "Every time I get near one of those Christians, I have to hear THAT VOICE!" Holding his hands over his ears, he was cringing in pain. Unable to tolerate the power of faith, the demons were tortured without the need for effort or even notice on the part of the Christians. Holding mundane interactions with these people, discussing everyday things, their faith spoke *for them* in energy. Having no hold on the Christians, despite their advanced spiritual abilities which had been refined towards the darkness and the deep, the demons were whipped just by being in their presence. Wow! Perhaps this is one manner in which the Lord marks the souls of the faithful.

****

Melissa, my daughter, had an experience (March 1, 2001):

"You, Dad and I were riding down a snow-covered hill upon a large inflatable sled. Before we knew it, we had suddenly gone into deep water and all had been submerged. Somebody was pulling me above the water, and when I emerged from the depths, I shouted out for you and Dad. Dad was walking towards me . . . on the water . . . but you were nowhere to be found. Going underneath the water, I found your body and lifted it up above the water, but realized that you had died."

"Up in the distance, Dad and I were stunned, as we watched your spirit walking towards the sunset, which was of an unusual brilliance. An outline of a gate, perhaps the gates of heaven, was outlined in the sky and lit by the light of the sun. Beautiful music of angels singing could be heard coming from beyond heaven's gates in welcome. Wearing a robe of gleaming and pure white, you turned to us and waved good-bye. Asking me to watch out for my little brother and sister, you shouted, "I love you!" as I shouted it back. "You'll have to look out for yourself now, and learn to handle problems without my guidance." Dad was just looking towards the scene with shock, as if he couldn't believe that this had happened so quickly and unexpectedly."

This moment marked the time that I decided I must push my doctors to figure out what was wrong with me, and when they finally identified the anomalous illness, a shockwave would burst throughout our home.

****

Entering into a brazen swoon, my soul began to experience yet another death, crossing over into the worlds of the beyond to witness the souls of those who had just crossed. All of these souls had made choices which had led them to a variety of states after death. Although none of them were to be sent directly to heaven, none of these particular souls had chosen hell. Realizing this led all of these souls into a transcendental swoon, as they became aware of how wonderful it was that they had not chosen hell. Angelic hosts placed them in an almost hypnotic state wherein they spiritually and energetically understood the wonderful grandeur of this moment.

Another interesting thing occurred in that there were a variety of parallel existence's coming to fruition in this realm, and thus, we were witnessing various aspects of all of these souls experiencing multiple death points. Other aspects of the soul which had come from parallel realities were experiencing synchronistic death points. As the primary aspect of the soul experienced death, the other aspects began to reach a death point, one after the other.

As this happened, each aspect experienced an almost identical death, with very minuscule and minute changes for each portion of the personality. Watching this phenomenon with a particular soul, I spoke of it with an angelic host. "It's very interesting," I thought to him, "how these different parallels each replay some aspects slightly differently than the previous selves, and how this seems to throw many people off." Primary conscious elements of the soul would become confused by these different experiences all intertwining and intermeshing into one another. Expecting identical experiences, they became confused when each aspect of their personality did not align in the manner in which they had thought. Because of their connection and attachment to the primary aspect of their experience, which they had chosen to be aware of during life, and thus death; they had trouble integrating and recognizing these other aspects of their soul as truly parts of themselves.

Turning to observe a particular woman, she was expressing deep regrets about her lifetime, in that she had not considered the status of her soul before death. Although she was not in a bad place - these souls were definitely not in heaven, but rather, some type of in-between state like purgatory - she immediately recognized that she had not yet made it to heaven and this distressed her. Despite the fiery and scary descriptions some have made of various parts of purgatory, this particular in-between state was not like that at all. (But that does not mean that such places do not exist.) Rather, it was much more like an extension of Earth, very possibly a fourth-dimensional overlay of our world.

Because of their purgatorial status, none of these souls could fly, as their souls were too heavy with sin. As a result, I soared towards the air in a sweeping gesture, and showed them the beauty of spiritual flight so as to seed them that this possibility could be ahead for those who purified themselves properly.

Another very profound occurrence happened after all the parallel existences had gone through their transition and the souls were now, in a sense, reunited. Very subtle things began to happen all around this arena which would remind them of the Lord. Whether it was a flash of light or a holy book found lying around, the souls were beginning to leave behind their mundane existence and begin to think upon holy things. One of these books was a very thick text entitled, 'Final Exit.' (Absolutely **no** connection to the Earthly title of the same name.) Looking upon its contents, I found it to be a very detailed instruction regarding this particular experience of the afterlife, this particular purgative state.

Two large angelic hosts appeared in white robes adorned with large white wings, and were now quietly addressing the crowd of about twenty souls. Speaking of their 'causes' for being in such a purgative realm, they said, "The bond is of the Earth." Many didn't understand what this meant, but I inherently and immediately understood that the angels were referring to the bonds of sin which had led them to this place, which was apparently karmic and/or mortal in origin; an attachment to something worldly. Speaking again, they said, "Jesus planned for mankind to keep the commandments . . . but some just didn't." Very matter of fact about this truth, these souls understood immediately that they had indeed chosen not to keep the commandments.

Once they realized this and took responsibility, it was now time to move onto the next phases which would include purification from those sins and attachments to worldly things which had led them to this state after death. Time over, I'd seen what the Lord had bid, and my soul disappeared into the ether.

****

Although I was not yet aware of what really plagued my potential corpse, my mortality was beginning to seem very real to me. Coughing uncontrollably for several weeks before, I was also experiencing severe chest pain.

As the death knoll began, I began to leave my body, immediately noticing an older man and woman quickly approaching my spirit. Emotionally wrapped up in the bliss of separation, I could still feel the pain of my body, however, as they came nearer. "We have to do something," the woman said, "she's leaving her body." Immediately I knew that she was not concerned about me taking a little journey, but that I might be leaving my body in a more permanent way through death. Without any further adieu, the man came towards me with a needle containing adrenaline and another drug which began with an 'F' and had a very long name. Interrupting his approach, I said, "Wait a minute, I think I'm having a stroke. Don't give me anything that would make that worse." Looking at me hastily, he conveyed that he knew what he was doing, and without waiting a second longer, he plunged the needle into my arm. At that very second, my eyes popped open in the physical realm.

****

Traveling through the dream world, an unknown voice began speaking to me as if to give guidance. Although I no longer remember the guidance given me, I immediately became suspicious and asked, "Do you come here on behalf of the Lord?" "Hell, no!" she replied. Intrigued, I asked, "Well, why then are you coming to me with erroneous advice?" "To test your soul . . . for the Lord wishes for your canonization." "Huh?" I said. Never believe anything such lost souls may tell you, because even if they don't *intend* to deceive you, they are receiving their *influx* from below. "I'm not interested in your flattery, which I know is intended to incite me to the sin of vainglory," I said, "but I am quite interested in your soul." Instinctively, I knew this was a lost soul as opposed to a demonic spirit. "Why don't you quit wasting your time allowing influx from the lower world into your spirit, and begin to seek after our Lord Jesus Christ?" With sincere befuddlement, she replied, "I don't know?" "I can tell that you are simply lost, and your confusion reflects that state. But it is really quite simple to find your way." "How would I do that?" she asked. "Seek after Jesus Christ." "How?"

Our connection was becoming weakened by the energetic intrusion of two of my children who were apparently unhappy that I was still in bed. Turning to my smaller daughter who was the cause of the greater disturbance in energy, I told her, "Stop! Do you wish to be responsible for this lost soul?" Nodding no, her unconscious self understood.

Turning to the lost soul, I said, "Think on Jesus, call on Jesus, ask for His help . . . it is really quite simple." Waning in and out, I heard a very innocuous response. "Oh." Praying that she might find her way, I awoke.

****

Having traveled a long journey on a bus to this unusual spaceport, I was awaiting entry into a magnificent building which I was told contained within it many mansions of the Lord. Within its confines were literally hundreds of floors, each of which represented a whole different world, a whole different understanding. As we had entered into the space portal, I noticed I was wearing the brown robe of a monk as I began to embark upon this journey of the spirit.

Before arriving at this intriguing world, we had traveled through what appeared to be an inner city floating in space. Placed within the dirtiest and most squalid place among the city, this large, square and white building which had appeared was a place of ritual passage. In the midst of this dirty, ugly, agitated and worldly ghetto, I saw a tiny ray of hope; a statue of Jesus stood before a storefront. Hoping to find a church, I found a sign for a psychic reader instead. My momentary joy had been dashed.

Entering the mansion worlds, it was easy to become overwhelmed because of the many places represented within its confines. Surrendering to the flow of the soul, my spirit was taken to a dark classroom where I whiled away many hours, sitting in meaningless fashion as the teacher of this class did nothing. Once in a great while, she would teach us for a very short time, perhaps five minutes, about an aspect of writing, such as verbs. Finding this to be all too shallow, I was trying to be polite and respectful. Finally, however, I decided it was time for me to move on. In a rude gesture, I stood up and left the dark room.

Wandering outside of the classroom, I found myself meandering through many mansions of the world. Realizing quickly that I had done the right thing to leave the classroom, I realized that the classroom had been a very tiny aspect of this mansion world. Still lost, I was now confined to a series of floors which were scattered, aimless and agitated. Comparative to the mass retain found in any busy business district of a large city on Earth, my soul meandered. Inexplicably, these city streets seemed to be enclosed in a very wide, white hallway, much like that of a university. Along the corridors, were neon signs, fast food restaurants, various businesses and the like. Chaos, agitation, and commercialism filled these mansions, as I accepted that these mansion worlds, too, were incompatible to my soul.

Car salesmen were shouting in one corner of the building while fast food restaurants were trying to lure me into their gluttonous calling by offering me free food. As I was very hungry, I accepted an offering of a chicken sandwich made by one of these establishments, but before I could take more than one bite out of it, I was approached by two large men who begged me to allow them to have it because they were quite hungry. Noticing that they had identical sandwiches in their hands with which they were gorging themselves, I inherently knew that they didn't really need what they had asked me to give. But I thought about Jesus, and what He would wish for me to do. So I gave it to them, and as I did, it became an epiphany as a corridor appeared before my soul.

Walking forward, hundreds of people were wandering through the noise aimlessly, but I and three other souls walked into the confines of the corridor, swept up into the mechanism of its establishment.

Now walking down a very narrow stairwell, quite a crowd was trying to make its way down and we were all packed together. All around this stairwell were hundreds of pictures and statues of Jesus and Mary. An almost invisible and transparent hand placed a small 3" X 4" framed picture containing the image of the Blessed Virgin Mary in my hand. Swooning in delight, my sigh left me in a glorious manner. A voice came from the invisible hand. "Blessed are those who are born into the mansion of Jesus and Mary upon the Earth."

As I quietly exited the stairwell, an amazing phenomenon occurred. Although the stairwell was narrow and led downwards into what appeared to be a basement, the moment I touched the floor after descending the last step, my spirit was elevated high above this mansion world into a mansion of God which resided at the highest level of the building.

Feeling the Presence, I immediately knew that it was the mansion of Jesus and Mary, and as soon as my soul walked forth, I heard the voice of the angel again speak. "Those who enter here, their robes will become white." As these words were spoken, I watched with ultimate delight as my robes slowly transformed in a wavelike pattern from top to bottom, from brown to white.

Looking before me, everything began to appear as vapor as all those who had passed before me were unseen. Translated suddenly from this realm into the heavens, I momentarily witnessed the soul of those who bore the robes of white walking in heaven peacefully. A huge smile lit upon my face as I ran towards them . . . but I was not to stay at this time, and was returned to form.
****

Alit with warnings regarding the dangerous state of my health, angels shouted in my ears, "*Emergency, Emergency,*" as they showed me a picture of my heart. Something was deathly wrong. "You must accept that you are very sick, and do *absolutely* nothing!" Appearing as if I was pushing myself too hard, I agreed as the angels disappeared.

Finding out the next day that I was in severe heart failure due to a condition known as Peripartum Dilated Cardiomyopathy, my heart was enlarged, functioning poorly, thinned out, and suffering from a generally terminal heart muscle disease, which they believed had been caused by a rare complication of pregnancy. Preparing to be evaluated for heart transplant, I allowed the news to sink in.
****

Amidst an astral gathering of souls who were instructing me regarding death, I turned to notice my dear friend who'd passed away fifteen years before in a car accident. Smiling, he appeared at about my age, the age he would've been today (about 36), had he not died at the age of twenty one.

Calmly, I looked at my smiling friend and shyly asked, "If I am to cross over . . . you will meet me, won't you?" Nodding 'Yes,' the peaceful loving smile did not change upon his face.

CHAPTER FIVE

"End of October, the sleepy brown woods seem to nod down their heads to the winter. Yellows and the grays paint the sad skies today, and I wonder when you're coming home." (From the song by Dan Fogelberg, 'Old Tennessee') My Uncle who had passed two years ago led a crowd of my family's ancestors in song. Currently, it was May, and it appeared they were telling my time might be up in October, but it also felt possible that they were just confirming that I didn't have a great deal of time, maybe a few years. (At this juncture, 85% of people with my specific condition statistically died within five years, although the numbers could be 50-70% for those with Dilated Cardiomyopathy from other causes.)

Floating outside, my three children and husband were playing in the sunny day while I was still asleep inside, my soul traveling the spirit world. Looking towards the deep blue sky, I watched intently as a cross began forming out of the clouds. Distantly, I heard the sound of a Native American flute, and my soul became mesmerized by its melody.

Walking over to my husband, I asked him if he could hear the flutes, but he was unaware of my presence, much less of the presence of the mystical malaise surrounding me in the ether.

An amphitheater appeared with about 1,000 spectators. Singing beautifully about Jesus, an intense black woman appeared. Beautiful and mesmerizing, she sang about the Lord. A couple in the audience was holding a glass enclosure, reaching out their hands as a flame spontaneously lit up within it. Getting very excited, I immediately knew that this flame was the Presence of Our Lord Jesus Christ.

As the flame was also within their hands, they began to touch other people's hands, which immediately lit up with this flame also, until everyone in the audience was aflame with the Presence of Our Savior. Walking towards them, they bid me stay back as this was not yet something in which I could participate. Asking Andy again if he heard the beautiful singing or saw this amazing spectacle, he wasn't even aware that I was talking to him or that my spirit was present.

Disappearing, the native flutes began their mystical melody again in the distance as I reached my hands towards the heavens and shouted, "I'm coming to you, Lord!" Lifting me towards space at the speed of light, the Lord allowed my soul to take in the celestial energies, before returning to my body.
****

Meeting the deceased brother of a very good friend of mine, (not the one who died in the car accident and has visited me for years), he said, "Because you and my brother have been like family in this life, you and I will be like family to one another when you cross over. I wish to do this for him." Realizing that this was a response to a prayer, I'd worried that I wouldn't know anybody on the other side because I was so young and would be the first to die. "By the way," he finished, "tell my brother that I watch over his sons, I'm one of their guardian angels."

****

Awaking from sleep, I noticed the presence of a male angel standing next to my bed. My doorway had been altered into a magnificent ascending starry passage into heaven, and the room was alit with sparkly light. "What are you doing?" I asked. "We are preparing the energies here so that when you cross over it will be an easier transition." "But my doctor doesn't believe that I'm going to die anytime soon," I said, confused. Flippantly, he laughed, "Yeah, we know, but that's not your problem." Pausing a moment before leaving, he said one last thing. "Andy will have to either fight for you, or learn to live without you." Looking at the astounding ascending passage, I dropped back off into unconsciousness.

****

As something went wrong with my heart, I immediately saw the tunnel and the light. Understanding the implications, I shot through it thinking, 'Uh-oh,' but then shouted in excitement. "Can I go see Jesus?!" As I said this, I began traveling towards Him. "Yes, you can do this," a voice said, "but if you journey all the way to Jesus, you will be unable to return." Shouting, I said, "Oh, no, I can't leave. I need to be with my kids." Instantaneously soaring back towards my body, I heard the voice of Christ in my head. "I want you to go back and fight to be with your kids." Conveying that our family needed to learn to value each other more wholly; not by function, but by mere existence, learning to care for each other's true needs, rather than 'using' each other, He stopped the strange happening in my heart and returned me to form.

****

"Padre Pio has accepted you as a spiritual child," the voice said, as an invisible hand gave me a relic of the saint. Awaking at San Giovanni Rotondo, I meditated quietly in a room alone all night.

****

Approaching me in liturgical robes of the purest white, I recognized him as a priest who had spent his lifetime fighting for the rights of the unborn. Coming to embrace me, he conveyed, "I am joyous that you are willing to sacrifice your life, so that Mary and Jacob may live." Because my illness had come about due to pregnancy, he seemed to understand that when my time of death did come, that it would be a sacrifice. In the meantime, my daily life as someone who had become greatly disabled due to heart failure would also be an offering to the Lord.

Looking at my three children through a clear pane of glass, an old nun was carefully watching over them. "If you are to die," she conveyed, "they will be all right."

****

Although my soul bore no memory of the journey to reach this highest of places, I awoke to find myself conscious in the top floor of what was presented to me as the highest building on Earth. Looking down, I noticed that my soul was adorned in a robe of the whitest white with a deep red sash around my shoulder and waist side. Knowing immediately that these robes were energetically linked to the Sacred Heart of Jesus, my soul became radiant with the light of the beatific vision, as all the scars of my worldly life had been removed. Because of the Lupus, I sometimes had visible signs of disease on my body, but these were now gone.

Reveling in this newfound freedom of soul, I received a phone call from below from someone in my current life who was very much caught up in karmic circling. Speaking with urgency, I listened to her with calm and peace, but noticed that as I did, my face began to break out in a rash. Exhaustion began to overtake me, as I politely hung up the phone. Quickly realizing that I must stay off the phone which was linked to those remaining below, communicating on that level appeared to drag me back into the world of death. Because they were trapped in karmic malaise, they had needs which they wished for me to fulfill which caused this affect. Souls who called wishing me well or desiring to know my status did not cause this phenomenon.

As soon as I understood this mechanism, I was led to the door. Looking below, I noticed that this 'building' was a way-station floating above the clouds in the sky. Without further adieu, I became unconscious.
****

Waking up in the back seat of a car, two other people were being driven around a ghetto with me. Stopping in an especially scary location, the driver asked all of us to get out of the vehicle. One exited the car immediately, while the other stayed put.

Looking more closely at the driver, I suddenly recognized him as Padre Pio. Because of this, I made a quick decision. 'Padre Pio wouldn't leave me here in this dangerous part of town,' I thought, 'I think I'll take my chances and remain in the car.' Not moving from my position, the Padre began driving quietly without saying a word. "Those who truly love you," Padre Pio conveyed, "will not put you in harms way." Referring to those who wished for me to continue to provide things to them that I had done before becoming ill, it was very clear that if they truly loved me, they would encourage me to fight for my life, and be unconcerned about the things I could no longer do for others.

Surprisingly, I felt more pressure to perform once I got seriously ill, than I had before getting sick, and it appeared to be due to people's general judgment of everything I did or didn't do. Now under close scrutiny, everything was subject to a general appraisal of whether or not I was fighting hard enough, being sufficiently positive, or feeling sorry for myself.

Because it is one of the worst things that can happen to you, I found that most people generate little compassion and can be quite insensitive to such serious illness. Although they seem quite capable of feeling compassion for much smaller issues, things they can relate to, death can be a very humbling experience, because the world lets you know that it'd be fine with them if you should slip quietly off into the night, not bothering them with the difficulties encountered in disability, or the grief you may feel about your own demise.
****

Awakened to the sound of grand celebrations ensuing 'in the spirit' within the confines of my home, about two hundred dead people were there praising God and talking amongst themselves about many of the small things they had done during their lives to assist the Lord. Gathering around to show me what I had done for God, they showed me homes which had been steeped in dark energies which now appeared as family cathedrals. Speaking of my writing, they expressed the great depth of meaning I had shared through my words. Feeling unconditional acceptance from these people, they were not judging me for being sick and possibly dying, which was quite a relief. Many of them had suffered lingering deaths, and they fully understood the frustration of losing your physical capacities, and accepting the loss of your Earthly life.

Standing in front of the crowd who continually praised the Lord in a jubilant celebration, the Lord Jesus Christ began to materialize directly in front of me. Wearing the dark robes that you might see in some of the Last Supper paintings, he stood before a small table reminiscent of that event and said absolutely nothing. His hair was luminescent and His face shone with light. Behind Him a huge scene of the crucifixion began to appear as I inherently understood that I was undergoing my own personal crucifixion at this time. Part of the crucifixion is the emotional aspect which comes to a person who is dying. Many people can be insensitive, although I'm sure unintentionally, when someone is passing from this world.

There are two things a person who is leaving this world needs to know: 1) that their existence had meaning, to themselves and to others, and 2) that their death will not go unnoticed.

People who are dying, especially those who are unusually young or leaving children behind, need to know that others consider their death tragic, rather than insisting that they must see something good and wonderful in their demise. Rather than being helpful, telling a dying person all the 'positive' ways they can see their own demise is insulting and negates the seriousness of their loss. Invalidating the meaning behind the person's life, it forces them to feel that their existence really doesn't matter all that much to others, and it shoves the soul prematurely into the humbling realization that they, too, shall die, and the world will go on as if they'd never lived.

Allow me to give you a listing of things that are always said to terminal patients, which should be abandoned: 1) Everybody's going to die, I could die before you do. 2) Everybody has their problems, just get over it and move on. 3) If only you thought more 'positive,' had more 'faith,' engaged in proper 'conduct,' practiced the correct 'religion,' thought 'properly' or took this 'supplement,' you would be healed. 4) Just get up and force yourself to go on, stop being lazy. 5) You are feeling better, aren't you?

Telling a person that anybody could go at anytime is insensitive and invalid. A terminal patient is facing death at *this* moment, and unfortunately, because terminal patients rarely know exactly when their demise shall come, death becomes an inseparable part of their lives; because it could happen at any time, or it could be delayed for years.

Aside from this, terminal patients usually face physical disability during this time-frame, and the pain and limitation they experience almost constantly, remains a continual reminder that their body is slowly failing and death will eventually occur. Somebody who goes suddenly, usually does not know that it is coming for more than a few minutes, and they are usually not already disabled and in mourning over the life that they've lost to the illness.

Subsequently, many terminal patients have no choice but to ask for help from people who may resent their need. Ironically, this resentment sometimes builds as the patient fights to live . . . and does. Because many people unconsciously project onto the seriously ill patient that it would be more convenient to others if they would either hurry up and have a miraculous and complete recovery or . . . die; survival, at the expense of remaining sick or disabled, can be used against you. And it is common to feel this from family, caregivers *and* medical professionals, as a patient may feel guilty about requiring assistance from the very busy medical profession.

Comparable only to a doctor telling someone that they *may* statistically die in a car accident or of a terminal illness sometime before they turn ninety-five, such analogies should never be used with someone who faces imminent illness and death.

Judged as having brought this calamity upon themselves either by wrong thinking, insufficient faith, or incorrect religious beliefs, they may also be regarded as lazy by those who have never experienced an illness which slaps you right down on your butt, making it impossible to do the things you once did with ease.

In order to insure that you don't express the sometimes sad reality which occupies most days due to your illness, people will say, "You *are* feeling better, aren't you?" As if 'not feeling better' somehow indicates a failure on your part, this is also taken as a warning not to 'go there,' so the patient behaves and says, "Oh, of course." Despite the obvious reality that a terminal illness is so because it has no cure, it will continue as is or will progress until you die (unless you are one of the people who is honored to receive a miraculous intervention from the Lord). Allow me to make this clear; it doesn't improve, the patient remains sick and disabled according to their disease, and it is likely to get worse, rather than better.

Because most people haven't experienced illness which does not go away, they keep wondering why you won't just get better, and in order to quell the terror they have of their own mortality, they revert back to the incorrect thinking which got you into this mess in the first place. After all, if you do everything wrong and they do everything right, than they are safe from this ever happening to them. Right?

Talking about death is absolutely forbidden with most people, even those close to you, and doing so puts you at risk of being accused of not 'fighting the good fight,' not being 'positive,' and being 'morbid.' Although this begs the obvious question, wouldn't you have to be a total moron not to *even consider* your own death, if you have an 85% chance of meeting it within five years? Perchance, it should be considered that our death is the most significant spiritual event of our lives, and in the case of a terminal patient, it is imminent and impending. Wanting to know the prognosis, seeking statistics, or wishing to discuss what will happen to your body as the disease progresses, is also a no-no; although most terminal patients genuinely need this information in order to battle their disease and prepare for what is to come.

A person faced with terminal illness faces the difficult task of balancing fight and hope with preparation for death. Because it is deemed a probability, those who shirk speaking about death to their loved ones, simply ignore a true, meaningful need. Although the living may not be comfortable talking about death, the dying *need* to talk about it, just as a bride wishes to speak of her upcoming wedding, and a couple needs to speak of marriage. People need to talk about what they are going through, and the very best thing you can say to someone faced with a catastrophic moment in their lives (whether it be a terminal illness, or another catastrophic loss or event) is that it sucks! As opposed to being negative, this validates the pain and suffering involved, and the loss of something as great as a life. When validated, tragedy can be processed productively. Invalidated, it remains as a searing pain upon the soul.

The most difficult aspect of a terminal diagnosis is that a patient must prepare for life and death at the same time, having no idea when the moment shall come. Losing their future, their dreams, and the plan they had for their life, the terminal patient must also prepare to lose *every single person* in their life. As opposed to the one loss that will be suffered by those they leave behind, the dying patient loses all their loved ones in one fell swoop, in this lifetime and this world. Anticipating a future in both worlds, accepting the limitation of disability, you must prepare to continue a fruitful and rewarding existence while living in a precarious limbo.

It is in these moments that true epiphanies arise in most every soul, things which those of us not yet at this juncture could gain from, true knowledge behind the mystery of our existence . . . if we would but listen. (Many souls are very compassionate to those in their suffering, but I share with you not only my own experience, but the identical thoughts shared with me by several other terminally ill patients. Because many people don't know what to say to someone who faces a catastrophic situation, I thought it would be helpful for people to understand what is going through *their* mind, and the things that can be hurtful if said at this time. Hopefully, this gives a better perspective on that which is helpful to a person facing a life crisis, and makes it easier to avoid the unintentional invalidations which occur regularly amidst our society.)

Shouting to the crowd, I couldn't hide my elation at the presence of the Savior. Everybody was in jubilation, and they praised all the more loudly in His presence. Looking through my soul, Jesus filled me with unconditional acceptance and love. Feeling more at home away from home, He began to disappear before my eyes, as I began to sink into a great sadness in our separation. Refusing to allow this, the crowd quickly grabbed a hold of my shoulders, turning me to join them in their praise.
****

Awaiting my arrival on the runway, the dark blue plane appeared normal to the naked eye. As I boarded, however, it opened into a mystical euphoric scene. Crystalline glass enclosed us as brilliant colors of the kaleidoscope appeared randomly all about the walls and ceiling which were formed into a large dome overhead. Rather than flying,

we began to glide very slowly across a large, calm body of water. Up ahead on the opposite bank, I could see a thick mystical forest. "Where are we going? What is that land ahead of us?" I inquired to no reply.
****

Traveling to yet a borderland, I found myself inside a small Catholic monastery amidst a wooded forest land. A lone monk sang mystical chants, the words speaking of death and crossing over. In a few moments, a young Tibetan woman entered the room, as a voice announced her as an emissary of the Dalai Lama. Several other people entered the room and circled themselves around her, as she began telling them of the next phase of their lives in service to God. Speaking to them of specific tasks, she turned to me and quietly said, "You don't need to think about further service to God on Earth for you are going to die." Nodding in understanding, I was unusually detached from this information, silently acknowledging the message.
****

Swirling through the ether, my soul had landed upon a desert oasis within sight of the Assisi Mountains on Venus. My old friends, the five Assisi Marauders were at my side, teaching me about being a spiritual guardian to souls. In the center of a large table were five conical, triangular-shaped crystals which I immediately knew to represent each member of my family including myself. Moving them around, I began placing them in positions which seemed appropriate for my children's further destiny.

Andy's soul was present in the Assisi Marauder with whom he'd blended into one, as if they were the same soul. For a moment, I also recognized other elements and identities within the Marauder, including the man whom I'd 'married' on the mountain. Feeling within me that I would have the presence of Andy with me in the after-life, I realized that many aspects of his soul remained on the other side, of which this was just one. Encompassed in the Assisi Marauder, they were all present within this particular manifestation, yet individually available through him, as well. Remembering who he was, we embraced in a quiet hug, as the red-headed aspect seemed relieved that I now understood his purpose.

Quiet and somber, they differed at this moment from their usual highly energized quality as it seemed that they were honoring my grief. Waiting, they were very patient with the fact that I was confused and learning to detach from the world, knowing this would mean I would have no choice but to leave behind my three young children, my jewels. Feeling God's will in all that was happening to me, we were peaceful.

Although they never actually removed the crystal piece representing my soul from the table, I felt the energy present indicating that this was what they were waiting to do.

For now, we waited . . . .
****

Although I had never played the trumpet before, beautiful and celestial music came from the instrument which now adorned my lips. My instruments had been the flute, bassoon, guitar and piano, but never the trumpet. Looking around me, I realized that I was playing with a celestial band of some sort.

A very tall man with short brown feathered hair was conducting, and he wore royal navy-blue clothing which was designed in galactic fashion. Rims around the shoulders to indicate high rank, the clothing itself had the consistency of vinyl.

As the band stopped playing for a moment, I heard a complaint from the back of the room. Noticing the person who expressed concern, I recognized him. 'Has he died?' I thought. "What's she doing playing the trumpet?" he protested loudly, "she's only played the flute in the past, she will ruin our sound!" Surprised by this unwelcome response, I was quiet. Replying immediately, the conductor said, "I have given her a special gift," he said very calmly, as I took notice of how well I had been playing despite my total lack of experience. "She is here because I wish her to be here. She has accomplished many things on subtle levels of energy which qualifies her to be here."

Boldly, I turned to the conductor who appeared so majestic. "Who are you?" I asked. Pausing a moment, he looked directly into my eyes. "Gabriel," he said, "as in the Archangel . . . Gabriel." Dumbfounded, I stared at him but said nothing more as my soul was whisked into a school building.

On the walls were hundreds of signs, all reading, 'Don't lose Hope. Remain Positive.' Walking over to the registration desk, I was fearful of acknowledging my status because I thought I was too sick to be accepted. "All who come here are in catastrophic situations," the lady said, "I believe you are here because you are waiting on a heart transplant?"

Looking at her with horror, my medications had helped my heart to function better. Although I'd been evaluated for transplant, and those with my condition almost always eventually need one (or die first), I was considered 'stable,' for the moment. Another possible obstacle was Lupus, in that it is a systemic disease which could disqualify me from having one altogether.

Saying nothing, I turned to notice that several people had arrived, including the person who had been unkind. Coming to apologize they expressed their loyalty to Archangel Gabriel. Apparently, it was their duty to apologize for their insolence. Quietly nodding my acceptance of their apology, I was gone.

Awaking in astral form in my bedroom, my spirit walked over to a mirror and noticed that my body had swelled up as if in acute heart failure. Returning to bed, I awoke.

Although my body was not swelling in any unusual way, I'd had a lot of chest pain recently and knew this to be a warning about the vulnerability of my body, and the need for caution and care. This began the now continual process which would be my life from here on out, going back and forth from relative stability to severe illness to the doorway of death . . . and back. For the remainder of my life (unless I got a transplant someday), I would ride the gateway between worlds on a daily basis.
****

CHAPTER SIX

Bright orange Bengal tigers with piercing black stripes wandered this high mountain abode. An old friend, Chinaman, sat inside this small oriental retreat cabin with his wife and two adult children, a young man and woman. Chinaman had been a spiritual guardian of Andy's many years ago, during the time in which we had begun to purify our karmic programs. Neither of us had seen him in many years. Although I was feeling fearful of the presence of the tigers, Chinaman assured me there was no need to worry.

All was quiet outside, and he told me we were 3200 feet higher than the highest mountain on the Earth. Although we were in the midst of a grove of oriental houses, there was no sign of other people being actively present. Assuming this to be because we were all in retreat, I made no mention of it.

Chinaman had assured me that it was necessary that I pull back from friends and family upon the Earth. "Their own issues about death," he conveyed, "are taking too much energy from you, which you desperately need in your battle to remain with your children." Having so little energy left for others because of my illness, I had pulled back so the little I had could go to my children. In order to do this, I had to sacrifice the many hours given to family and friends for their problems. Making it clear, Chinaman nodded that this retreat was good. Having felt guilty doing this, his assurances were helpful.

Chinaman handed me my guitar and led me to begin strumming an old song I wrote long ago, 'To Retrieve a Golden Angel.' Lyrical pathways in the song speak of the light trail home to the 23rd dimension from where I had come, the realm of the golden angels. "Remember where you came from," Chinaman said, "and how to get back." Mystical winds surrounded me as wisps of memory filled me with his words. Assuring me of salvation, Chinaman gave peace to my tormented soul, which had become obsessed with its eternal destiny.

As I again momentarily felt the impulse of the 23rd dimension, the realm of the golden angels, I saw little Chinaman smile, his family behind him in supportive fashion.
****

Standing in a borderland, I watched the spirits of the 'dead' fly, going about their heavenly business. Wearing Earthly attire, many of them were dressed in business suits and casual wear, flying through the skies. A deep yellow hue patched the skies of this vista, and although it looked much like Earth, it held a vibrance and light which was absent in mortal spheres.
****

Arriving in a splendid array of light, the angels came to tell me that it was time for me to make my journey. The top of a huge mountain completely isolated from the rest of the world was my destination, a border-world.

Directing me to board an old western train, it waited silently at the side of a wild rushing river, white from the gales of the current. Walking quietly towards it, the angels disappeared.

Boarding the old train, my spirit was immediately made aware of the presence of one soul, a cowboy wearing the customary garb of the 1800's. Wearing an old worn cowboy hat and light brown western wear, I stared at him rudely before approaching. Looking outside the windows, the train stood no more than a few feet from the banks of wide and deep rushing river.

Engaging the cowboy in conversation, I asked, "Where and when does this train cross the river?" Knowing I could not reach the mountain top without crossing this great divide, I also recognized its impassibility by any other means than the train. "We can't cross the river at this time of year," he said, "we'll have to wait."

After fighting for months and making progress with medication, it was October 29 . . . the end of October. Could I have averted and received pardon for a potential time of death?

Turning the train around, he started me back towards my home in the foothills.

Standing amidst a large auditorium, I noticed that there were many ovular, metallic tubs filled with warm water. Souls of people who had crossed over from life into death were fully immersed in these tubs, as if in meditative baptism. Uncomfortable at the prospect of getting into one of these tubs, I couldn't get the idea of not being able to breathe out of my head. Although these souls had no need of breath while underneath the water, I turned to the man in charge. "Is the water too warm for a heart condition?" I asked. Allowing me to feel that the water was lukewarm, he asked me wait my turn.

Scheduled to go last, I watched the others immerse themselves. While meditating under the water, the souls of the people began to display and be surrounded by inexplicable aspects of the Trinity. Dumbfounded by the beauty of this transformative process, I remained unable to understand it.

Before I could enter into the waters, my soul was taken from this fascinating border-world.
****

Exiting an elevator, the doors opened and one of my deceased grandparents was waiting for me. Without saying a word, he led me towards a truck, planning to take me on a drive somewhere. Noticing a troubled look upon his face, it appeared that it was unclear at this juncture whether or not I was going to die, and he did not wish for me to die. Worried about his great-grandchildren, he continued his duty despite his displeasure at my fate.

As time would progress, I learned more about my condition, and how to remain more stable. Keeping myself away from the crisis of imminent death, I learned how to balance activity and rest, so that I wouldn't visit death's shores quite so frequently.
****

Had a very involved experience with many of my dead relatives where they didn't seem very happy with me. It seemed that they felt I had misjudged a family

member unfairly, and upon reflection, I felt very ashamed. Taking steps immediately to repair this damage, it was my hope that my relatives could forgive me at some point.
****

An elderly person had come to me in the astral state, his soul terrified and confused from the battle it now waged. Close to death for quite some time with a form of dementia, he was living in a netherworld because of the absence of his physical mind in his body. Suffering from an illness which can cause great lingering, he came to me in the spiritual world followed by a host of about 300 demons.

Upon his arrival, he said, "My soul has been condemned to hell, and I've made a deal with these demons. They've agreed to allow me to come to you for help on the condition that they be given the opportunity to have at you in an attempt to overcome and possess your soul."

Because there was an active war for his soul, he would go in and out of a demonically controlled state. During the brief episodes while he was not demonically controlled, I was pleading with this aspect of his soul for his own eternal salvation! Actually quite frightening, he was a big man and very intimidating while possessed.

Given leave to torment me, the 300 demons took my soul down a literal road of perdition. An intensive spiritual battle ensued along a highway ten or twenty miles long, wherein every aspect, nook and cranny of the roadway was permeated with lures, temptations, torments, and terrifying tricks. Led by the demons through a highway of temptations, after passing through literally tens of such things, my exhausted soul finally reached the end of the road. In front of me was a white line which had been painted across the road. Given to know that this line represented the final thrust of demonic interplay, as soon as I crossed, I could claim victory.

Unfortunately, inside this small space there was a multitude of demons filled with every vice, deadly sin and discharge. Looking upon the demons who stood next to me with disdain upon their faces, I smiled at them with gladness. Those who stood beside me had already lost the battles from which they had waged war for my soul. "I think I get it," I said, "I have to get through that final passage, cross over that line, and if I do that, I win, right?" Nodding with dismay and sadness at their loss, I shouted, "See ya." Flying past the final demonic entourage, it was over in seconds.

Returned to the home of the soul who had come for my aid, the prime demons had been forced to leave. A small band of demonic influences had been given leave to stay within him, however, and these demons raged within him occasionally as he sat on the couch. "I came to you," he said, "because you're the only one who cares." Because he came from a family with atheistic alliances, no one within it knew how to help him. Nodding, I acknowledged that I cared very much about his soul having been condemned to hell. Walking over to a chair, he sat down.

Demons began to rage within him, and I began using the name of Jesus in various forms of prayer to help to exorcise his soul. Nothing happened, so I continued without avail. For a moment, the part of his soul which desired salvation re-attained control and said, "The name of Jesus will not work with me." "Why not?" I asked.

"Because during my life, the name of Jesus was never on my lips." During his life, he'd been a good person who could care less about God. "Because His name was never on my lips during life, it will not work for me now." Referring to scripture, Christ had said that those who confess of Him before men, He shall also confess of them before His Father in the judgment. But those who confess Him not, He shall not confess of them before the Father. Presenting me with a new dilemma, I was quiet. "Oh, then we'll have to think of something else."

Watching and praying quietly, the holy spirit came over my soul and lifted me up to the center of the room as I began to very slowly and quietly, almost a whisper, recite the 'Our Father.' "Our Father . . . who art in heaven . . . hallowed be thy name . . ." As I did this, the demons quickly gave way of his soul, and he sat alone in the room with the knowledge that he had been saved from eternal damnation.

As my spirit began to be sucked back into my body, I awoke still reciting the prayer. As I returned, I shouted to him, "I will offer my sufferings for you for as long as you need. I will offer your continuing sufferings on Earth for your soul, since you are not physically capable of doing this for yourself. I will offer prayers for you, for as long as you need."

Leaving him, I knew that he had been saved from condemnation to hell, but that his soul was still in great need of assistance as it embarked upon his own unique purgatory, a state of undefined dementia. His soul would learn 'in the spirit,' that which he'd neglected to care about while still of the Earth. Wondering if much of his purgatory would be done on earth, as he suffered from this lingering, long-term illness which left him unaware of Earthly reality, I began to question whether the Lord was doing something similar with my own soul. Could my illness and possible death be an opportunity for purgation? Was this perhaps the purpose of my own illness? Was I in purgatory?

****

Looking up from my bed, I realized that I was now lying upon it underneath the stars. Grandpa appeared sitting at the foot of my bed in a small wooden chair, watching quietly. In the distance, we could see through the walls of the house as Andy and his family were looking for an outfit for me to wear for my funeral. Grandpa remained silent while I lay convalescing from my latest brush with death.

****

Surrounded with an aura of yellowish-white light, my old friend who'd died in a car accident had appeared. Although surrounded with such brightness, I'd remembered many experiences I'd had since his death which had indicated to me that his purification was incomplete. Demonic tendencies which he struggled with in life had been shown to me in his death.

Laying near-death, he said, "Don't worry, you can come with me." Shocking myself, I was surprised that my response did not shock him. Reaching his hand to me, I replied, "Please do not take offense, my dear friend, but when I do indeed cross over, it is my intention to go directly to Jesus. Did Jesus send you? Do you intend to take me straight to the realm where Jesus reigns?"

Lowering his hand, unsurprised by my discernment, he began to slowly disappear without saying another word.
****

As people prayed for me, I began to experience visions of roses. Singular roses, tapestries of roses, gardens of roses, and they all seemed to precede a recovery from a close brush with death. One night, Mother Teresa stood over my bed for several hours, waiting patiently for me, as if she had something for me to do.
****

Showing me the scene of a massacre, it clearly represented what had happened to our family since the diagnosis. As it was completely restored, I felt the presence of someone very holy.

Catapulted into the presence of Padre Pio, I couldn't see him, but *felt* him filling every corner of the room. Enveloping me in love and acceptance, he conveyed to me a certain peace about my condition, and that it was, indeed, God's will. "I implore you to be at peace regarding your illness. I, for one, am elated and joyful that you have been allowed to share in the sufferings of Christ, totally without merit on your part."

An angel came down from the sky with a gift for me which I *knew* to be from Jesus. Handing me a beautiful medal of Padre Pio, it slowly transformed into a Padre Pio rosary which was identical to the St. Francis rosary I currently owned. Feeling his presence around me, he conveyed, "You are following the way of the cross." As it was an honor to share in the sufferings of Christ, he was guiding me through his letters which contained much advice regarding suffering and the holy state with which we can be endowed when we come to such a juncture in our own lives.

Unexpectedly, a life-size statue of the Virgin Mary appeared in front of me in the image of 'Our Lady of Guadeloupe.' Having been painted rather sloppily, I thought how disrespectful this was of its benefactress. Around the eyes, the paint overlapped and bled into the cheeks and there were no clear lines in the paint job.

Having immediately bowed before the statue, I knew that Mary was present in the room. Within the distorted image, I felt the full presence, power and fullness of the Mother of God, despite these flaws. Mary wished for me to see that an imperfect body does not disguise a soul reaching for perfection. The suffering demonstrated on the image of the Blessed Mother, represented the spiritual transformation which we undergo . . . through the sufferings of this world.

Without warning another full-size statue appeared, this time in the image of 'Our Lady of Fatima.' Exquisite and painted to perfection, I again bowed, realizing that the true beauty of a soul is always realized by God, despite the horrific image which suffering may make upon our bodies at the time of its fruition.

Whole and complete, Mary's immensity filled me yet again, as I stayed on my knees in the power of her presence. "Your suffering comes about through the absolute will of God, and you are to be at peace. I am pleased with the manner in which you have endured your trial, and the Lord is pleased in that which you are learning." Love, peace, joy and calm came from the Creator, through the Blessed Mother and Padre Pio.

Giving thanks, I lowered my head in humility at her presence as they disappeared.

****

Coming to me in disguise, the evil spirit had approached me in hopes that I might pray for his soul who had died twenty years prior. Great pity emerged from my loins, as he had been killed in the process of committing a robbery/attempted murder at the age of nineteen by a man who had killed him in self-defense. Praying for him, I'd hoped that perhaps doing so might release him from purgatory and allow him to enter heaven. Going on the assumption that he had been a misguided youth who was paying for his torrid years in a hellish purgatorial existence intended to prepare him for heaven, I was deathly wrong.

A young boy, literally a toddler, had been having nightmares about a 'demon who had tried to take him away,' and I entered into his dream with the permission of the Lord to find out and hopefully take care of this problem. Turning out to face the grandchild of the man who had taken the life of this soul, I entered into the city.

Dealing with the city where this young man had once lurked, I ascertained that this soul had been damned and was now an evil spirit who had been given some type of permission to leave hell on the twentieth anniversary of his own death to roam the world and tempt souls. Rather than doing this, he had decided to make a claim on the 'third generation,' a grandchild of the man who had killed him in self-defense twenty years prior, referring to the biblical admonition that the sins of the father are visited upon the third and fourth generations. As this third generation was a baby boy . . . I was immediately enraged.

Marauding through the streets, this evil spirit was harming and attempting to kill everyone in his path. In this most horrific of cities, a young adolescent black boy had been influenced by this spirit and was beginning to follow evil. As his father prayed for his soul, he asked that he might be liberated and follow Christ, but it was too late. Losing his life in the act of committing evil inspired by the evil spirit, I quietly and unobtrusively began to pray with the father for his son's soul. Becoming aware that his son's soul was saved, the Lord Jesus was now calling me to take out the evil spirit who had violated eternal law. Crossing boundaries forbidden him in the freedom given him to tempt souls, he had not been given leave to murder and maim.

Everywhere this evil spirit had been; chaos, murder and death reigned. Catching up to him as he was driving away in a pick-up truck, he was sitting casually in the passenger side. Using the gift of the lightning which the Lord had given me years ago within my hands, I directed fifteen bolts directly into the area of his heart. Ironically, he had died from a gunshot wound to the heart. Receiving the discipline from heaven, the Holy Spirit filled me with words. Shouting, I revealed, "You have no quarrel or claim to this family, for you died lawfully. It is true that if this man had not killed you in self-defense, somebody else would've *had* to take you out. Most likely, this would've been a SWAT team during one of your many violent and criminal acts. The man who took your life holds no sin for your life, but in fact, is responsible for saving many other lives of which you would've taken. You have no claim to him or his descendants, and because you have violated the boundaries of your freedom to roam the world as an evil spirit and violated eternal laws in such a manner as to go after and attempt to harm children, the Lord has decreed that you will again be returned to the pit of hell, where you will be locked up and chained. You will be given no reign to harm the souls of the earth!"

With this, he fell as if dead from the lightning bolts which had taken him out this second time. A friend of his began shouting at me that his legs and ankles were swelling up, and there was great anger in his voice that I had ended their 'fun.' Ignoring them, I turned away . . . and he was never heard from again.
****

Amidst the spectral universe, my soul was led to several classrooms where I was given inexplicable knowledge regarding astronomy which lay beyond my comprehension. But as this class commenced, another spirit entered the room with the purpose of inflicting upon my soul some lurid sexual temptations. Because I was so mesmerized by the teaching, I didn't even notice that there was somebody at my side attempting to lure me into insidious behavior.

When it was that I finally realized the presence of this individual, but not his intent, I turned to him and kindly asked him to go away. Rather surprised that I didn't respond in any way, shape or form to this, the guardians appeared stunned.

As the man who behaved inappropriately disappeared, the guardians of the rite looked at me and said in a very quizzical manner, "You didn't fall for that temptation." "What temptation?" I replied.

Remaining stunned, it appeared that few souls passed through this rite. Walking towards a door which emitted much light, as they opened it, you could see nothing but an indescribably bright, white light which blared through our souls. Walking alone, I proceeded to enter this light, and then it was that I awoke.
****

My body had been placed in a white casket inlaid with gold and taken outside to the driveway. As my spirit waited inside, I spoke to Andy. "I think it's inappropriate for my casket to remain in the front yard. You'll never live this down with the neighbors if you don't quickly call somebody to pick it up." Timidly, he agreed, but mentioned he'd put it there because he didn't want the kids to see it.

Another night, my soul was taken to visit a decomposition doctor, who measured my body parts as they were now, so that they might be compared to a future time when I might be decomposing. In this way, they could monitor the process. During this experience, I was given to look in the mirror and take note of the fact that my hair was turning gray and squalid like that of a corpse, although this was not yet the case in real life. And much like a corpse, there was very little hair hanging onto what was remaining of my skull.
****

An angel of the Lord had been given charge to show me a woman who had been

given much in the way of religious training. Allowed to witness the true outcome of her life beside what could've been the status of her soul if she had made good use of the graces provided by God, the angel described her current manifestation as that of a 'meaningless bimbo,' while next to her stood the beautiful image of a woman looking towards heaven emitting a great degree of holiness. Exhibiting great disgust at what she had become despite the great workings of the Lord, the angel regarded her with sorrow.
****

In another realm, Andy had been convinced to accept this man's offer of trading our small home (not our current one) in a usual neighborhood, for his huge mansion set aside on a piece of land which was quite secluded and serene . . . at least in appearance.

My suspicions were very high, as it made no sense to me that this man would make this offer unless there was something wrong with the house - first suspicion being that of a haunting. Andy had been impressed by the four Steinway grand pianos, and a very large gym which contained a basketball court which he considered to be something wonderful for our son. Admittedly, I was impressed with the grandeur of the home and its privacy, but it was clear that something was amiss.

The individual rooms in this house, in particular the living room, were each larger than our entire current home as this was truly a mansion. Planning to go through the home, room by room, and fix it up according to our tastes, there was a great deal to be cleaned up as many things had been stored up and taken care of in somewhat shoddy manner.

Because of the suspicious nature of this interaction, I wasn't surprised that the man and his wife left the house in an abrupt manner, but their manner of leaving held interest to me. A beautiful and ornate horse-drawn carriage carried the two who were dressed almost as royalty, perhaps extreme upper class, of those who might have lived during the time of the Russian Revolution, early 1900's or so. As they departed, a crowd suddenly appeared all around the grounds bidding them adieu with gratefulness and joy. This was the first sign that we were not alone.

As I worked my way through the rooms, I'd begun in the very entry of the house and worked towards the other end. Being a true mansion, I'd accomplished the reordering and cleaning of the first three to four rooms, but still had at least thirty to go. These three or four rooms were immense, and the process began to make me aware that perhaps I didn't have the energy for such a huge task. Living in such a huge mansion might not be so desirable to me (and perhaps Andy, as well). As we'd just looked at the Steinway pianos in a storage room which was larger than most houses, and were peering in on the gym, something happened.

Looking around this large, ornate fitness area, I noticed that there were people hiding behind stashes of storage items and in the rafters. Because they noticed that I had seen them, many began to come out of their hiding places, approaching me. My middle child, Mary, was with me at this time, and one man approached with what appeared to be malicious intent. "Back off!" I said, holding my hand up in the sign of 'stop,' "In the name of Jesus Christ, leave her alone!" Obediently, he pulled himself back, lowered his head, and placed his hands before him in penitential manner. Within moments, I began to realize that these people were obliged to obey my every word, and did so with the very least of promptings.

My first inkling of their presence had been that they were servants, but this theory was quickly becoming evidently incorrect. Without warning, a gale wind assaulted Andy, Mary and I which began to bring us up towards the ceiling much like a gigantic ocean wave filling the room. At this moment, I turned to Andy and said, "This house is haunted, that's why they wanted to leave." Conclusions premature, the gale wind subsided and we were let to the ground, as I began to walk around the house suspiciously.

Noticing that it was now full of people in every room, this formerly empty house had become lit to the full with at least four to five hundred souls. In one room, I found about fifteen spirits who were clearly criminals. Without any resistance, I ordered them to turn themselves into their police immediately. Doing so, I noticed that their police were also spirit beings who were dressed in the attire of police officers of the early 1900's. Taken out of the house to an undisclosed location, I began to notice something very unusual which began to shed light as to my purpose here.

Beginning with a woman who made an inappropriate sexual gesture to a gentleman, before she could take this seemingly minute act of lust any further, her body and face began to transform into the pinkish-red, reptilian face of a demon. Horns began to protrude from her forehead and within seconds, she disappeared. Those around her went on as if nothing had happened, going about their business, trying to behave in a most upright manner.

Seeing this happen again and again . . . and again, those who made overtures towards others which were lustful or inappropriate in the slightest of ways, turned into horribly disfigured demons, disappearing from the scene. A man who had quickly reached his hand towards me in a very vulgar manner . . . also turned into a demon and disappeared, at the very moment I ordered him to back off.

Looking towards a very tall man dressed very astutely and with obvious prestige, he tipped his top hat and bowed to me very politely. "This house isn't haunted, is it?" I asked him with grave concern. "No," he quietly said. "But you people are not servants, either, are you? You are all dead, aren't you?" I asked timidly. "Yes," he quietly said, with no change of expression on his face, except for a very subtle smile coming from the corner of his lips. "This is a purgatory, isn't it?" I asked. "Yes," he quietly replied. "This purgatory is kind of a last resort for those souls who struggled with lust on Earth, isn't it?" I asked. "Yes," he quietly said. Pausing a moment, I thought deeply. "Those who turn into demons and disappear are being sent straight to hell, aren't they?" At this time, his head lowered a bit in sadness. "Yes," he said quietly.

Suddenly, I understood why these souls were so obedient. Because this was their last resort, if they showed that lust remained in their hearts to even the slightest of degrees, there were no further chances. Approaching an older black woman who was dressed as if from Cajun country in the early 1900's, I listened as she began to tell me about her life. As I listened, my mind couldn't help but wander to the others in the room who were acting with great gentility in an attempt to save their soul. Interrupting this very charming older woman's story, I shouted out to Jesus for help. "This place needs transformation!" My soul was transported to a heavenly highway outside of this realm.

Sitting at the side of a wide cosmic tunnel, the light formed a roadway through space. Andy and I sat at the side, watching in the distance as a huge vehicle began to approach. Six times larger than a fire engine, and in the color of the whitest white, it held within it transformative assistance which we knew would be arriving at the purgatorial mansion. Lifted from the spinning lighted tunnel, I was returned to my body on Earth.

CHAPTER SEVEN

Fond of the darkness, these unusual men who lay before me, about to become my quest for the night, were Satanists. Abhorrent and violent people, it only made sense that I should be terrified of them, but by a special gift from the Lord, I wasn't.

Beginning in a darkened sideway behind some large trees and near two very big rocks, two people with a knife approached me and Andy, who had joined me only for the beginning and end of this quest. Asking us to participate in a ritual with them, they promised not to hurt us if we would do so. However, I inherently knew that they would attempt to hurt us either way. Despite couched terms used to deceive us as to the motives of their ritual, I was very much aware of the fact that these were members of a satanic cult and their ritual was dark, disgusting and blasphemous to God. Never specifying this truth to their followers, they always used terms which were vague and misleading. In truth, they were the darkest of the dark, as evil as souls may get, and their master was Satan. Sad . . . so very sad.

Threatening to cut Andy with the knives, I approached them, grabbing the arm of the guy who did not have a hold of Andy. Repeating their intentions, they said, "If you participate in our 'ritual,' we won't harm him." Pausing, I very quietly replied, "You see, we have a little problem with that." "What's that?" he asked. "Well . . ."I paused, "I . . . looooooooooooove . . . Jesus."

Silence permeated the place for several moments, and then you could hear a faint growl coming from his mouth. Holding my ground, they still threatened Andy, so I shouted to him. "Run! Get out of here. I'll take care of these two," but Andy wouldn't leave. Realizing I would have to aid him in departure before I could deal with the souls of these Satanists, I used heavenly gifts to attain our freedom. Even so, I sustained several energetic bolts to the chest which took some time from which to recover.

Returning that same night, Andy was no longer with me and it seemed that I was being energized to seek out and find this cult for the purpose of infiltration, dismantling and disposal. What would eventually happen, however, would be much greater than this.

Bidding my soul to arrive in a large older house, the Lord placed my buns in an easy chair in the living room where I proceeded to act as if I owned the place. Several women were on the first floor, most of whom were completely deceived as to the true nature of their 'guru.' But there was a select group of mostly males who were apparently the 'right hand men' of the high priest, who very much knew exactly what it was they were doing. Most of them hung out on the second floor of this house, plotting and colluding in various evil and dark schemes against their enemies.

Beginning to talk to the women, I became aware that the high priest was scheduled to arrive shortly and that my time with these particularly deceived souls would be short. Mincing no words, I told them exactly who their leader really was, but they didn't believe me. So I told them to watch closely all the things he said and did when he got back, so that they might be able to discern the truth for themselves.

Walking in the door, he immediately observed my presence on the easy chair. Under his breath, he growled, but tried to maintain a good appearance to the women in his charge. Making some nebulous comments about some rituals and procedures, he directed his followers to come with him into another room where these would take place. As a master manipulator and father of lies, he often made misleading statements or those which were completely untrue and this time was no exception. Turning towards me, he said, "Well, after all, I once trained to become a Catholic Priest . . . but you know that I left the seminary because it wasn't exactly my calling." This was completely untrue, but he had said it to give credibility to his 'techniques.' Sarcastically, I looked at him and said, "Well, I'd love to join you . . . after all . . . I . . . looooooooooove . . . Jesus! But perhaps I'll wait here."

Growling again, his followers made note of his strange response to the mention of Our Savior's name, but still continued after him. Standing outside of the door, I waited only a few minutes in which time he had all of them in a state of total satanic mesmerization. Running into the room, I shouted and pushed them over onto the floor. "Oh, this is wonderful!" I said, looking towards the high priest, "Christian Meditation!"

At this point, he was really pissed off because his subjects were now coming out of their strange trances and asking me what had happened to them. Quietly, I said, "Oh, nothing like a little satanic memorization to control your wills and minds." In their faces, you could see that they were beginning to realize the deception which had been perpetrated upon them. Continuing, I said, "Oh, but don't let it bother you, it's just a form of *meditation*." Stating the word 'meditation' with much sarcasm, I said it very slowly so that they would understand my intent in speaking it.

Looking at me with a very quiet and subdued growl, the high priest whispered under his breath. "Leave," he said. Responding very loudly and again, with sarcasm, I said, "But I don't understand . . . I . . . looooooooooove . . . Jesus! How can I leave this intensely spiritual gathering when I love Him so much and we have here a great master of the Christian path to teach me all the ways of My Lord?" Every time I talked about my love for Jesus, the high priest and his inner circle were very much disturbed and, although they hid it on the surface, it was throwing them into an inner tizzy. Many of the less involved followers, those ignorant of the satanic nature of this cult, were becoming suspicious of them.

Following me back to the easy chair, the high priest had anger and suspicion in his eyes. Indeed, he was well aware of who I was and Who had sent me, but he couldn't say or show this outwardly because it would affect those under his charge. Sitting down, I made my intention of remaining in the house very clear, which displeased him.

Momentarily, my spiritual vision was expanded to view the activities of the upper floor where the hard-core cult members were gathered. All were dressed in black ritualistic garments, and their conversation was putridly evil. Amongst their topics of discussion was that of mutilating a human corpse, which they intended to do in a ritual they were preparing to attend.

Suddenly, my spiritual body materialized in their presence, and I was led to act in a very ignorant manner of what they were truly planning. "Oh . . . this is wonderful . . . are we preparing to celebrate the Eucharist together?!" Looking up with disgust, I ignored them and said, "Great! You all know how very much I . . . loooooooooooove . . . Jesus!"

After my disappearance from the lower level, the high priest had assumed I'd been sent to this upstairs gathering. As a result, he entered the room just as I was concluding my declaration of love for the Lord. "It's time for a final battle between forces," he stated to me very calmly. Giving me directions to a location where we would all meet, there would be a showdown. We were to meet on an island, and it was to be me against about forty of them. "Okay," I said, "I'll be there."

Flying over the waters towards the island destination, I fully expected that this battle might not be winnable. Considering the possible injuries I might endure, I was assessing my losses ahead of time, so to speak. When I arrived, however, there was a great shift in energies and things began to go very differently than I had anticipated they might.

Thirty to forty of the darkest and most evil members of the cult had shown up in full dress black. Standing before a patch of bare ground piled high in a mound, they stared me down with their eyes. Intending this mound to be my grave site, I was completely unmoved or unafraid through an inexplicable gift from God. A presence could be felt all around us and literally in the molecules of the air which I could not yet identify, but I knew that I was surrounded by heavenly protection, and even more than that, I was filled with peace and a sense of complete safety. Perhaps I had not come by myself after all, but had been given the invisible assistance of legions of angels from heaven.

Kneeling before the patch of ground, I began to continually repeat, over and over, the words which caused them so much anguish. "I love Jesus, I love Jesus. I . . . loooooooooove . . . Jesus." As I did this, six roses emerged from the ground in three rows of two. Single stalks with singular flowers, they appeared in the colors of white, pink and red. Growing as if from a heavenly light, they began to expand into bushes as more flowers bloomed.

As I'd been ignoring the cult members, I was shocked to notice that the high priest had fallen to his knees, followed by several of his cronies behind him. As they did so, you could see demons leaving their bodies, coming out of their mouths in the form of black mists shaped as diabolical images. Floating upwards, they dissipated as they entered the heights of the skies. Becoming limp after the expungement, they instinctively had fallen even further forward, bowing to the ground.

Turning to him, I very cautiously said, "You know, I really do love Jesus." Looking up, his eyes were almost blank. A new energy began to surround and fill the skies above us, that of the Rosary, a Catholic prayer in honor of the Virgin Mary and the mysteries of the life of Jesus Christ. Sparkly lights began to fall from this energy into the blank eyes of these former cult members who were still almost lying forward on the ground. You could hear whispers in the air like thousands of people praying; "Hail Mary, full of grace, the Lord is with thee . . ." Beginning to fill with something new, the eyes of the high priest looked towards me and spoke. "You know," he said under his breath as if almost embarrassed to admit it, "I think I love Jesus, too."

Shocked at his revelation, I was stunned at what my soul was about to witness. Many of the others expressed a similar feeling under their breath, and all began to comment at about the same time. "Yeah, me too!" "Uh huh, yeah." Without further adieu, they all began to get up and follow one another towards the church which stood conveniently nearby where they intended to receive full baptism! As they began to walk away, I reiterated to them under my breath, "I really do love Jesus." But I did not move from my kneeling position as this amazing conversion took place.

As I'd come expecting to infiltrate, dismantle and dispose, I was shocked that I'd actually witnessed a *conversion* among the most evil of souls.

Moments later, Andy and I were driving through a small town in a very bright and sunny oasis. Colorful, bright and pretty, there seemed to be a sense of lightness and good. Suddenly to my left, we came upon a building which was quite different than the bright surroundings. Dark and misty, the building appeared gray and black covered with statues of gargoyles and other demons on its eaves. For a moment, the Lord bade me to witness the building as it appeared in the physical realm, which was just as bright as every other building in town. But in the spiritual realm it was quite evidently 'possessed.'

"Interesting," I said under my breath towards heaven, "do you want me to go in?" Receiving a definitive verification, my spirit was made to know that this would be my next mission. "Okay," I said.

****

Entering into a religious bookstore which seemed to be placed in a happenstance manner along the parkway, an old woman approached me. Showing me a white casket, she spoke in a very serious tone. "Your grandmother has a burial site for you." (My grandmother is deceased.) Placing a medal around my neck, I observed that it was an image of the Divine Mercy, a special Catholic devotion especially suited for the suffering and the dying.

Awaking in a dream, I instinctually looked downwards towards my feet which were pitch black, much like that of a decomposing body. Surrounded in light and wearing a gown of the most subtle and pale blue, a woman stood at the foot of my bed quietly. Though her skin was fair and very beautiful, she lifted her hands which had been hidden at her sides. Upon her palms was a thick layer of black paint which resembled my feet. Showing them to me, I understood.

It has become interesting to me in my journey of death to realize that between illnesses, accidents, malfeasant acts, etc., that there are a great many people on this Earth who do not live very long. Some die in childhood, and others sometimes pass during their twenties or thirties. Despite this constant reminder of our own mortality, I have noticed that very few people seem to actually contemplate their own death, but rather, they are constantly thinking of their future plans in this world. This is interesting because any one of us could be standing at the judgment seat of God within one or two minutes of any given moment.

If you were to die right this minute, would you be ready to stand at the judgment seat of God . . . right now?! Though we must take care of matters which deal with our continued existence upon the earth, we must never forget that this is a temporary abode from which we can be snatched at any given moment. At that moment, all that we have upon this earth will be spontaneously taken away. Only those things we have done which hold eternal value will come with us, and all of our future plans will be irrevocably altered.

As the bible states so very clearly, death is appointed for all . . . and then the judgment.
****

Standing before me as a radiant beauty indescribable in human terms, the Blessed Virgin Mary had greeted me as I'd left my body, watching my physical form lying down with my youngest son below. For a moment, it seemed that I might be experiencing death, but the Virgin directed me to observe my sweet baby boy.

Coming from inside of his spirit, I could see a stirring, as if he were perhaps praying for me in some way. Inside of him, I could see my two daughters and their prayers for me also.

Suddenly, a very thin light beam came forth from his body directly into my soul, pulling it back into my body. Knowing this beam was the result of my children's prayers, the Virgin allowed me to witness this event over and over again. Showing me that I was not incorrect in determining that my situation was quite tentative, she conveyed that I was still alive because of the prayers of my children.

Wearing a veil of dark blue with stars around her head, her face was filled with light and appeared pale because of the effect of the light coming through her. Upon her breast she wore a lighter blue robe which contrasted that of her outer garment. "Thank you for allowing me to see you," I said excitedly, "I am honored." Without words, she raised her hands as I was sent back to my body.
****

Amidst the crowded astral streets, my spirit was approached by a young woman who claimed that her house was haunted. As she came towards me, I offered to help and handed her a business card which said, "Marilynn Hughes - Ghost Hunter." (In the physical world, I do not have such a card, so I found it amusing.)

As I'd discovered over the past two years, many hauntings are actually caused by three different types of phenomenon; demonic spirits, lost souls, and those doing their purgatory upon the earth. Each of these three types of hauntings or poltergeist phenomenon requires different spiritual approaches in order to affect a successful outcome.

When entering the home, I was unable to discern of which type we were dealing with, because of the excessive poltergeist activity in the home. Poltergeist activity can often be linked to demonic spirits, but on occasion, such extreme forms of haunting can be perpetrated by lost souls or purgatorial wards. If this is the case, it is usually because the soul is still carrying a great deal of anger about something. In this particular home, there was a lot of flying objects and it was what I'd term to be a very 'unfriendly' haunting.

Having met the woman's husband who was now waiting inside the house with me, his wife awaited the results outside. "Are you ready to go to work?" I asked him as he nodded that he was. Repeating several Catholic prayers over and over, we entered the house.

Starting with the Apostles Creed, my voice slowly trailed through the room. "I believe in One God, the Father Almighty, Creator of Heaven and Earth, and in Jesus Christ His Only Son, who was born of the Virgin Mary, suffered under Pontius Pilate, was crucified died and was buried. He descended to the dead." Pausing for dramatic effect, I turned and walked around the room before continuing. "And rose again on the third day, returning to judge the living and the dead. I believe in the Holy Spirit, the Holy Catholic Church, the communion of saints, the forgiveness of sins, and life everlasting." Tentatively observing me, the young husband didn't quite know what to think.

"Hail, Holy Queen," I began to recite the Catholic prayer of the same name, "Mother of mercy, our life, our sweetness and our hope. To Thee do we cry, poor banished children of Eve. To Thee do we send up our sighs, mourning and weeping in this valley of tears. Turn then most gracious advocate, Thine eyes of mercy towards us, and then after this our exile, show unto us the blessed fruit of Thy womb, Jesus. Oh clement, oh loving, oh sweet Virgin Mary, pray for us, Oh Holy Mother of God, that we may be worthy of the promises of Christ."

At this time, I began a sermon about Jesus Christ. Pounding on a table to give emphasis to my words, I spoke of His majesty and the fact that our salvation comes from Him. My spirit cannot remember the details of this fairly long endeavor, however, but as I finished my sermon my spirit quickly returned to prayer. "Hail Mary!" I shouted, beginning the prayer of the same name, "Full of grace, the Lord is with Thee. Blessed art Thou among women, and blessed is the fruit of Thy womb, Jesus! Holy Mary, Mother of God, pray for us sinners, now and at the hour of our death. AMEN!" At this moment, two spirits materialized clearly in front of me completely de-energized in their violent activity. Lying on the floor, I approached and sat down with them.

Sitting upright, a middle-aged woman had appeared whose garments were changing from their former color which I could not discern to a very light beige. A young oriental woman was lying beside her, and her garments had changed from their former color, to a gown of whitest white. Immediately, a young baby boy appeared at her side, and she directed me to pick him and cuddle him.

Although he appeared immediately upon their materialization, he had not been a part of the haunting of this home. An angel was waiting at his side, a luminous, clear, whitish being with large wings. Clearly, the baby was already in heaven, but was taken to his mother's side at the moment of her redemption. Conveying to me that this was her child, the young Oriental woman expressed her deep anger and regret at the young husband who lived in this home who was apparently a former boyfriend. His guilty look made clear his sin against her, but he honestly hadn't known that she was pregnant, or that she and the baby had died.

Doing her purgatory on Earth, she had joined together with this older woman who had chosen to assist her in engaging in poltergeist activity. Directed towards the one whom she held accountable for her wasted and lost life, she knew she'd sacrificed her potential on the altar of the vice of lust. The many prayers I had offered for them had begun to purify their souls, which had manifested in new garments of white and beige, respectively.

Inherently, I understood that they were both now prepared to enter into heaven, although the older woman apparently still had some purification to undergo. Despite this need, she was to be released from her purgatory upon the earth and taken to a higher purgation site very near to the entrance of heaven where she would go shortly. The young girl, however, was ready to join her tiny baby in heaven. Calling the young man over, the two souls had a moment of atonement with one another. Forgiveness seemed to be given and all awaited what was to happen next.

Directing them to kneel with me on the floor, I said, "Now it's time for us to pray you into heaven." Bowing their heads, we commenced our prayer. Joining me as they slowly learned the words, they disintegrated many minutes later. Above them, I saw the angels in whose hands they had been given . . . and I bid them a wondrous journey to the ultimate place of bliss . . . our heavenly homeland.
****

Pounding fiercely to demonstrate my palpitations, the metallic body also had an approximately one and a half foot in diameter metal patch in the center of the chest which protruded outward from the body to demonstrate the enlargement of the heart and the power of the palpations. Next to it was a metallic body which represented a normal, healthy person. Pointing to the metallic form whose heart was pounding, the scientist standing next to it said, "How long do you think *that* can go on?" Despite reassurances from my doctor that I had a while to live, it seemed I was being warned that my future was not so set in stone. Vowing to be more careful so this status would occur as infrequently as possible, I heeded the warning.
****

Having appeared to me in the splendor of white, I was stunned by His presence, and overwhelmed by his purpose. Throughout the night, the Lord Jesus repeatedly took me out of my body to observe what my husband and children's lives would be like when I was gone. Literally driving me somewhat crazy, I would try to bring myself back and wake up my spirit so that I wouldn't have to bear witness. "Don't you understand? I don't want them to grow up without me!" I shouted at the Lord, as He responded in understanding and patience. But each time I returned to sleep, Jesus calmly took me back out and allowed me to observe my family in my absence. Ironically, they seemed okay despite my loss.

Very calm throughout, the Lord had wished me to see that my family would be okay without me, and He also filled my spirit with an indescribable peace about the will of God. Conveying that this experience was vital to the spiritual formation of my children, it was an experience which would help form their destiny in adult life. (As always, the Lord never revealed if or when I would truly die, just that whether I or not I died or experienced disability for years, it was the will of God.) Wishing for me to know that my family would be fine if I did pass on, this was very hard for me. Because I most certainly wanted them to be okay, it was hard for me to accept that I may not be present at least while they were growing up. Frankly, I was afraid of being forgotten by my children, and of being replaced by somebody else who might enter their lives as a step-mom. Feeling tremendous guilt for this, I knew that if I were unable to be there, I'd want them to have a motherly figure to love. But I'd always assumed that it would be me . . . apparently arrogantly so.

Waking from this traumatic event, I accepted the peace Our Lord was giving to me as a gift, and I understood that when the time had come in which it was appointed for me to die, that I would be grateful to know that they would be okay, despite the fact that they would be okay *without me.*

That very morning, my middle daughter shared that she had a dream where she was playing in the front yard. A man with long brown hair, a beard and moustache, dressed in white and red robes came walking up the street towards her. "Are you Jesus?" Mary asked. Replying that He was, He played with her in the yard for some time before taking her back into her bedroom where He watched her while she slept, disappearing only in the morning when it was time to get up.
****

Standing amidst a tannish pink horizon, I came across a very close friend of mine who held incorrect views regarding spiritual matters and issues upon the ground. (Having been terminally ill for several years, she was close to death.) Believing herself completely, she was unable to get outside of herself and her distorted thinking long enough to discern that she had misperceived and misinterpreted various aspects regarding the spirit and God, and thus, various aspects of occurrences within her own life. As a result, she actually had incorrect perceptions of events within her own life; believing things to be true which were not, believing things not to be true which indeed had been so. As I explained this to her, she looked at me with a blank and confused expression upon her face, because she was so distorted she couldn't even comprehend that her false views were not true.

Sweeping my hands into the sky, I called to Jesus for assistance, as He parted the skies to reveal the heavens. As the entire horizon opened and the heavens appeared, eternal truths were depicted to her energetically. Although demonstrated clearly, she still could not *see* them because of her own biases and delusions which had actually prevented her from being cognizant of the parting of the heavens which lay in magnificence before her.

Remaining in her delusion, unable to *see* the tremendous truth which the Lord had deigned to show her, I observed the tragedy of those who remain unable to hear the truth because of their attachment to false views.

Although I had no idea at the time, her appointed time to die would come within two weeks, and afterwards, she would share with me her after-death journey.
****

Appearing amongst a coven of witches who also practiced deviant sexuality in ritual manner, they were demonstrating rituals in an attempt to convince me that there was nothing wrong with their practices. Disgusted by the blatant nature of their evil, I called for the help of Jesus.

As it had been their purpose to demonstrate the power of darkness by casting spells and performing evil and lewd rituals, I waved my arms to the sky and Jesus parted the heavens to show them eminent and *true* power. Clouds parting and rumbling to the sides, a pinkish bright white light had come down from heaven. In majesty and might, there was no doubt about the energetic truth behind what lay visible for all to see, the *truth of God revealed.* "I don't know!" I said in a very sarcastic and mocking manner, placing my hands on my chin as if I were thinking, "Which should I choose?" Because it was *so* obvious, I was making fun of the huge contrasting chasm between the heavens opened before us above, and the lewd acts of vice and evil for which they were participating on the ground.

Despite this, there was no legitimate response. Although the witches present were actually capable of *seeing* the heavens bared open, it did not move them, not in the slightest degree.

As God's display of majesty pulled back into the heavens, I called out to Padre Pio, asking if he might appear and talk with these people. No response came, however, as I began to consider that even asking this after such a bold demonstration from the Lord, could be considered overstepping my bounds. Having presented them with an undeniable pronouncement of the truth, they made a decision to reject it. It was as simple as that.

If such a catastrophically grand event had no effect on them, it had been arrogant and presumptuous of me to think that any further display of God would prove any more fruitful. In asking the Lord to present more signs and wonders, I'd asked him to throw pearls before swine. As it says in the bible, they loved their sin more than they loved God.
****

After entering the retreat center, I was taken to a back room and guided to look upon a large statuesque mountain of stone outside the window. As the sides of the mountain were steep, there was no vegetation and it was brownish red. Twelve pillars stood from the top of the mountain about twenty feet high.

Inherently, I knew the mountain represented death and the pillars, God. When I reached the pillars, the Lord would meet me there and take me the rest of the way. But in my weakened condition, I could see no feasible way to get to the top and was exhausted just looking at it. Noticing that there were three people in the room with me, I observed an old woman with long gray hair wearing a night robe, a younger woman who came to me and handed me a small porcelain angel, and a quiet priest who appeared to be reading quietly while sitting in the corner. Turning to accept the porcelain angel, something inexplicable happened.

The priest tapped my shoulder as I again looked in the direction of the mountain to see what he might have to tell me. Miraculously, the mountain had been painted from top to bottom in the colors of red, orange and brown. "I understand that you need some help in accomplishing your task," he said. Energetically, it was if I had already ascended the mountain and reached the summit because he had painted it. This is inexplicable, I know. "When the Lord tells you that its time for you to travel towards death and reach that summit," he said, "you won't have to do it alone. He will send help."
****

An angelic being stood before me holding an image of my heart in her hand. Allowing me to observe its appearance, I was able to note that it was large and thin. Without warning and before my eyes, the heart exploded and burst. "This is the way you will probably die," she said. (Since that time, however, progress has been made on size and thinning.)
****

Standing amidst a heavenly abode, my soul began to float upon the ethers in a state of perfect bliss. All around were celestial sights, which confirmed the status of where I had traveled. Music was penetrating me at severe depths, as I allowed it to fill my soul with warmth and light.

Suddenly an inspiration came upon me. Knowing that the next song to play in the celestial spheres would be an answer to a question I'd asked in prayer, I remembered what I had asked of the Lord. 'For what have I been placed upon the Earth, and what is God's purpose for my life.' A musical symphony began to fill me as I began to listen to the words of a woman who sang with force and dignity. At first I began to think I was listening to a Christian song because it spoke of the salvation of men, but then I realized there was a great deal more. As the song progressed, it became clear that the words being used were similar to the type I use in my own writing. She spoke of 'being the light,' and 'taking salvation to a higher level.' My soul actually experienced the two levels of salvation of which she spoke in the music. There is a salvation which comes to a Christian based on redemptive suffering of the Lord, and there is a higher salvation which comes to a soul after this who overcomes himself.

As her voice continued and my soul was filled with a huge awareness and bliss of God's will and purpose for my life, a tremendous light came from the sun of heavens towards my spirit. "The purpose of your Earthly existence is to take salvation to a higher level, which is encompassed within 'The Mysteries of the Redemption." Unable to be clearer, I was thrilled to know this. Surrounded in the cosmic energies of bliss in the heavenlies, I felt utter peace, realizing that though my words do not coincide perfectly with Catholic teaching, they define purification and purgation within the Earthly sphere. Reincarnation and redemption are inextricably bound on Earth because our world *is* one of the purgatorial realms, wherein a soul must continue to return until he gets it right.

In the larger sphere involving the actual mechanics of existence, there was no contradiction. Knowledge and mechanism are one, and they operate in a continuum beyond Earthly dogma.

Waking from this experience, I was filled with peace, and I *knew* beyond any shadow of doubt that the path I was following had been ordained by God for His greater glory.

****

Beyond words described how I felt when I found out that my closest friend had died suddenly in the night. Although she was terminally ill, she was expected to live possibly many more years and all were taken quite by surprise, especially her family.

Having met her years before at a book-signing, we became fast friends. Early in our relationship, she told me of a dream she had in ancient Egypt, where she was young girl of about eight, and I was her grandfather, a member of a priestly class who worked on the pyramids. Most profoundly, she recalled in her dream the moment of his death. Lying on the ground, the little girl was kneeling at his side crying. Grandpa said to her, "Wherever you go, wherever you may travel, I'll be there. And when you're ready to learn the mysteries of the spirit, I will teach you. Whatever time and place that may be." She repeatedly told me that she knew from this experience that the time had come, and we had been reunited so that I might be able to teach her of this world beyond. Because of her intensive belief and emotional tie to this experience, she always called me grandpa, which I enjoyed immensely. (However difficult it was to explain this to others, since we were both women of similar age.)

Our union was predestined, and our parting seemed to also be so. For two nights after her death, I didn't feel her presence at all, and this disturbed me to no end. Because of unusual circumstances at the scene of her death, there was a question of whether or not she overused her prescription drugs, and this made the loss even more painful. On day three, however, she came to me in an afternoon dream. My spirit was looking out the back window of my house where a huge brown wooden table appeared with two chairs. Immediately feeling her presence, I felt a peacefulness which gave me serenity regarding her status. Conveying to me, she said, "I will be sitting down and talking with you *very* soon." And then she disappeared.

Again feeling her presence that night, she took me to an astral computer screen. Immediately, she went toward a web-site which was called 'accidental death.' Conveying to me that she had been in such a state of severe agony that she had taken pain meds earlier, and when she awoke in the night, she didn't remember that she had taken them already and took some more. Apparently, she took too much.

Taking me to a monastery somewhere in the heavens the following night, she immediately introduced me to an older Chinese monk. Because she had been Buddhist in her lifetime, she'd been taken to this monastery which offered a combination of

Buddhism and Catholicism. Frantic, I was somewhat afraid for her, although she was without any doubt in a good place. Approaching me, she said, "I've entered into a state of purgation and am now in need of prayers to help me through this process. Can you pray things like the Rosary or the Divine Mercy for my soul, and ask my husband to learn them also so he can pray for me, too." It was interesting that she was asking for Catholic prayers, because she'd been a Buddhist.

The Chinese monk explained, "Because she suffered from some level of mental illness stemming from severe childhood abuse, she's beginning her purgation with the aspects of mental illness she had faced during life. Many of the things she believed to be true were falsehoods, and are now being demonstrated energetically in a manner which is undeniable in its truth and unnerving to a soul when it just begins." Promising to pray, I began a quest to get everybody I knew to pray for her, but especially our family and her husband.

Two nights later, I was honored to witness the power of such prayers as my dear friend stood upon a large rock amongst a desert oasis. All alone at this time, you couldn't see anything for hundreds of miles. Aloneness filled the air and my very special pal was sitting in a lotus position on a rock continuing the purging process as a total of six screens were coming out of her spontaneously and consecutively. Three screens were on each side of her body, lined one on top of the other, and the images within them changed continually. Much like watching a disc download, various difficult memories, terrifying moments, and incorrect thinking as a result of such experiences were coming out of her spirit very peacefully and with calm. Completely at ease during this process, she no longer displayed agitation or fear about this purgation.

"Thank you for the prayers you've offered on my behalf," she conveyed, "they helped me to get from the state of agitation two nights ago to a peaceful purgation, and an acceptance of purification." Nodding my honor, I turned to go.

In preparing for my own death, I had also prepared for hers. Now our special union had created an energetic link-up between us which had brought about a unique opportunity to explore the journey *after* death. God's ways are mysterious.

CHAPTER EIGHT

Absorbed in prayer, I had been begging for my life due to a serious setback in my condition. Drifting into the world beyond, my spirit came into a brightly lit bookstore sitting inside a mountain oasis. Although I didn't see Him, I felt the distinct presence of the Lord Jesus Christ who proceeded to communicate. "Okay," He conveyed, "I am going to help you to get better again, and with the extra time I am going to give you, I am going to give you work to do."

Directing my attention to several books lined up one behind the other on top of a shelf, I noticed that they were written by me. Although my current manuscript was one large text at this time, he indicated that it was to be broken up. Each of the books I'd written taught of a particular spiritual concept, and together, they became unified into a clear cohesive understanding. Intrigued that some of these concepts were Eastern, Christ reiterated His sanction of my work in uniting the East and the West.

Nodding my understanding and excitement, He conveyed, "You *will* be healed at this *time*, but the road ahead will be *very* rough." Speaking of my latest downfall, rather than a healing of my condition as a whole, I agreed to His terms, I felt peace surround me. In this serenity, the presence of my recently deceased friend became felt, as she encouraged me to fight and live.

Thus I would continue to follow the road of my fate, being prepared to live . . . and to die . . . at any given moment.
****

Displaying before my soul the holocaust of our time, Our Lord Jesus showed me a gruesome scene. Bloody baby corpses fully formed, and tiny hands and feet ripped from bodies were floating in a sea of blood. Spiritually bereft of any appropriate response to such horror, I looked at these images given to me by the Lord with horror and great sorrow. The holocaust of my time, that of abortion, and the full tragedy of its evil, was displayed for my soul to look upon in disgust.
****

After preparing for my funeral 'in the spirit,' I was sent to spend the evening with a group of souls who had already crossed over to watch my future funeral from above.

Commenting on the messages I'd written for loved ones and the music I'd selected, they said, "We really like what you've chosen to do for your funeral because of its uplifting nature for those you will leave behind." "Thanks," I replied.

Having selected a series of musical renditions with three themes, they were: 1) How the heart of our existence is Jesus Christ and our lives are really about Him, 2) Great praise and thanksgiving to the Lord, and 3) finally, the continuing spiritual journey of the soul after death and the never-ending eternal nature of every soul. Messages to my family and friends were those of love, joy and release, with the assurance that the Lord had generously prepared me for my transition and of my continued watchfulness over their lives.

Enjoying the funeral service, at the end I was instructed to play my guitar and sing the song I had written years before, 'To Retrieve a Golden Angel.' Ending in quiet reflection, our joyous celebration filled me with peace in knowing that I could now focus on other things with the knowledge that I'd prepared for my death well.
****

Appearing very excited, my deceased friend had come to show me some of her experiences in the after-life, and she was anxious that I record them.

Journeying through death had taken her into yet a new phase of travel wherein she was no longer in the confines of a monastery undergoing purgation, but had moved into a period of spiritual discovery which had now moved beyond the bounds of her Buddhist and my Catholic faith. Traveling now in Universal knowledge, she was learning of the mechanism of the evolutionary journey of souls. As she began conveying to me, she repeatedly mentioned the number twelve in regards to her journey, but I didn't understand. (It occurred to me that it might have something to do with the twelve pillars on top of the mountain of crossing.)

But because of my excitement, I could remember no more of what she had said. Shouting towards her, I said, "It's you, you're here to talk to me!" Smiling, she surrendered to my inability to hear her further, but she was able to convey to me a sense of peace regarding her children. Having a certain 'foreknowledge' about their future, it gave her total and indescribable peace about their welfare, although she did convey that it would take a lot of time.
****

Walking towards the horrible scene in the spiritual realm, a certain peacefulness came over my soul. Allowing me to look upon the dead body of my friend, the Lord had done so for the purpose of deeper understanding of the meaning of life's end. Blue and surrounded in vomit, it was very hard to look at.

Hearing her voice above me, she called me by a different name which intrigued me. "Mary," she said, "Don't be afraid to pray, don't be afraid to ask about me." Renewing my covenant to pray for her, I knew that she was also making reference to my fear of the mystery of death.

Lying on the back porch covered in the signs of my own impending doom and decomposition, worms, maggots, dirt and various molds were attached to my legs as I tried to scrape them off with a large comb.

Walking down a valley road which represented the various directions that my life had taken, I cautiously walked towards the distant town which represented my present life. Observing several junctures of that life upon the way, there was a certain smallness to my life, a simplicity which encompassed appreciation and understanding of the little things which give life meaning. Clearly, I had followed my path in life which included a deep investigation into the matters of the spirit, but a contrasting goodness was shown to me. In order to provide a balance for those who read my writings whose lives are meant to serve a different, but just as exalted, cause, I witnessed many areas of our world which allowed a soul to be in the forefront of scientific advancement. Witnessing, those in medicine, geology, biology, physics, mathematics, astronomy, computer technology, and every other field of science, my spirit felt the grand importance of these callings, and the great expansion that participating in such advancement allows a soul, and the gift it offers to the evolution of humanity. Great importance filled the air and surrounded the souls of those engaged in such works! Science and spirit should not be separated, for the knowledge of both combines wisdom from two worlds (physical and spirit) into one; worlds encompassing very different laws of existence.

Off in the distance, I saw what appeared to be a rocket trail going from the ground into deep space somewhere in the area of my present home. Looking somewhat like a cloudburst, it resembled that of the smoke and steam you might witness when watching a rocket being launched, except that it bore the color of a deep brilliant pink. This rocket trail didn't diminish over the passing minutes, but remained as a testament to that which my soul was bade to witness.

Speaking above my head, a man's voice began to speak of the journey of life and death as I continued walking towards the rocket trail. "We live our lives from day to day as if it will go on forever," he said, "but then, all of a sudden, we have a death date to carve upon our tombstone, and our life is instantly over." Remembering my friend, I nodded in agreement as he then conveyed the possibility that my life might be over soon, as well. Giving me a time frame which I would not see the end of, I became very sad at this realization, but also knew from experience that terminal illness provides a variety of possible death options, some of which may be able to be avoided, and others . . . which cannot. At this time, I didn't know which kind of death date this might be, but made note of it within my soul.

Looking off at the distant rocket trail, I instantly knew its meaning. Representing the ascension of my soul into heaven, it was a reminder of what the heavenly world is truly about . . . . GALACTICA!

****

Terror surrounded Andy and I, as we were running from the villains who sought my life. Although it hadn't yet occurred to me that these murderous and violent people might actually represent the violent and destructive disease which was trying to take my life, we continued running for cover, over hills, valleys, tunnels and buildings. Emerging in a large art museum from several escape routes below ground, the battle continued raging all around the building, but for the moment, we were well hidden from destruction's force.

Coming upon a room filled with huge paintings, they emanated peace. As the battle had not yet reached this room, and I quietly looked around at these paintings which were hung on the wall, and those which were lying around on tables still waiting to be displayed. Surrounded in ornate frames of silver and gold, the paintings themselves were filled with bright colors and were somewhere around ten by twenty feet in size.

Gazing upon them with wonder, I quietly picked up a large painting waiting to be displayed which was lying on a table. Filling with tears of joy, I called out to Andy, "Come here, Andy! You must see this!" Upon first inspection, you might have thought it was a very beautiful painting of a mountainous scene filled with color and delight, but upon further view, you could see that there was an image painted in the lower right hand corner, an old man dressed in the robes of a priest. Hair the color of mostly dark gray, the colors within his soul betrayed his youthful vibrance. Even so, Padre Pio was filled with energy and light.

Becoming animated, he remained rather still, but seemed to wish to convey something to me. As the violent battles continued all around us, Andy and I were filled with peace and silence as we gazed upon the infinite beauty of this holy man. Nodding towards me, Padre Pio's gaze gave me strength and filled me with a sense of wonder in knowing of his watchful protection over my body and soul. In his face was a grand sense of acceptance, as if he knew of my mission in this life as in regards to writing, and he approved. In his heavenly abode, he knew that what I was doing was indeed the will of God, despite the apparent contradictions previously discussed. Encouragement filled his face and a certain sense of perseverance in the battle for my life, as well.

As Andy was about fifteen feet away facing me from behind the picture, Padre Pio turned towards him, motioning him to come forth and nodding at him in approval, as well. Filling me with serenity, the Padre's nod at Andy gave me a sense of peace in knowing that his watchful protection would also be with Andy, especially at the time when the battle for my life was lost. Because of my children, this became all the more important. Directing us to go and participate in the battle which raged on all around us, we ran for cover from the forces of evil which were now gaining on us again.

Boarding a bus towards my childhood home, we began to think that perhaps we were home free, but in fact, we had only just begun.

As we came upon the road which led to my past life within my current life, the long road of about two miles which had led to the house was overridden with dirt. Old friends from my past appeared who were to assist me in covering this road in rock, to make it beautiful and complete. But the old friends who had appeared happened to be the ones who had been somewhat dark at the time (who knows where they may be today, they may be transformed in light!) and they quickly began to display murderous intentions as they snuck up behind me and smashed rocks into my head.

Turning in self-defense, I knocked one of them out with a stone and then lay beside her with great remorse and sorrow. Although I had been defending my own life, I was now very concerned as to whether I had taken hers. As I waited for her to show signs of life, I wandered the street which was now miraculously paved with stone for a quarter of a mile, and I gathered all the remaining stones which appeared to be large enough or shaped in such a manner as to be able to be used as weapons. Upon her waking, I quietly sat beside her and talked to her about the importance of peace and love. Although she initially seemed open to such matters, within moments she had found one of the stones which had a very distinctive weapon quality. Looking upon her with disappointment, she put it down, "I will honor peace," she said.

No sooner had she made a commitment to do so when hundreds of black snakes appeared upon the part of the road which had not yet been completed. Both of us knew that it was impossible for us to pave this entire road without anybody else's help, so we looked in horror at the scene before us. At this moment I realized that my battle was not just against the violent forces within my own body which wished to take my life, but also against the very dark forces of the Universe.

As the black snakes were very large, about five to ten feet long, and because I was easily able to take a stick and push them away, they began to grow arms and legs. With their new limbs, they began to reach towards me and attack. Without further adieu, I realized that because of the location of these battles and the now obvious signs of the presence of the dark side, that the battle to save my life was also a battle between my destiny and the dark intentions which had been placed upon my soul by those I'd left behind in my past.

Putting my stick on the ground, I gazed upon the rock pathway and the now thousands of black snakes which slithered along the dirty part of the road. Sitting down, I ignored them completely, as wisdom began to come upon me like a torrent in the night. "I understand," I said to myself, but out loud, "I cannot build this road from the light which is my present to the darkness which is my past. It is not I who need to build this road, but many others who have chosen not to help with this task . . . . I'm not going to work on this road anymore." As I said this, I was no longer there.

A holy nun stood before me in a place of solitude and rest. Placing within my hands a picture of a sainted medieval nun, she directed me to place it on the wall of my spirit.

In a moment, I was with my friend who had recently parted this world as she was leading my soul into the home she had been living in while still upon the Earth. Wishing to share with me several things, she began by expressing her sadness that her family was still renting their home. Through her purgation process, she had become aware of the fact that her indiscriminate spending had given rise to this condition which had prevented her family from saving for the future or buying their own home. Leading me to the medicine cabinet, she pointed out to me the many medications she had taken for very legitimate and intense pain. Despite this legitimacy, she expressed her sorrow at having used such dangerous drugs so indiscriminately and without due caution. Taking me to the kitchen, she opened the cabinets and refrigerator doors, showing me some of the unhealthy foods she had eaten all too regularly during her lifetime. Expressing sorrow at her lack of discretion in such matters, she now realized that she had placed her body at more risk because of unhealthy habits.

As we finished our task in the kitchen, she handed me a curly straw, telling me she had used a lot of straws to drink during her life, and wished to give this one to me. As we were both laughing, I took the straw and placed it on the counter. (Her husband later confirmed that she had a special curly straw that she used for the last few years of her life.)

Finally, she directed me to the bookshelf where she guided my eye to a set of old Catholic books. Although I didn't realize it at the time, she was guiding me to a gift she wished to give me, a set of classics I'd wanted for years which would show up the very next day at a thrift store for almost nothing. At the moment, however, I just acknowledged them on the shelf.

Nodding to her, I knew our time for parting had come. Promising to share these very important words with her husband, her presence disappeared in a wisp of wind. Shortly before her death, she had been shown the truth, but could not see it because of her own distorted perceptual thinking. Because she was now seeing that which she had been unable to in the past, I was very proud of her. Purgatory had been good to my friend, and she was beginning to understand a great many things.

****

Taken into the reality of someone who expressed a different angle on the issue of incorrect views, I flew into a room which represented their spirit. Led to a table which displayed three very beautiful and exquisite paintings, they represented this person's spiritual search. Each of the paintings represented a different religious viewpoint of which he had studied; Judaism, Buddhism and Hinduism. As I looked upon them, I understood immediately that this person's spiritual journey was very sincere and quite serious.

Gazing upon the room around me, it was filled with clutter, and I understood that there was more to this story. Scrap papers were thrown around the room, sheets and blankets thrown over furniture and a general pattern of disarray permeated the room. Being led to a kitchen, it was conveyed to me that I would observe that upon which this soul spiritually feeds. Observing the same sort of messiness which had encompassed the other room, an invisible presence led me to observe something which had been very well hidden at the side of the refrigerator.

As I pulled it out, I began to look upon the pages of what appeared to be a magazine. Inside, were images of people having sex, and as you continued through the magazine, the images became more lewd and deviant, indicating that the deeper you went, the more this vice manifested in this person's soul.

Although this person's spiritual journey was very sincere and serious, he had not linked his spiritual search with his life; with the choices, decisions, vices, and issues which made up his true self. In a sense, the spiritual journey was an intellectual exercise which was intentionally kept far away from the actual spiritual substance which was his soul.

Another manner in which souls can be unable to see the truth, when a soul separates the spiritual quest from who he actually is, ignoring vice, choices, responsibilities, etc., the search will not bear fruit. Because our vices, issues, responsibilities and choices *are* **the way** for each one of us, ignoring them to focus on intellectual truths has no purpose. Difficulties in our lives are most often the means which God gives us to prune our souls, if we attempt to ameliorate them and avoid the truth that they provide, we miss the point.

In this man's case, he very much wanted to discard of the responsibility of a wife and children in order to pursue his spiritual journey. What he didn't realize was that his wife and children *were* his spiritual journey, and to discard them to find himself would be pointless and empty. Substance lies within those things which are difficult for us to do, the very responsibilities which can appear to hold us back are the doorways to our freedom.

****

Pulling my stretcher up the road, Andy was trying to bring me home, but my limbs were heavy and my body weak. Unable to move, a caring neighbor helped him to pull my stretcher up a hill. Embarrassed, I surrendered to it and let it go. Moments later, I woke in a hospital in an environment which felt so real, I truly thought this was physically happening . . . although it was not happening in the physical world.

A nurse was attending to my sick body, "You've been unconscious for three days," she said, "under normal circumstances, we would not release you from the hospital like this. But because you have children and they aren't able to see you in this ward, we are going to send you home so you will be able to see them." Taking care of various tasks in the room, I nodded. "Before you can go, you have to see your doctor one last time." Expecting my cardiologist to enter the room, I was shocked when my priest came instead and referred to himself as my doctor. Immediately thinking of last rites, I wondered if it were possible that he'd come to impart spiritual healing.

Before I could figure this out, I was instantaneously flying out of my body down a hallway in the morgue. Listening to various conversations of doctors along the way, I noticed the bodies which were laid out for autopsy in each room.

****

Taken to a warehouse, many things had been stored here, but I immediately noticed that amongst the various garbage of this realm . . . were huge statues of exquisite beauty representing the Way of the Cross! Approaching, the first one I noticed was a bigger than life size depiction of a scene of the Blessed Virgin Mary bowing before the tomb of her son as two twenty-foot high angels stood before it. But as I looked upon this, I noticed that others had been well-hidden behind other things. Looking upon them, statues began to materialize all over the place. Life size, the Way of the Cross appeared first in complete order. Touching the thorns upon Christ's head on the statue which depicted the crowning with thorns, I found myself especially drawn to Jesus Carrying His cross.

Internally, it was conveyed that the hugeness of these statues represented the prime force which suffering was now taking in my own life, my own Way of the Cross. As this path was forged all around me, life-size statues of various saints began to appear and I mused in wonder at them.

A band of roving thieves had come upon the warehouse with evil intentions to cause me harm, and I began shooting them with a tranquilizer gun. As they lay sleeping on the floor before me, a voice said, "You may fight your disease and put it to sleep at times, but you cannot destroy it. It will come again."

Gazing upon Jesus Carrying His cross, I fantasized about having such a marvelous remnant in my own yard to constantly remind me of the glorious nature of this path of suffering. Perhaps, I could gather these stone figures within my soul to remind me of such things. "God is good," I thought, as I continued to repeat this over and over even as I awoke. "God is good, God is good, God is good . . . "

****

Dark and occupied by two other nuns, the cell in the medieval monastery seemed confining. As we were praying, I immediately recognized one of the nuns as a friend of mine from this present life. Mother Superior was directing the two of us, as we were kneeling on the floor praying before a blank wall adorned with a single crucifix. Praying for hours, I began to feel restless. After several more hours passed, I could no longer take it.

Getting up, I began walking towards the doorway of the cell. Joining me, my friend and I walked through the doorway and into our present life.

Our souls seemed to be lighter without the weight of the habit, but we said nothing regarding this sudden miraculous transition from one world and time zone to the next. In our hearts, we understood very clearly that what we'd experienced had demonstrated an intense extreme, and it was now our process to restore proper balance. Prayer is a very important thing, when done in the context of living your life fully. What had been missing in that former time zone was *joy*, and we had quietly and unobtrusively walked into the future to find this elusive quality.

CHAPTER NINE

Blissfully taken away, I found myself standing in a room with my dear friend who'd died recently, as she was all aglow in her new garment of sheer white. Happiness exuded from her face as I ran towards her, tackling and sacking her in a fierce hug. As we fell to the floor, we laughed and hugged together in a joyous reunion. At this time, I noticed that her husband and two boys were in the room, but unable to see her. Pointing out to her husband where she was standing, I followed her as she took me towards a bookshelf.

Several items were upon the shelf for me to peruse, the first of which was a hymnal similar to the one I'd written with my first book, 'The Mysteries of the Redemption.' Pointing inside, she showed me a song she had written for me which spoke voluminously of our deep friendship and her love for me. Honor and bliss poured forth from me as she handed me the book, saying she wanted me to have it. Although her husband was unable to see our interactions, at this moment he had a similar inspiration, and also asked me to take the book, because he believed his wife would've liked me to have it.

Directing my attention to a small Buddhist book which spoke about saints, she said, "Don't buy into all the stories written about the saints, because some of them were portrayed as being more perfect than they truly were. Doing this will prevent you from accomplishing your own work, because it requires you to speak in opposition to certain established doctrines."

Showing me the Gnostic texts of the Christians, ancient texts written by followers of Christ which are not included in the New Testament, she also had the Apocryphal books and other books which were considered heretical.

Looking upon them, I *felt* their true holiness, and as I held them, they energetically reinforced my purpose which would take me outside of established dogmatic parameters. "You must do it! You mustn't fail the Lord!" she said, fiercely adamant about my destiny.

Pulling away, she directed my attention to her children for whom she had expressed concern recently. Unwilling to talk about her death openly, she had said that they needed to express their deep grief.

Everything suddenly became awkward, because I didn't know what to do to help them. A sudden inspiration led me to run towards a bed, where I began pounding with my fists and shouting, "THIS SUCKS! THIS SUCKS!" Asking them if they'd like to join me, they approached and we all began pounding on the bed and shouting out to the heavens our extreme dissatisfaction at the fate of their dear mother and my wonderful friend. "It's important for there to be humor involved in the grief process," she said.

Turning to one of her kids, I casually made a joke about seeing a bug on him, and used the opportunity to start tickling him uncontrollably. As they laughed, my friend began to direct me towards her husband.

Expressing concern over my illness and potential fate, he felt very badly about our shared fates. As I thanked him for his caring, I began to tell him that I had a strange feeling that God might be willing to give me another extension on my life, and as I did this, my friend again appeared behind him with a great big smile on her face. Knowing what she meant to say, I was very much aware that she had been interceding for me before the throne of God. Although it wasn't clear yet what the answer might be, it seemed that another extension on my existence might be in the works.

Conveying to me a deep sense of importance regarding my work, she bade me to know that she was now helping me to accomplish it from the other side. Another smile lit up her face as she expressed gratitude regarding the painting I had done of her experiences in purgation. "The first few weeks were very difficult for me, but I am now more at peace and able to enjoy the fact that I'm no longer in physical pain." In her eyes, I could see the pain of separation from her children, but she was coming to terms with it. At that moment, she disappeared.

Because my latest death date was coming up within the week (and I would surpass it due to her prayers), I found it a most amazing thing to witness that the dead pray for the living, and that their prayers can be efficacious if the Lord so deigns. Receiving the extension, my limbo was not to be lifted as my heart function had begun decreasing again.
****

Joining two older men we gathered together in a solitary room as the angels explained that we were all currently scheduled to die around the same time. One of these men was the soul who had been saved from condemnation to hell. Because of this intercession, his destiny had been altered, but he had a great deal of time left to do in purgatory because of his continuing angry nature. Although he had not been violent during his life, he'd been very mean, at times. Having an angry nature would give him an extended journey through purgation, although what had condemned him to hell was his total and complete disinterest in the Lord during his life which he acknowledged at the time of the battle for his soul.

The other man had also led a questionable life, but his faith in the Lord had saved him, and his soul was not in danger of hell. Purgatory would also be prepared for him, but despite his bad life, it seemed his time there would be shorter than the other man because of his true love for the Lord. In his youth, he'd not only engaged in anger, but violence. But in his old age, he was mellow and passive, no longer the man he had once been. On his face, you could see his fear and respect of the Lord, which had helped his plight.

Leaving the room quickly, the angry man did not wish to communicate with us, so I turned my attention to the other, who was greatly afraid of death. Suffering from an extended terminal illness, the angry man was aware of his eventual fate, but the other man had no reason to believe he was close to death before this pronouncement, other than his advanced age. Death would be sudden and unexpected for him, and he was truly terrified.

Approaching him, I placed my arms around him and said, "We needn't be afraid. At this time, we must think of our heavenly homeland." Beginning to sing a traditional operatic aria version of the 'Our Father' prayer, I sang quietly, "Our Father . . . . Which art in Heaven . . . Hallowed be Thy name . . . " Slowly joining me, we sang together. "Thy Kingdom Come!!!!!!!! Thy Will be done!!!!!!!!! On Earth . . . as it is in Heaven."

Calming down significantly, my spirit's attention was drawn to members of my extended family who had not shown much sadness over my imminent demise. As they appeared in the room, they noticed my deteriorating status, and in this realm experienced their full grief before me. Overwhelmed with sorrow for me, I was truly stunned! Because of the way they had behaved in regards to my condition, I had quite honestly perceived that some of them really didn't have any feelings about my death. A great gift, this moment allowed me to see that, despite their own unique ways of handling grief, they did truly love me and were very saddened by my imminent parting from this world. Moved, I began to disappear from this realm, awaking again in my physical body.

"Do not wait for death
To reveal the great mystery;
If you know not your Heavenly Father
While your feet tread the dusty soil,
There shall be naught but shadows for thee
In the life that is to come.
Here and now
Is the mystery revealed.
Here and now
Is the curtain lifted.
Be not afraid, O man!
Lay hold of the wings of the Angel of Eternal Life,
And soar into the paths of the stars,
The moon, the sun, and the endless Light,
Moving around in their
Revolving circle forever,
And fly toward the Heavenly Sea
Of Eternal Life."

The Essene Gospel of Peace, Book Two, Page 52 – 53, (Translator: Edmond Bordeaux Szekely, Words of Christ)

****

Surrounding my spirit were a plethora of holy crucifixes of many different sizes, shapes and designs. Standing in a battered and run-down old country store, I gazed upon each one carefully. In the center there was a huge crucifix which bore the image of Christ, but the cross itself was translucent. Jesus was obviously suffering, but the instrument of his torture was invisible, much like my own illness. Amidst this wide assortment of crucifixes, I came across a statue of Our Lady of Grace which portrayed her lying down amidst a field of flowers. Rather than the usual demon underfoot, the many colors in bloom serenaded her feet. At peace, the battle was over and she was surrounded in her victory, much like my own death.

Gazing upon it with wonder, I heard the voice of a male angel who surreptitiously appeared at my side. Native American, his long black hair framed his deeply dark face, while white wings protruded from the back of his bare chest. Eminence came from him, but I was so drawn to these images of the crucifixion that I only looked at him for a moment.

"The time has come," he said, "for you to speak for my people." Nodding, I remembered that several years ago I had been told I would speak for 'my' people, the Native Americans, who were 'mine' through the benefit of many past lives living as one of them, but I had never been told what I would say or when.

'How do these images and the words he just spoke interact?' I thought, looking at what appeared to be a contradiction. "This is what you will say first," he said, "The Native Americans were very much like Jesus Christ . . . "he paused, as I tried to understand the meaning of what he was saying to me. With unction and extreme stillness, he said the final words he would utter very slowly and quietly, almost a whisper. "Lambs led to the slaughter . . ." My heart literally fell as I immediately understood the connection and the profundity of this comparison.

Native Americans suffered at the hands of an invisible instrument of torture, racism, and their graves now bore the fruitful bloom of the martyrdom of a brave and tortured people. Understanding, I disappeared.
****

Given to witness how another person might respond to the level of pain I experienced on a regular basis, I was surprised to see that this male individual for whom I was given to watch was screaming out in agony. "You are a very strong person to be able to endure such increasing levels of pain," an angel said, "and others might very well be shocked to feel what goes on beneath the surface while exteriorly you are able to conceal the pain as if you are in perfect health." Grateful for this, I nodded.

Several days later, my spirit was led through the experience of a 'sudden death.' Within less than a moment, my transcendental nature had been separated from my body and I was hovering in a very soothing dimension imbued with the color of peaches upon the horizon. Despite this environment, I was anything but soothed, as I began to fight to return to my bodily form in the other world. Knowing I must return to my children, I fought with my entire strength, but the divide was sealed and there was nothing further I could do.

For this moment, I experienced the amazing shock of sudden death. Lamenting the loss of my life with my husband and children, a voice echoed across this peach-colored horizon. "Your chest pain is not 'Nothing,' it said, in response to what I'd been told by my doctors, "Your doctors have missed something, and you are at high risk of sudden death. Be very careful . . ."

Feeling the presence of my friend trying to protect me from this imminent destiny which had taken her, the divide opened and I turned to cross.

****

Sitting quietly in the hospital room where she now received treatment and help for her mental illness, my departed friend was wearing her garments of white and staring off into the distance with great sorrow piercing her face. Family surrounded her, those of the living and those of the dead, as they had gathered this evening to visit and give her comfort and support. Pointing to an older man and woman in the room, she said "'Mom and Dad' are here with me." These were her Aunt and Uncle, who had been much like parents to her.

Two cowboys were hanging around, although not in the center of the family fray, one of which was her departed brother, who had died about two years prior to her death. Although the two looked much alike, I didn't know who the other man might be, but was later able to confirm that another brother had died during infancy, and the two had since reunited beyond the veil.

A succession of children came forward walking in succession in front of my friend. Five or six of these souls appeared before me, each jumping successively into a pool of water . . . knowing that they were going to drown. Each of them had made this sacrifice willingly to serve a greater good which would come of their gift. Beginning to wonder if these souls were the babies which my friend had miscarried during her life, I recalled how she had lost about that many pregnancies to miscarriage because of an incompetent cervix. Finally, the doctors found a way to help her be capable of carrying to term, and she had her two living sons.

Given a special opportunity to speak with one of the children, a small, blonde little girl with pigtails sat upon a chair manifesting at about the age of four. Immediately, I learned her name was Molly, and we began a lengthy conversation. "What do you do in heaven?" I asked, "Do you pursue careers?" Quietly, she said, "No, you just follow your heart at any given moment as God leads you." Nodding my understanding, a nurse approached, allowing me to hold and rock one of the other babies while I continued to talk with her. "Can you tell me," I asked boldly, "the time in which I will die, or that of my husband, children or my friend's husband?" Turning to the side, I realized immediately that I'd asked a forbidden question. "Is that something you are not allowed to tell those of us in the world of the living?" As she turned her gaze back to mine, she nodded, 'Yes.'

Now my attentions were turned to my friend, who remained despondent, sad and quiet. Conveying many things, I sat next to her and held her as her sorrow was expressed. Having watched from above to witness the consequences of various actions she had taken in life, she was learning about the true impact of those decisions on those that remained behind.

In particular, she had left behind a financial disaster for her family to clean up. In her newfound state, she was able to see the line of energy in the choices she'd made which had led to this condition, and was feeling 'convicted' of spirit, so to speak. Although she was accountable for the damage she'd left behind, she was less accountable than she might have been had she not suffered some level of mental illness.

True delusion was involved in some of these choices she'd made, and it was only at this time in her after-death journey that she was able to truly understand the ramifications of some of these choices which had been made so haphazardly during her life.

Expressing great concern for one of her children upon the Earth, her manner of accidental death was of concern to her and the heavens because she had modeled to him a certain way of handling difficulties in life which could lead him to handle future problems in a similar way. Great sorrow filled her in this regard, for she hadn't realized that this issue she'd had regarding the use of prescription drugs, could indeed be passed along to her children. Giving pause to great warning, she asked that I convey this to her husband, so that he could be extremely watchful in preventing this sort of fruition from ever taking place.

Because she was now in the heavenly spheres, despite her status in a mental hospital, she shared with me that her capacity to love had been greatly increased and that she hoped her husband could know that she loved him even more in this new place than she had been capable of in the world. Further, she expressed her hope that he could someday offer her his forgiveness for the financial disasters she had left behind, and that he might be able to separate in his mind her love for him, from some of the very harmful choices she had made. Asking for understanding of her compromised mental state during life, she made clear that she had truly been mentally ill.

A great deal of her sorrow was generated from the fact that she knew that some things can be undone, and others only endured. Many of the problems she'd left behind could only be endured. Because she'd crossed the great divide in such an unfortunate and untimely manner, she felt a certain impotence in being unable to assist in cleaning up the mess she had left behind. It's always easier to deal with our issues and problems while still in the world than to wait until we are no longer of it, and thus, no longer able to affect it in a full and complete manner. Purpose exists in this life, and it is best to fulfill it while still in this world. Fulfilling it from across the divide is much more difficult. Walking alongside her family, it was vital that she assist in helping to resolve these matters, even though she must now do so from beyond the grave.

Finally, she conveyed a final few words regarding her practice of Buddhism during her life. Far from being a conviction of the religion itself, she convicted herself of not allowing her practice to become penetrating. Becoming more of an intellectual exercise, rather than a process of transformation, she'd actually allowed it to become a crutch in the assessment of her life. Much like the other person of whom I'd witnessed earlier, who had not allowed the truths of his religious practice to penetrate into his personal issues in life and the actual things he was doing, and she was confessing that this had been a fault she shared.

Buddhism, ironically, is a religion of renunciation and could have very adequately provided her with the tools to conquer the issue of misuse of financial means. Separating spiritual or religious practice from the actual life is a misunderstanding of the true purpose and destination of Earthly life. Religious practice cannot be separated from the actual life, because our actual life is the *true practice*. Religious practice, of whatever faith it may be, all centers upon transformation from within. If your practice is true, your faults and issues will naturally arise from it as a result of your devotion.

In many respects, this true practice leads to a continual process of 'convictions' of the spirit wherein the soul witnesses the view of its soul from the heavenly spheres, rather from the limited point of view of itself. By doing so, it recognizes those cravings and fetters as the Buddhists would say, or the sins and vice as Christianity might term it, which linger within. Issues arise because they are the fetters which tie a soul to the Earth, matters for which mortal realms have been created to serve. Souls do not part from this realm until those issues have been resolved in a mortal context. So, as you can see from this, there is a purpose in this life of which you must fulfill while you remain in this realm . . . otherwise, you will return until it has been resolved within the context of time. Timelessness is not the proper context in which this particular purification of a soul may be completed.

As we hugged tightly, I was aware that my visit was about to end with my dearly departed friend. Sadness filled my soul, although at the same time I felt a joy at her newfound wisdom and understanding of that which is true. But watching this process can be a double-edged sword, because truth is only attained through the suffering which comes to us when we deign to see things as they really are, rather than what has proven to be convenient for our conscious minds to peruse.

Because we witness our own delusions which have caused suffering for others, there is sorrow and regret. But we must never forget that it is the seed of sorrow and remorse which are the soil and earth upon which every spiritual transformation takes place, and without it, the grandiose heights cannot be reached.

So we gather in sorrow together as a human family to comfort this wonderful soul who now looks upon her life with regret, so that we may assist in this grand process which leads to purification. With this knowledge we may go in peace, because sometimes what is best for us to know is not the most pleasant thing for us to hear. But the unpleasantness lasts for but a moment as a soul begins to generate true loving compassion penetrating to the core of the soul. Penetration leads a soul to harmlessness, wherein a soul truly seeks only the good of all sentient beings, and further, has the clarity of vision to pursue it in every action, thought, word or deed.

No journey worth taking is without flaw or difficulty. Smiling at her, she remained quiet, but seemed content in the knowledge that she had been able to express to her family her love . . . and her sorrow.

About a week later, she again appeared to me wearing her white garment sitting behind a table looking at a book. Expressing her immense gratitude in having been able to share her sorrows with her husband on the Earth, her soul was able to experience peace as a result of having been able to do so.

****

Standing amidst the galactic heavens, my soul awaited that for which I had come, although I was unaware of what that might be. Because I'd recently considered getting a job due to financial matters, I had been thinking about things I might still be able to do in my current condition. Suddenly surrounded by a crowd of very colorful spirit beings, I looked among them. Recognizing them as the prophets, saints, mystics and sages of all ages and from all over the world, I was honored and quite amazed.

Feeling a powerful rush of energy, they all began to enter into me energetically, like a bolt of lightning. But this power burst lasted for only a moment as I began to hear above me a resonant and holy voice which came across as 'a mouthpiece of God.', "You are the voice of the prophets and saints. You speak for us in the physical world . . . and this is your occupation." Demonstrating how they were able to use me in the physical world to accomplish the will of God, I was a vessel, a sieve. Without saying so, I knew that I was being directed not to pursue any type of job at this time, and it was further shown to me in another manner that most of the jobs I might be able to acquire would be too physically demanding in my condition and put me at risk of death.

Gazing upon this amazing gathering of souls, a vortex of energy began to circle around and through them into me, as my soul became a rocket burst of light! An incandescent smile lit upon my face to imitate the grand smiles coming from each of them. Marveling at the gathering, I was able to observe that there were prophets, saints, mystics and sages from every world religion represented. So many were there, I felt sure there were those representing smaller sects present, but I wasn't as familiar with what these special souls had looked like during their lives. Among them were Babaji, Paramahamsa Yogananda, various Old Testament guys, some very amazing Jewish sages, a particularly interesting Sufi who I believed might be Rumi, some Buddhist monks of whom I knew to be among the saints of that religion (one of them I believed to be Milarepa and others among the patriarchs), and various monks, saints, nuns, mendicants, hermits and priests of the various religions, as well. In this whirlwind of energy, my spirit was rushed away to return to the Earth and remember my incredible journey this eve.

****

Raging through the darkened night, my spirit was in a hurry to arrive at the monastery in the galactic heavens which I knew would give me and my ward refuge. As we'd entered, I was excruciatingly aware of those who were quickly following behind, with the intention to harm my ward. As a result of this knowledge, I continued further and further into a catacomb-like structure beneath the building.

Bearing this tiny unborn baby in my hands, the Chinese baby could be no more than five inches long and perhaps several months along in pregnancy. Swelling feelings

came from within my soul for this child, as if she was my very own, but I knew I would be giving her up soon. Those who were following me were taking a journey deep into themselves as they ventured into the catacombs, wherein their souls were undergoing transformation. As it was my duty to protect this baby until the threat of abortion was no longer present, the parents arrived moments later. Opening my hand and showing them the fragile and tiny little child, tears came from their eyes. Handing her back to them, I inherently knew that she would be safe now and that this child would not be harmed by abortion.
****

Journeying through the countryside, I was gathering my things to embark upon the next leg of my journey in this life. As I packed a bag of clothing near the house, I noticed in the distance a huge, perhaps twenty foot long, electric eel approaching. Very thick, this eel was perhaps a foot and a half in diameter, and I immediately knew it to be a demonic force. Slithering about six feet into the air, there was a hump in the center of its body.

Grabbing my things rapidly, I ran to the truck with Andy, desperately trying to get out of there before the demon could get near us. But we weren't fast enough, and I did the only thing possible to protect myself, which was knocking the creature to the ground with my arm. Inherently, I knew that this creature had come to kill me, and that it was going to use its electrical properties to throw the electrical systems in my heart out of whack. Running, Andy had the key in the ignition and we were off.
****

Having been a very normal day, there was no reason to suspect that it might be 'the one.' Waking in an unfamiliar place, I was lying in a hospital bed completely unaware of how I had gotten there. Quickly, it became clear that I wasn't feeling very well. "How did I get here?" I asked the nurse standing beside my bed, "What happened?" He calmly replied, "Oh, you wouldn't be expected to remember that. You ran into problems while you were sleeping and you passed out." "Well, what happened?" I asked again. Although they refused to be more specific, it was very clear that something had happened with my heart while I was sleeping which was apparently quite serious; serious enough to force my soul to cross over into this borderworld.

For several moments, I became quite anxious, wondering if I had experienced sudden death and was irretrievably dead, but found fairly quickly that my spirit had been sent to this borderland hospital in order to receive spiritual assistance to *prevent* my crossing over . . . at least, as of yet.

Hooked up to several I.V.'s, my spirit remained there for four days, although when I returned I came back the next morning chronologically. "Don't feel bad about having to come here," the nurse said, "you may need to come back here many times during your illness, because it is necessary to keep you alive and may very well give you more time." They seemed to know how long I had left to live, and although I got the impression that I may only have, at most, a few years, those few years appeared to be quite important in the larger scheme of things, and thus, they wished to intervene in any way they could to insure that I didn't expire prematurely.

When they were finished with me, I felt significantly better. But when I attempted to return to the body, I found resistance. Experiencing severe chest pain, my heart and breathing were going very fast and it was pounding so hard it felt like it might explode. Making several efforts to return, the angels and nurses from the astral hospital intervened with my physical body and were eventually able to shut down the problematic behaviors within my body. Shaken up, I went about my day.
****

Standing before me was a large emblem of green, a great expanse of wings emerged from its sides, and the centerpiece held what resembled a family crest with a very prominent eagle inside. Representing the various layers of the soul, it conveyed the importance of awakening these layers while remaining upon the Earth. As I gazed upon this intricate symbol, a melody and words began to replay over and over again in obvious reference to the awakening process of the soul beneath the soul. "Born beneath the soul, born beneath the soul, born beneath the soul, oh oh oh, the soul is waiting." For a moment, I felt the tragic nature of the human soul, in that so many remain asleep on every level throughout their lives, missing the sole purpose of their existence in this realm. Sad it is, how sad . . .
****

Standing before the ancient patriarch, his ochre robe was draped over his body all the way down to his feet. In his hands, he bore the 'Catechism of the Catholic Church,' from which he was teaching me. Focusing primarily upon the entries regarding Abraham and the patriarchs, he was having me read the inter-dimensional version of the Catechism which explained the metaphysical and multiple mystical meanings which were hidden within the words. Looking upon the inter-dimensional text, some of it would wave in and out of view, and therefore, I was reading slower than usual. Meanings were hidden within the words, deep, mystical and difficult to comprehend. As he finished, the patriarch was pleasantly surprised to realize that I was indeed listening and taking in the words of his teaching, because he was unsure if any of it was penetrating. Although I would be want to explain any of these deeper meanings, my soul went into a meditative state contemplating these new understandings.
****

Lying in bed, I looked up to notice that the ceiling overhead had begun to swirl. As it did so, the walls of the room became transparent and my vision soared to that of the now swirling clouds above my home. Parting, the clouds opened to reveal an image of the heavens as a parade of bluish-white, life-size statues appeared in succession. Showing the history of salvation, it began with the Old Testament patriarchs and prophets and continued through the life of Jesus, finalizing at the ascension of Christ which was portrayed by a bluish-white statue of Him ascending to heaven with a large white-winged angel standing aside.

After this final statue was depicted, there was a large cliff which fell fifty to one hundred feet below. Above the statues was the entrance to heaven which was clearly in view and depicted as a bluish-white, swirling cloud with light. Below the statues and standing below the cliff were thousands of people all reaching to the heavenly gate. These were souls in purgatory, who regretted the missed opportunities in life which would have allowed them to enter heaven immediately upon their death. Although they did not appear to be suffering in any obvious physical way, they exhibited very clearly that they were undergoing a mental suffering in being able to see the gate of heaven, but being unable to penetrate it as of yet.

Following the exquisite salvation history of mankind through the parade of statues backwards and then forwards again, I marveled at this grand plan of the Lord.
****

Chaos had ravaged our part of the Earth as the most extensive wildfires in hundreds of years continued to burn very near to our home. As we were evacuated amidst the tumult, my heart did not respond well to the strain, and although we had been honored to be taken into the home of a stranger who accepted our whole family during the crisis, it felt very clear that I was in deep jeopardy of losing my life. Two days prior to being evacuated, I'd been informed that my heart was declining.

Appearing to me in the usual white dress with a globe of light shining from her heart, my deceased friend appeared as my heart was pounding rapidly during sleep. "If you don't want to join me any sooner than you're meant to," she said, "you need to get out of here and go to a hotel." Having tried to keep up appearances with our hosts, I was wearing myself ragged, and a hotel room would allow me to 'direct traffic' from the center of the room and stay in bed, rather than being required to socialize while I was doing so badly.

But now that she stood before me and I had an opportunity to question her, I grabbed her and asked, "Why did this happen now?" We'd all wondered about this, because she'd taken an overdose. Embarrassed, she didn't want to respond, but I insisted. "You *need* to tell me this!" I said with urgency. Quietly, with reserve and embarrassment, she said, "Because some people and I weren't getting along." Having been confronted with her spending issues which were driving the family to bankruptcy, she simply chose not to deal with them. In doing so, she dealt a death blow to herself and her family in a momentary whim. Able to call it 'accidental' because of her mental illness, the status of her delusions made her choice less intentioned in the eyes of God.

That day, we transferred to a hotel, and I believe it saved my life. Several more days into our evacuation, my heart was still very traumatized but making small progress daily towards stability. As the fire raged for weeks more, the stress of the situation would continue.

On the night we returned home, my spirit was taken to witness a huge, 200 foot high Eucharistic Tabernacle shining in gold amidst a barren desert. Inside of the Eucharistic Tabernacle where the host is usually placed, I saw myself being beat up by an unknown force. "The suffering and violence being done to your soul at this time, has purpose within a divine context," a voice said. 'Impermanence,' I thought.

Concluding many things, I observed several truths which are relevant to us all. Firstly, until somebody has truly undergone the purifying fires of suffering and death, either through their own mortality or that of somebody very, very close, they simply do not understand the catastrophic nature of terminal illness. Secondly, people choose not to go there because of their unwillingness to face mortality and death in their own life, and being judgmental of those who are walking this road is a very convenient method of denying that death, too, comes to us all. Thirdly, to face such things is a true gift from God, because it completely severs our belief in our own self-sufficiency, and makes us render to God what is His. Fourthly, to experience the loss of life and the loss of property simultaneously creates a very healthy awareness of the impermanence of this life and everything in it, reminding us that our heavenly homeland is our true destination, and that we must not rely or allow ourselves the delusion of feeling safe in a world which guarantees only one thing, that no one will get out of it alive.

Continuing to observe my soul being battered within the confines of the Eucharistic Tabernacle, I gave great thanks for this unusual experience, because it carried with it the greater knowledge of life . . . and death. And as I sat observing this phenomenon, it became clear to me that we truly had been blessed above all others in our suffering, because it had been in this journey into losing everything, that we had become whole and our love for one another had increased tenfold. Detachment was now a daily aspect of our lives, and in this we had brought eternity into the confines of our family from what had previously been a limited, confined and selfish love. Agape had come down from heaven and entered into all of our hearts. God is always good, and infinite in His wisdom, and it is wonderful to realize this amidst tragedy when we are usually confounded rather than enlightened.
****

Meeting my deceased friend, her husband was feeling tremendous guilt in trying to come to terms with their relationship during life and now after, because he felt that he would be dishonoring her if he was simply honest about the good and bad within their lives.

Coming to me in the morning, she didn't speak. Beginning to talk to her, I said, "You know, my friend, that the only way your husband is going to be able to get through this and process it successfully is if you allow him to reflect upon your lives together and the manner of your death honestly and truthfully, with the confidence that *you* still know that he loves you and honors your memory. Do you think you could give him permission to process this experience with this kind of honesty, knowing that by him doing so it will not make him love you less or make your importance to him change in any way?" Very calmly, she nodded, 'Yes' and sent a rush of energy through me, because she very much wanted him to be able to get through this, despite the fact that reflecting honestly might sometimes be painful or not paint her in the best of lights. "I accept full responsibility for everything," she said, "and tell him I love him . . . and I know he loves me." Pausing, she finished, "By thinking of me as I truly was, the good with the bad, he will honor our special relationship as it relates to eternity."

With a rush of energy, she was gone.

****

"Thunderbird," the heavenly host said loudly as he handed a long-ago worn out ring with the sign of the thunderbird upon it to Andy, who then gave it to me. Repeating his words, Andy said. "Thunderbird." Describing the fiery quality my soul possessed which energized new programs on the Earth, the heavenly host allowed me to look upon the Phoenix, the harbinger of change. Smiling, he disappeared into the ether.

CHAPTER TEN

Traveling the galactic heavens one fortnight, my spirit noticed a familiar soul wandering the heavenly pathways ahead of me. Running to catch up to him, Paramahansa Yogananda immediately seated himself in a lotus position in midair and looked at me expectantly as if waiting for me to pose a question. Bowing before him, I got on my knees. "My question to you, Master, is this. Over the last year, I've experienced and understood that many people die young, either through illness or accident, and don't seem to get the opportunity to finish what they start. Because of this, Master, I am struggling with the feeling that life appears quite meaningless to me."

Calmly, and with no change of expression on his face, he replied, "You must lower your desires and relinquish all things. Allow God to lead your soul to where the meaning lies." Our beatings within the Eucharistic Tabernacle served the purpose of impermanence, renunciation and detachment. Nodding that I would do this, I got up onto my feet and turned to go.
****

Honored to encounter my deceased friend, she came with urgency to explain several issues to my yearning spirit. Because she wished to convey several things to her husband, he sat with us in the room but was unable to see her. Conveying to him immediately her words as soon as she expressed them to me, she addressed several issues. Firstly, she loved us both and was very sorry. Secondly, she was now taking very good care of herself, and regretted that she had not done so during life. Further, she regretted not doing all that she could to help herself in her condition. Because she had been unwilling to try non-drug therapies to help alleviate pain, she had become highly addicted to dangerous narcotic drugs. Altering her state of mind, she became less lucid, and this contributed to her untimely death. Although her condition could not have been cured or much alleviated by such things, they may have made her pain more tolerable, and her need for dangerous drugs would have diminished in part.

Attempting to discuss further the issue of the manner of her death, she refused to discuss it and began to disappear from the realm. "Okay, Okay!" I shouted, "We will not go there." Direct and with purpose, she had something disturbing to tell me.

As her soul remained in purgatory, she conveyed, "I must remain her a very long time, primarily because of the manner of my death. Although it is not a 'bad' place to be, and in a lot respect is similar to Earth, it is not good, either." Nodding, she continued, "Most of my time will be spent doing purgatory on Earth watching over those I left behind prematurely, and the rest will be spent in this realm which is always overcast because of the absence of the presence of God, the sun of light. This is my greatest suffering. Knowing that I could have made different choices which would have led to my immediate entrance into heaven and uniting with God is a continual torment to my soul." Vowing to continue to pray for her, we parted ways with a loving smile and my promise to her that I would continue looking over her family on Earth.

Before she left, she said, "I'm very jealous that it is so much easier for you to talk to my husband now, than it is for me. I miss being able to just sit and talk to him more than anything else."

****

Appearing with a distressed look upon his brow, the middle-aged man appeared and began speaking very rapidly as if there was not much time. Immediately, I *knew* that this man was a soul in purgatory and I was very interested in what he might have to say. "You have to replace all the *peace* you didn't make, conflicts you started, unhappiness you generated, agitation or just general discord that you put into the world." Finding his words rather profound, they seemed to generally sum up the true destiny of mankind, the meaning of life, in a way that I'd never fully thought of before.

Going on, he said, "We need to create a wall between us and the living because we have to focus on repairing for what we have lacked and what we could've done, but did not." Again, he repeated, "We have to repair for all the peace we took from the world . . . it takes a lot of energy to do that."

Beginning to ask him a question, I stopped myself as he continued speaking. "You always knew what your passion was, knowledge of God, but my passions in life were other things. I have a lot to make up for." Looking down, I replied, "I am very guilty of taking peace from the world, in many instances." Casually, he replied, "I hadn't known that."

Interrupting, I asked, "What happens when you die, do you reunite with all your loved ones, do you all travel the journey of death together?" Remaining very serious, he replied, "The people you knew before are in the room 'above the bedroom.' You meet them directly after death and then go on your separate ways of purification." "But what about . . ." my words were interrupted, by a rapid yet quiet voice, fading quickly into the night. "We need to create a wall between us and the living, it takes a lot of energy . . ." Then he was gone.

We can do much in this world to make it a better place, but against the enemy of life, which is death, we shall all fail. Our powerless is complete, and we shall all share the same fate. Rather than this being sad, it is liberating, because we are then free to enjoy the moments God chooses to give us without guilt, shame or fear; or the pressure that we must solve this problem, as well.

There comes a time in every life, whether it be the oncoming plane is in view, the terminal condition has taken hold, the car is on its way over the mountain, the volcano has erupted, the tornado is here, the flash flood came too fast; when the soul sees his undeniable fate approaching - and it is death - a ripping away from all things known and seen in this creature's short life, and the soul knows that it is powerless to change the outcome.

Surrender occurs, and it is in this moment that a soul truly lives with eternal life in mind, bringing meaning to the pronouncement held by all religious faiths that we should *all* live our lives with its end in view.
****

Lying down in my home, the normal low ceiling no longer existed and in its place was a large, open cathedral ceiling composed of hundreds of blocks of crystal. Grandpa was standing there as I looked upon it. "You built that," he said, "it's pretty neat isn't it?" Understanding that it represented what I had built in the cathedral of my soul, I nodded, 'Yes.'

Grandpa and my Uncle were suddenly vacuuming the house, as I realized that they were trying to help us with our mess. Asking them to stop, I said, "Don't do that, we should clean our own mess up ourselves," but they ignored me. Feeling the sudden presence of my ancestors, I noticed that my little dog from my childhood had appeared. 'Joy' had died over twenty years prior. Picking her up, she seemed very happy to see me, and it was mutual. Becoming very caught up in my childhood puppy, I forgot about my relatives vacuuming the house for a few moments and just enjoyed my dog.
****

As my eyes opened to the spirit world, they took in a sight unimaginable in the human terms of my own day. Perhaps a future time would not find this vision quite so unusual, but during my time, it was astonishing. Circling my home and filling the clouds around my house were spaceships from many different star systems, apparently having come to give welcome. For a moment, my spirit was lifted out of my body and began flying around the room under the power of the extra-terrestrial beings, as I laughed in the pure joy. Returning my soul to form, they conveyed, 'When it is that your time comes to die, we shall be there to bid you welcome to the galactic heavens.' Honored, I thanked them and bid them adieu.
****

Unable to conceal my annoyance, I'd been taken to the top of the Himalayan Mountains. In my momentary spiritual blindness, I could only think of how difficult it would be to get back down these mountains in my weakened physical condition. Because of my circulation difficulties, I was always cold; and I was absolutely freezing in this location, despite the fact that I was in my spiritual body which usually feels temperature as constant.

Standing amongst a group of Buddhist monks, my deceased friend appeared. As the monks had indicated that I would be studying many ancient texts, different ones each week, my friend looked quite radiant in her white dress. Running towards her and hugging her, as I let her go, I looked deeply into her eyes and said, "I've missed you so much and I love you so much!" Smiling and reciprocating this emotion, she quickly gave me an indication that she had a purpose in being here. Beginning to guide me down the Himalayan Mountains, we walked through the wilderness as she conveyed energetically the wisdom for which she had come to impart. "Buddhism is a little bit more detached and unemotional about mistakes and incorrect views, and this will be helpful to you at this time." Energetically, the understanding of what she was saying pierced my core and I intensely grasped her meaning. "It seems like what you're trying to tell me is that Buddhism is a little bit less judgmental than Catholicism and that this approach might be helpful for me at this time." She nodded, 'Yes.'

As we continued down the mountain, it seemed like we had been together a very long time, and I began to be complacent in realizing that at some point, our visit would have to come to an end. Asking her how I was doing in the spiritual life, she said that I was doing something incorrectly, but she wouldn't be more specific. Making reference to the concept of the 'rapture,' she showed me an image of myself disappearing with just a little pile of clothes remaining, and then moments later, the pile of clothes disappeared just as quickly as had my body. Although I didn't grasp this at the moment, I later realized that this was a demonstration of 'emptiness,' a Buddhist quality I needed to revisit in the spiritual life.

Not understanding her meaning, I just gazed at her expectantly and again asked her to be more specific, to tell me directly what it was that I was doing wrong. But for some reason, it appeared that she did not have permission to do this, and as we got to the bottom of the mountain, another spirit had come to get her. Quietly, she walked away with this spirit and disappeared.

****

Gazing about the room, there were about fifty spiritual children flitting about, all in robes of white, and many with flower garlands draped about their heads like halos. Understanding them all to be prophets, I also inherently knew that they were there on behalf of my children; their purpose in my home had to do with the spiritual formation of my little sweethearts. Despite their childlike stature, their presence was filled with great holiness and power.

An older man was standing next to me, as we were awaiting the arrival of the sub-conscious soul of a man who resided on Earth who was known for his spiritual gifts, in other words a 'psychic.' Chuckling, the older man said, "Won't it be interesting to see if this man will be aware of the presence of so many prophets in your home." Although he didn't say it, he conveyed that oftentimes those with such gifts are so competitive about their abilities, that they completely block out those of a holier nature than themselves, rather than have to humble themselves before more sanctified beings, especially those of such small stature. By doing this, they negate the need for their own further development and can claim that they are already 'there,' simply because of the nature of their gift. Such gifts are given in the hopes of greater cultivation towards holiness, not just the use of the gift in its most primal form.

As he arrived, his response to the room was quite agitated as it was very clear that he was aware of the presence of the prophets, but was very uncomfortable acknowledging that these 'little people' encompassed a holiness greater than his own. In order to reduce the need to speak of them, he turned to us and said, "Gee, you know . . . I believe that I've already given the required amount of time to your reading as I was entering the room. Go . . . ask the guy at the door, he'll tell you. I'm afraid I cannot give you more of my time for a reading." We both looked at him quietly and nodded.

As he was leaving, the older man next to me gave me a knowing glance as I began to disappear and return to form. Honored to have seen the 'little prophets,' I wondered at their greater meaning, but could only speak of having seen them without fully understanding their import.

****

Entering into the fiery monastery, I could not believe the surrounding holiness which filled my soul; fiery in the sense of the Holy Spirit, rather than any physical phenomenon. A lone monk stood before me, his hood draped to cover his forehead. Speaking slowly, he mouthed words very slowly, but as he did, concepts of great magnitude filled my understanding.

Premonitions of my own death filled his concepts, and beyond this, great understandings of the journey of my soul and the souls of my children and husband. Bestowing on me knowledge in regards to my own children, he conveyed that whatever might happen from this point on, was destined to be and was an integral part of their spiritual formation. Sensing that I might have a few years left, I was also deathly aware that this could be wishful thinking. Premonitions are changeable. It could be more . . . . it could be less.

"Are you not aware that your spiritual journey has just begun?" he said, with an ominously exciting look upon his face. "When death comes, your soul will be just beginning the eternal journey for which it is destined to embark!" As he said this, I energetically understood that I was an infant in this great powerful process of God, and there was much for me to learn and discover beyond this world.

Around me were the sounds of a music I cannot describe which filled my soul with such peace and absolute tranquility, I did not want to leave. Fire of the Holy Spirit filled this heavenly space in such a way that it was felt but not seen. The presence of the monk in his aloneness poured out a sense of utter sanctity and I relished in this amazing fire of God's love that I was allowed to feel this night. Candles were lit all around me in the monastery as if this were a medieval holy site that had been preserved and kept throughout timelessness. Vibrating with power in the holy place I'd come, every word came from the mouth of the monk as if in slow motion and caused my spirit to vibrate. "Be at peace with your death," the monk conveyed, "for all is well, and all is as it is meant to be."

Guiding me to a corner of the room, I began to see my obsession with holy writings and relics played out as if in a movie on the wall. Watching as I rummaged through piles of secular books, only to find the one holy book which had been sacrilegiously strewn there, the monk pointed out to me that my ability to recognize and honor that which was holy, was a gift from God.

For hours, I languished in the spirit of this holy monastery amidst the heavens and would have done anything to be allowed to stay there any longer. But as the night progressed, I found my spirit walking along the streets of a heavenly city where people were reading ancient sacred texts in every corner; in restaurants, on benches, in buildings . . .

A very tall man adorned with dark hair, a moustache and beard approached me as I was walking quietly along the stone-encased roadway. For a time, I'd noticed that he'd been following me, and he was showing up in almost every location I happened to traverse. Heavenly lights poured forth from his eyes, and I inherently knew that he loved me. "Don't you recognize me?" he said, as I gazed upon him seeking remembrance. A great knowing filled me, although I could not place it. I *knew* that I knew him. "Do you *not* know that what God is giving to us is the greatest gift in all of heaven?" he said with great fervor. Actually, I hadn't known, so I did not reply.

Leading me down the street, he took me to a tiny corner building. Leading me inside, my eyes filled with wonder as I gazed upon a room filled to overflowing with ancient sacred texts. Running towards a stool surrounded by piles and piles of such texts, I sat down and began to look through them, as my newfound friend looked upon me with a wide grin.

Continuing to look through these old and tattered books, the man patiently awaited my inquiry. "This gift from God you speak of," I asked, "please tell me . . . specifically . . . what it is." Asking this, I wondered if his answer might be knowledge, or perhaps eternal love itself which permeated every cell of this heavenly city. Finally, the thought occurred to me . . . 'He must be speaking of the Redemption!' 'Of course,' I realized, 'he's speaking of the fact that we are saved!' As he smiled a knowing grin, I began to disappear and return to form.

****

Accompanied by a male angel, the woman who had died of heart failure came to encourage me to fight. Showing me a heart transplant in progress, it was indicated that two major complications could arise in my case, but I should accept a transplant if it were to be offered. "Do this for your children," she said.

****

Having died young, a woman came to visit me. "I was afraid to die," she said, "but then I was given entry into Heaven." Pausing, she looked deeply into my eyes as she said, "I was sent here to tell you that Heaven is SO beautiful, that I've never regretted having died so young since." As she began to pull her energy back, I asked her, "Do I have ANY chance at all of going to heaven?" Looking at me with a blank stare, it was clear that she had said what she had been sent to convey, and she didn't have permission to respond to this question. Within a moment, she was gone.

****

Spending the night on a ranch with my grandmother and an Uncle who had passed in the previous two years, another young man was sitting very casually in the kitchen. My Uncle kept referring to him as my 'other Uncle.' Finally, it occurred to me that my father had a brother who had died at the age of five after being struck by a truck while sledding. Excited and exuberant, my newfound Uncle and I went horseback riding along the Galactic mountain range which existed in the heavenly spheres. Expressing

ambivalence about my presence, he shared, "Your condition is very unstable, but you are not necessarily destined to die quite yet. Perhaps if you were to be more careful, you could be assured that you would fulfill every moment of your life. If not, you might die prematurely." Understanding, we returned to the ranch house and I disappeared.
****

Soaring into a wonderful Galactic convent, it was filled with nuns of every age, young and old, who wore modern clothing which appeared to be from my time. An old woman with short, curly gray hair was my guide for this evening, and as I sat and rocked my children who appeared on my lap as if they were babies, they all gathered around and allowed me to listen as they spoke of various things.

Three very holy priests entered the room and sat at our table, beginning to speak of the gifts of the spirit. As they spoke of the Anointing, they made mention of a modern day healer who was not Catholic, but who was blessed with a true gift of the Holy Spirit. Showing unity amongst the denominations, I listened with interest. Because I had been so sick, I didn't move, but the nuns understood.

Leaving the room, the priests retired to a holy sacristy which we were not allowed to enter. As they had been drinking milk, several of the nuns gathered around their glasses and began drinking what they had left behind, conveying that this would fill them with the spirit of holiness that had filled the priests. But I was not allowed to sip from their glasses, because I was of the Earth.

Before I left, the nuns conveyed to me of my holy purpose as a mother, and that although I was very compatible in *visiting* their convent, I wouldn't be so in *living* there. "Go to your home and rock your babies," they said, "for this is what God has ordained for you." Finally, they gave me the sense that I must rest and attain to more stability, because my true time of death had not yet arrived and they wished for me to fulfill my full aeon upon the Earth.
****

Having sat down to play the guitar, I was very surprised when about thirty monks began to literally come out of an old jar which was sitting on the floor about twenty feet in front of me. Wearing a brown habit with their hoods draped over their heads, I immediately knew that they were Essenes. One stepped forward quietly, as he handed me a book which was titled, "The Lost Books of the Essenes." Nodding, I allowed myself to take in their energies as I understood that much of their contents could be found in the Dead Sea Scrolls.

Emerging in my physical body, a single monk stood about five feet from my bed, his hands held in prayer and a hood covering his head. Praying over my sleeping soul for several minutes, he disappeared slowly as I came back to consciousness. Completely silent, his presence conveyed power.
****

Having sat down to talk with this young woman who had recently gone through a bout of non-invasive cancer, I found that my words were not very effective in my attempts to guide her. Next to her, an image of a person began to slowly materialize into the realm in which we occupied, and I became quiet to see who it might be. Within moments, Pope John Paul II had appeared in his white robes with a simple white cap, sitting next to the woman very quietly. "You can not talk to her," he said, "because she has not yet discovered her destiny." Understanding, it was clear that it was pointless to try to talk to this person at this time because of her spiritual status.

****

Filled with knowledge of this incredibly dark soul, he had been involved in a horrendous act of violence, and was now working his way through the court system trying to figure out what to do. Having been offered a plea agreement which would punish him appropriately, but give him a chance at a life in a reasonable amount of time, he'd turned it down, despite the fact that such a choice placed him at risk of being in jail for the rest of his life.

Standing before me, he had just been shot dead energetically. As he resurrected before me, it became clear that by choosing not to take responsibility for his crime and pleading guilty, he had cut off his soul from any future potential.

Good aspects of his soul were shown to me, and the great potential that had been misused and lost because of his horrendous choices. At the very core of his soul was a large pocket of evil, which was very dangerous, unpredictable and violent. Despite these good things, this man was a threat to society, and without a conversion experience, his soul was now officially damned.

Now exiting this soul's symbolic death, I came upon this man's sub-conscious spirit and those of his violent and vicious friends who proceeded to come after me and my children in a gun battle. So that we could not escape, they slashed my tires. Evil exuded from their very pores.

Turning to the kids who I protected with my body, I called to St. Michael for help as we immediately became invisible to all of them, except the defendant. My children began to disappear from the scene, and I was left alone with the main defendant who was now standing at the door of my car inciting me to get out and fight him. Realizing that I could not get away from this confrontation, I got out of the car and stood with my arms folded in front of this man's soul, which was now bare and exposed before me.

Challenging me to fight him, I refused to do so, inciting his rage all the more. Beginning to shout, his voice rang out, "Why won't you fight me?! Why won't you fight me?!" Folding my arms, I looked directly into his eyes with no fear. As my face exuded disgust, I maintained calm and composure as I spoke to him quietly. "Jesus said we should turn the other cheek," I said. With that he tried to punch me in the face, but his fist went right through me. "Love thy neighbor," I said as my voice began to get louder and more insistent, "Do unto others as you would have them do unto you. If you love Me, do as My Father Wills!"

Getting more and more angry, he started to wimp out and walk away, but I followed him with continuing disgust at his violent cowardice. "You're just angry because you *know* you aren't living your life right!" Running after this bully, he was now running away from me. "You know that you are *not* doing the will of God, and that you're screwing up your destiny!" Stopping for a moment, his head turned halfway as if he was listening to my words but did not want to admit them to be true. For a moment, a look of melancholy came over his ashamed face.

"It just drives you crazy that you know you could turn your life around, but you haven't done it! You *know* you are *not* doing the Will of God!" At that moment, he turned to look me in the face for just a moment. His gaze was uncertain, for he had chosen the evil path he wanted to walk, but he *knew* that the choice he had made was wrong, and he *knew* . . . he just *knew*. At that moment, he decided to change his plea. Without any further adieu, my spirit disappeared and was gone.

****

After a series of very violent attacks against strangers in another city, I was given to witness in the astral state the nature of the perpetrator. Portrayed as an envoy of Satan, this person was spreading evil and mayhem in such a manner as to make it seem as though it might never end or be salvageable.

As I gazed upon the sad state that had been caused by this evil soul harboring no brilliant thoughts as to how to solve it, I suddenly witnessed something of stupendous magnitude. From the ground and the ashes of destruction caused by this very tormented and evil man, came a surge of light. Coming from the depths of the Earth, it spread outward as it funneled high into the sky into a wondrous beam which now cascaded with brilliant orbs of sparkly light. A white dove flew from the depths of the Earth, directly into the highest heights of heaven, and a holy feeling overcame my soul.

At that moment, I knew that the evil would be overcome through the intercession of God, and that this had been affected through the prayers of multitudes of people. Awaking the next morning, the beltway sniper had been captured.

****

Wandering through the starry heavens, my soul was alit in the wonders of a great and holy monastery. Gathering to share their joy that I'd arrived, the nuns took care of my every need. A great holy energy filled this place, which was reminiscent of the Essenes. "The Lord does not wish for you to worry about whether or not your works were published, for this does not matter. All that matters to God is that your soul remains 'energetically' in this monastery." Feeling the presence of the Essene monks who had recently come to visit, I understood that they resided in the 'deeper recesses' of the monastery.

****

My oldest daughter (Melissa, now 15) had an experience after praying for me. Worried because I'd recently been put on nighttime oxygen, somebody had come into her room. Looking up to see who they might be, two men in turbans had entered; one black and the other white. Distinctively holy, the black man was clearly the mentor of the other. Both men wore all white garments with the ballooning pants in the tradition of the Sikhs, with the exception of a lime green sash which was worn by the black holy man.

Following them, they peeked into her siblings rooms; they then walked towards my room and stood quietly at the foot of my bed with their hands serenely held before them. Giving me something that I very much needed 'energetically,' love, caring and support, such things had been lacking during my illness because of the normal manner in which terminally ill people are isolated from others. Expressing the great holiness, peace, serenity and powerful silence which occupied their presence, she mentioned that she fell asleep in her dream, only to awaken later to watch them as they left the house quietly. She felt they had come both to assure her that her mother was being watched over, and to let me know that despite the rejection of the world, I was on a correct and holy path. She said they had displayed a calm satisfaction in my spiritual state.

A few weeks before, she had a similar experience where she had been given to go to her brother's window within a dream. Outside the window stood one of the Essene monks wearing a garment of pure white facing to the side with his hands in prayerful repose. Again, was the quiet, silent picture of great power and holiness, of which energy she felt so strongly that she fell to her knees in response. Above him and all around, were the spacecraft of extra-terrestrial civilizations, which emanated power, might and the great vibration which accompanies such crafts 'in the spirit.'
****

Entering into a house, I saw four people I'd known in the past arrive at my door and leave something underneath it. When I went to retrieve it, I was surprised and moved to find that it was a set of cards with lists of hundreds of names of people I had known throughout my life, many of whom had recently found out about my condition, all expressing concern and sorrow. As I held the cards, I felt their concern deeply and realized some very important things.

Although people may say or do weird things in such a situation as this, it doesn't necessarily mean that they care any less. Even those who say things that come across as hurtful probably don't really mean the things they say. Because it is an awkward situation for both parties, the sick person feels like they must constantly validify how they're handling it, what they're doing about it, and whether or not they have the proper mental attitude; while those who come to visit have no idea what they should say. As a result, the *oversensitivity* of the terminal patient can make the visitor feel more *self-conscious* about their words, and that *sensitivity* can make the terminal patient more *self-conscious* about every word that is said. People do really care, which is what is truly important, although the way they show it can sometimes appear otherwise.
****

Coming across a wise old lady who was waiting for me in a house, my dearly departed friend sat across a table from her. Learning from this wise old woman who had gained much knowledge during her life in regards to matters of the spirit, the psychic gift and the path of virtue followed by religion, my friend was here as her pupil. My friend had always been interested in the psychic aspect during her life, but had neglected the path of virtue which is vital to true spiritual unfoldment.

As I awaited word of the purpose for my visit, the old wise woman opened her mouth with a joke. "It seems that your friend here thought she was older than she was," she said, as my friend chuckled under her breath, "she apparently still had some time left in her." Laughing at this reference to the part she had played in her own death, as I told my friend I was jealous that she was going to get to learn from this wise woman and I couldn't. As she seemed to be doing better and better, I was grateful to see her in this light.

Within moments, she was gone.

****

Having wandered through the small town and gone through several ritual passages to receive permission to enter the tiny building, my spirit was elated to finally be given the go-ahead to open the door. Another woman was with me, and had participated in assisting several souls this night, as we gazed upon a building no bigger than an outhouse with a mystical doorway.

Opening the door, we were excited to enter into a grand palace of ancient texts, much larger than the size of the entrance could have inferred. Six floors of white and gold gilded stairwells, each level filled with the ancient knowledge from throughout time. Gathering books, we slowly made our way from the sixth floor downwards. As we prepared to enter upon the first floor, we heard voices and mystical music coming from below. There was an exit available between the second and first floors, and when I heard the sounds, I said, "Perhaps we should quietly leave so as not to disturb anybody." "No, no, no," she replied, "when you hear Kabalistic music, it is an invitation. It would be considered rude if we didn't introduce ourselves." Nodding, we proceeded down the stairs to the first floor.

Astounded by the ancient sacred texts, they were huge and voluminous, the oldest in the building residing on this floor. In fact, some of them were scrolls. Standing before us were a husband and wife with their four grown sons who introduced themselves as the 'Keepers of the Ancient Knowledge.' Honored and amazed, a Jewish woman was singing Kabalistic music 'live' in the corner, and they all welcomed us with the utmost of kindness.

After sitting down with them to eat what they called a 'Pearly breakfast,' consisting of knowledge from the texts being energetically instilled within my soul, one of the sons took me over to a special section that they wanted me to see. Two huge volumes, at least three to four feet in height and a foot thick, were on the shelves next to several scrolls. The first was entitled 'Ave Maria,' and the second, 'The Mysteries of Our Lord.' Allowing me to open the second of these texts, I found mingled within the writing, a fabric banner which was a symbolic image.

As I looked upon it, the young man explained to me that the fabric banners of the cross which I made in the physical world held hidden meanings and were actually textual images. (One of my hobbies was to make fabric images of the cross with various symbols and designs.) Bouquets of flowers moved upwards through the top and above the cross, each blossom representing graces coming from the sacrifice of the cross. Placed upon each blossom were the sayings of Christ, forming a bouquet of the Word.

Showing me a set of keys, he made reference to my own library of ancient sacred texts, comparing it to this counterpart on the other side. By doing so, I realized its importance, even though it sometimes appeared to me to be just my own personal hobby. "You are also a 'Keeper of the Keys,'" he said, "Continue this task in the physical world, and when it is that you cross over, you will continue it in the next . . ." Motioning with his hands the vast expanse of the library, I was so excited that I would work here in the after-life.

Taking me to a large picture window, I was amazed to see a huge city. Skyscrapers made of diamonds could be seen off in the distance, while emeralds and pearls made up much of the rest of the expanse. Literally glowing with light, I was most entranced by the diamond skyscrapers which loomed in the distance. What a beautiful heavenly city! Handing me the keys, I began to disappear from the scene.
****

Undergoing a life review, my spirit walked the pathway of my life and looked over in a very detached manner all the places I'd lived, things I'd done and the general path I had taken this time around. Rather than being a *critical* life review, where my life was scrutinized in regards to things I'd done wrong and right, it was simply a *detached* 'looking over' of the general pattern of my life with no feelings expressed or felt about any events.

After undergoing this journey, my spirit was returned to the beginning and I watched again as another pathway was overlaid above my life. It was a pathway of ancient sacred texts which overlapped the path of my life. After observing the pathway of texts, it was conveyed that I would be returned to my life at the point I was currently occupying. Expecting to go back to the mountains, I was surprised to awaken on the shore, as waves crashed and fell in the sands before me. Observing the oncoming tide, I wondered if this would be an Earthly transition or a heavenly one.

CHAPTER ELEVEN

Having come in response to an urgent prayer, the priest had appeared in a room which resembled the showroom of a modern car dealership. One exception existed, however, in that all the signs and advertisements which would normally be hung and free-standing about the room about cars and trucks were about St. Patrick and St. Nicholas. In the center of the room was a sign which read, 'Don't do anything that pulls you away from Catholicism.'

Sitting down at a table which had been set up for confession, I faced the priest and began to share my usual list of sins, but then quickly stopped myself. "The books I have written speak of reincarnation which is not an accepted Catholic doctrine, what should I do?" I asked. Directing my attention to several books which were displayed on a bookshelf, I noticed that they explained Catholic doctrines. "Some of the views expressed by denominational Christians are incorrect." He said. "These books will help you to see where they are in error."

Leading my attention to life-sized cardboard cut-outs of St. Patrick and St. Nicholas strewn about the room, I observed that they were all depictions of the two saints expelling demons. Showing me a large white book about the life and virtues of St. Patrick, he began speaking in great detail about the *ten heroic virtues* of St. Patrick. "If you study these ten heroic virtues of St. Patrick," he insisted, "you will know what to do."

St. Patrick had expelled demons, converted pagans and attempted to document his amazing mystical life, though he was not gifted with words. But what seemed to be the most important information about the saint was that he had been a follower of the original Nazarean sect of Christianity, who later became the Gnostics who clearly taught reincarnation. During the time shortly after Christ's death, Jesus' brother St. James had expressed a different doctrinal Christianity than St. Paul, who despite his great holiness had never actually met Christ during His life. St. Patrick had followed the Nazarean sect, and this was one of the reasons for his many difficulties with Rome.

"The disciples said to Jesus, 'We know that you will depart from us. Who is to be our Leader?' Jesus said to them, 'Wherever you are, you are to go to James the righteous, for whose sake heaven and earth came into being."
The Nag Hammadi Library, The Gospel of Thomas No. 12, (Christianity, Gnostic, Words of Christ)
"When the blessed one had said this, he greeted them all, saying, 'Peace be with you. Receive my peace to yourselves. Beware that no one lead you astray, saying, 'Lo here!' or 'Lo there!' for the Son of Man is within you. Follow after him! Those who seek him will find him. Go then and preach the gospel of the kingdom. Do not lay down any rules beyond what I appointed for you, and do not give a law like the lawgiver lest you be constrained by it.' When he had said this, he departed."
The Nag Hammadi Library, The Gospel of Mary, No. 8-9, (Christianity, Gnostic, Words of Christ)
****

Taken on a journey through many purgatory realms, my spirit was shown something inexplicable. Many levels were represented; beginning at 100 - 300, but going on to around 100,000. Souls who were in the purgatories numbered 100-300 were much more likely to be released in a short amount of time, while those above represented higher and higher levels of vice which required long periods of purgation from which it was much more difficult to be released.

Shown to me in comparison with the stories on a high-rise building, an elevator was accessible to ascend or descend from levels 100-300. While the other levels above this were accessible to be ascended by this same elevator, souls in these realms were not able to descend or leave these realms without strict orders from the Almighty.

Souls worked themselves down from their level of vice, under strict divine supervision, and those who inhabited the levels above 300 appeared to have been there for a very long time, while souls in levels 100-300 had a regular and timely turnaround and were allowed to operate with a great deal more personal freedom.
****

Watching in the distance over the desert oasis, my spirit observed as six fighter jets approached their target and bombed a city. After the place was obliterated, they flew away while I continued to watch the clouds of destruction dissipate.

Finally, a huge craft of obvious extra-terrestrial origin appeared and flew over the scene several times, sometimes slowly and sometimes very fast. Emitting great power, the craft was shaped somewhat like an Earthly airplane, long and conical; but it was completely silver, had no wings, and was covered in a variety of metal plates which resembled the exoskeleton of a grasshopper. Overseeing events in the world, I knew that they were watching carefully the decisions of mankind, but that only my eyes were able to see them at this moment. (A moment of great import, the world was in the midst of making the decision of whether or not to invade Iraq which was being ruled by an evil dictator.)

Returning to form, an obviously demonic presence manifested before my face, that of a woman with black hair and canine teeth. In annoyance, I calmly said, "Get a life, Satan."

As she instantly disappeared, the image of my white-winged horse, St. Harmony Crystal Fire, appeared before my vision, wings flapping in the wind. Feeling the immense power, St. Harmony Crystal Fire passed by me in a wind of ethereal power as I reached to touch a feathery wing which swept across my face as he passed.
****

Cascading through time, my spirit was taken to visit a group of souls consisting of many I'd known throughout my life. These were the souls of those who had stayed in my life, but had never embraced a spiritual path, many of them atheists or agnostics.

Gathering for this profound reunion, we spent many hours talking and reminiscing about times spent together, but as the evening wrapped up, I wandered alone upstairs. As the gathering was being held in the home of a soul who had been previously revealed to me, I remembered that her home had once been infested with many demons, almost like a haunted mansion, but now I was grateful to note that the demonic presences were gone and the home was clear of any forces.

Profundity filled my vision as I ascended the stairs to notice a grand picture displayed before my eyes. Amongst this home filled with items displaying a love of the world, was a magnificent portrait of Jesus and Mary. Gazing at it, I could not believe that it was hanging on *this* wall in *this* house. Running downstairs, I found the person who lived in the house and another of her friends. "Where did you get this?!" I shouted expectantly at their confused faces. "You mean you really don't know?" her friend asked. Nodding that indeed I did not, they both led me upstairs to a bedroom that I had not yet seen.

As the door was opened, I watched in amazement and shock. Adorned with magnificent holy relics, every wall was covered from top to bottom with religious artwork, crucifixes, statues, medals and holy books. "Oh, my God!" I said. "Where did you get all of this stuff?" "You mean you really don't know?" they both asked me again in unison. "No, I don't."

"You began sending us these things about twelve years ago, don't you remember?" Immediately, I realized that although the impact of my words through the years had appeared to be of no import on a conscious level with these souls, they had been received as heavenly gifts. Stunned, I walked around the room, admiring the beauty of these magnificent pieces. For a moment, I was almost a bit jealous because I would have loved to have these beautiful works in my own home, but realized that such thinking was very selfish and admonished myself for such thoughts.

Taking me back downstairs, the woman showed me a large picture window which was now adorned with the most exquisite curtain of roses. About 500 individual stained glass roses were formed and joined together as a large window-covering. Pointing at the spectacular vision, I turned to the woman of the house. "That was a gift you made for me before you died," she said.

****

Within a moment, my soul was looking upon the most spectacular light and I chuckled when I saw what lay within its confines. Although my dog, 'Joy', had died twenty years prior, she stood at the gateway to the light waiting for me, looking brilliant and joyous. Wishing to embrace my childhood pal who had been with me for about fifteen years, I knew that I could not, for doing so would irrevocably take me into the light and beyond the gateway of death. "I'm sorry," I said to my dog, "I can't come with you now because my kids are just too young."

In total understanding, she remained in the brilliance of the light as a book appeared in my hands. Looking at its title, it said, 'The Palace of Ancient Knowledge.' 'Oh, okay," I thought, as I gazed upon the cover art and its depiction of this grand place within the realms of ether.

As I gazed upon the page, it transformed itself into a written message from Christ, whose Presence could now be felt powerfully at my side. "You need to pray more for a quality of which you are lacking." Displayed on the page, the quality was written down and I recognized immediately that it was something for which I should strive.

Despite this, I was unable to recall the quality upon return.

Led to a porch, I observed that the steps leading to it were of different heights. The one on the right was waist high and complete, and the one on the left was built only to the level of the bottom crossbeam. Immediately directing my attention to the one on the right, Christ conveyed, "This one represents your soul, and as you can see, it is complete." Directing my attention to the one on the left, He continued, "And this one represents the souls of those you will leave behind, which are incomplete." Looking at him, I said nothing, but questioned Him with my gaze as to what had caused this deficit. "It is incomplete because of selfishness," He said. Directing my attention to the light which still contained the essence of my childhood dog, He began leading me towards it. As He did, I heard somebody screaming at another person somewhere nearby. "Thus is the nature of this world," He said, "Even as you cross over, they will be thinking only of themselves."

Gazing at the light, I felt a sense of total peace and welcome, something which was unfamiliar in my past near-death moments. For in the past, I had encountered an energy of uncertainty, as though my dying would be premature if I were to go in that moment. But at this time there was total serenity because my soul was complete.

Because of this shift, I had an epiphany as I stared at the light. At some point, my time would truly be up, and I would go to sleep and wake in another world. Death became more real to me than it had already been due to my illness, and it really 'hit' me that I was really going to die . . . and it might be soon. In this welcoming grand gesture of God, in the light which stood before me, I was beginning to feel that my journey upon the Earth was coming very close to its end. Someday, and perhaps soon, I would no longer have a choice.

As I realized this, Christ filled me with peace about this eventuality, in that I had completed that which I had come to do, and it was just time for me to go. Before my eyes, I saw the image of the books I had written as Christ conveyed, "You must pass the torch onto Andy, and make sure he realizes the importance of this task. He must finish your work when you are no longer able."

Directing me again to the bright tunnel, Christ conveyed that He was giving me the final option of entering into the light. "I cannot go to the light, yet, Lord, for my kids are too young." Nodding, He honored my willingness to remain for their sake. In a flash, I was back.

"And five hundred and fifty days since he had risen from the dead, we said to him, 'Have you departed and removed yourself from us?' But Jesus said, 'No, but I shall go to the place from whence I came. If you wish to come with me, come!' They all answered and said, 'If you bid us, we come.' He said, 'Verily I say unto you, no one will ever enter the kingdom of heaven at my bidding, but (only) because you yourselves are full.'"

The Nag Hammadi Library, The Apocryphon of James, No. 2, Verses 20-35, (Christianity/Gnostic, Words of Christ)

"Then he said to his disciples, 'Have I not told you that like a visible voice and flash of lightning will the good be taken up to the light?'"

The Nag Hammadi Library, The Dialogue of the Saviour, No. 38, (Christianity, Gnostic, Words of Christ)
****

Whisked off to the grand city of the palace, my spirit waited in a small house in a neighborhood before they came to take me. While I was waiting, I looked around the house, honestly perceiving that this was an Earthly home in the spheres, but was shown several labels on construction supplies used to build the place, which all exhibited dates from the future, most of them 50 years beyond the current date.

Two extra-terrestrial spirits arrived and quietly led me off, out of the neighborhood and into the city. Taking me to a small room, I was shown a set of five papers which explained my interstellar journey to the city and that with which they were about to embark. Changing my clothes, I was being adorned in the attire of the galactic heavens; a pair of shiny pants and a large shirt which was long sleeved and closed to the neck. After dressing appropriately, my spirit was taken to a square in this magnificent city of light.

Standing at a counter, a young man said nothing as he gathered up four very old ancient texts from behind the desk and placed them in front of me to view. Intrigued, I noticed that they all appeared very old, but was surprised to notice that their publication dates ranged from 1991 - 2058. (In my present time-space continuum, it was currently 2003). Reading their titles and taking note of their contents, I remembered that one book was deeply ingrained in Native American spirituality, while the others were mysterious spiritual commentaries on various subjects. Bringing me another book, it was written in a language I didn't understand, and a man appeared at my side to explain its meaning.

From the title, I could glean that it was about the mysteries, but nothing more. Looking to my right, a tall man with a cowboy hat was gazing at the text, as I immediately realized that both of us were galactic archaeologists, and it was my task in this next life to 'translate' texts which were written in my native tongue to an inexplicable galactic language of the spheres. Rather than being a librarian in the 'Palace of Ancient Knowledge,' it was going to be my task to translate, as did this other man who spoke a different language, from what I recall, a European tongue.

Walking towards a boardwalk, I entered into a small glass-encased room which held sacred relics. As I entered, I noticed a large head of Christ on the cross, the 'Ecce Homo.' Several crucifixes were displayed on the glass walls, as well, but my spirit was led to a remarkable object which lay ahead. A life-size sculpture of Mother Teresa in her death casket was carved out of the purest white stone, as I immediately understood this to be symbolic of my own death in some way. Gazing upon the serene and holy image, somebody had come to take me on a tour of the city.

What ensued was entirely inexplicable and I have only been given to remember small snippets of this wondrous and exciting adventure. Taken through the city, we were on our way towards the Palace of Ancient Knowledge, but we made about eight stops in different locations where various souls were waiting for me to tell me of different secrets of the spheres. Having many beautiful terms to share with me of galactic things and heavenly attainments, I was unable to remember a single one, despite the fact that I wrote each of them down on a note pad in the spirit. One small snippet that my memory retained was of a galactic being who in answer to a question I posed, replied in a lengthy scientific discourse about molecular structure and galactic knowledge. In a state of total awe, I took a tour of this city as the hosts made welcome to my soul. Knowing I would be coming to this city upon my death, I was so very excited; I cannot even put it into words.

As we made our way through, my guide took me to the edge of the city of light where I noticed in the grand distance the 'bad part of town.' Looking like a 19th century towered city of London, great darkness oozed from the distant place. Hearing the screaming and yelling of the dark ones, my tour guide bade me to know, "When you arrive in this city, do not ever venture beyond this point, for what you see beyond is a point of darkness, a purgatory realm of great discord and to do so would put your soul in great peril." Understanding, I nodded in agreement to never do such a thing as I was whisked off through another corridor.

As I entered, another familiar face came into the room. The man who had 'married' me on the mountain had come into the room with several friends, and was so engaged in what they were doing that he didn't notice my presence. Taking note of this familiarity, I turned to my guide, a tall thin man with black hair, and asked, "Are you going to be taking me to the Palace?" Smiling, he replied, "We are on our way there." Pulling out several pictures, they held images of notable people who had lived in this city and done important things for God. Most of them appeared to be from a different age, as the men wore top hats and the women wore bonnets. Taking my hand, we began walking quickly through another corridor, presumably towards the Palace.

Placing his arm around me, a sudden familiarity came over my soul as he smiled at me in recognition. "Who are you?" I asked, wondering if he might reveal our ancient connection. "I can't say," he replied nonchalantly. "You're not allowed to tell me are you? None of you are allowed to reveal your connection to those of us still on the Earth, are you?" Nodding, 'No,' I asked, "Why?" "I can't say," he replied.

Stopping, he pointed off into the distance as I felt the wondrousness of this holy city, and the imminent nature of my demise. At this moment, it felt that my time on Earth would *really* be coming to an end and that I was being introduced to the world I would attend to at that time. Any concern that I might have had about my readiness was quickly dispelled, as the same message that had been conveyed to me by Christ about my soul having reached completion was repeated and felt deeply within. But knowing my own unique path and that sometimes I underwent spiritual deaths in order to bring in new knowledge, only time would tell. "The Palace is up in the distance," he said, as he pointed towards something I could not yet see. Excited and amazed, I looked with anticipation as something began to materialize in the ether. But before it could, I was whisked away. "No, let me see it!" I shouted, but it was of no avail. It was time for me to go.

Was my soul preparing for a true death? Or was I being initiated into yet another realm of knowledge beyond the gates? Either way, my journey would continue . . .

Waking, an inexplicable and very intensive heat began to pour through my chest, arms, abdomen and hips which continued for three hours. So hot, I checked several times to see if the electric blanket was on high, but found it to be detached from the bed. 'Could the Lord be bringing me back in some way?' I thought.

"And he sent for the merchant which had brought him, and for the apostle, and said unto him: Hast thou built me the palace? And he said: Yea. And the king said: When, then, shall we go and see it? but he answered him and said: Thou canst not see it now, but when thou departest this life, then thou shalt see it."
The Apocryphal New Testament, Acts of Thomas, Second Act, Number 21, (Christianity, Gnostic, Words of St. Thomas)

"The Savior said to his disciples, 'Already the time has come, brothers, for us to abandon our labor and stand at rest. For whoever stands at rest will rest forever. And I say to you, (be) always (above) time . . ."
The Nag Hammadi Library, The Dialogue of the Savior, No. 1, (Christianity, Gnostic, Words of Christ)

CHAPTER TWELVE

For several nights, my soul was given to observe aspects of my next task. Frantically writing, the energy seemed somehow different. Entering into the Palace of Ancient Knowledge, gold and white filled the space which was ornately decorated. Staircases of a grand whiteness were inlaid with gold as the oldest scrolls were kept on the first floor.

Taken immediately to a place within the palace I had not yet seen, my spirit was surrounded by filing cabinets stacked from the floor to the ceiling which was about thirty feet high. Every available space in this basement was filled, and I looked upon the cabinets with expectancy. A man and woman were waiting my arrival, immediately showing me a set of two smaller filing cabinets. "I've been summarizing all of these filing cabinets into two," the woman said, "and I'm almost finished. I'll be giving them to you very soon."

Allowing me to look into one of them, there were tens of manila folders, each labeled with deep aspects of many manifold spiritual mysteries. An element of science emanated from them, as well, which excited me. Looking at lists of spiritual/scientific concepts which were to come, I nodded that I would be patient.

Suddenly, my attention was drawn towards the other direction which was no longer part of this enclosed building, but a scene from somewhere . . . sometime. A man wearing the uniform of a revolutionary war soldier was running frantically across a grassy field towards me, calling out to me as if I were his daughter and he was trying to get to me before it was too late. Before he made it across the field, however, a shot rang out and he fell, almost as if in slow-motion, to the ground. In that millisecond, he was gone, and the mystery of his beckon would remain so . . . . for now. Before long, such ancestral surges through the mists of time would again emerge to reveal their purpose.

The following night, a tiny animal which looked like a furry version of a prairie dog scurried in front of me, and as he passed, a series of ancient texts appeared. Encompassing the greater secrets hidden within the mysteries, he conveyed, "Although such things are available in your world, they are not well written. You are going to write about the mysteries and make them understandable to mortal men." Nodding in acceptance of this new task, he finished, "Remember what I said, it's important." Scurrying off into the night, energetic loops entered into my spirit from the ancient texts which lay before me, filling me with the energy of mystery . . .
****

Gathering amidst the ancient library, I found my soul drawn towards a large set of old texts which were about 8 inches in height and off-white in color. At the side of the room, a set of about twenty exquisite and large ornate Catholic statues of Jesus, Mary and various saints, were lined and painted with the utmost care and beauty. Observing their holiness, I continued towards the texts.

Appearing to be a series of papers on the mysteries, I walked towards them, suddenly noticing that upon the wallpaper of this deep cellar, an image of a secret door was opening. White and blue stripes lying vertical from the ceiling to the floor began appearing, overlaid by a mystic image in the shape of a square filled with angels, cherubs, gateways, golden ribbons, and other mystical mirages moving on the wall, as if it were a doorway.

Reaching towards it, I turned to notice that many of the Catholic statues had disappeared and only a few remained. Of those few, the paint was dripping off of them as if they'd been kept out in the rain before the paint had a chance to dry. 'I understand,' I thought, 'in my journey into the mysteries, I must be very careful not to lose the truth, not to allow it to be *watered down* by nebulous intellectualisms in my inquiry.' Loosening, the gateway which merged into the wall became fluid and penetrable.

Beginning to open the secret door, I suddenly noticed a man in a business suit approaching. *Instantly*, I *knew* he represented pure evil, but before I had a chance to respond, I was hit. Shuddering from the force of the attack, I awoke and began vomiting violently. Somebody, or perhaps some dark force, did not wish for me to enter into the mysteries and reveal them to the world.
****

Running through the canyons, I was deep in the crevasse of rock. Another angelic guardian ran beside me, repeating over and over, "Keep pushing! Keep pushing!" Continuing to run, my spirit wasn't finished until the end of the night. As I finally had run all the way back to the top of the deep canyon, my spirit and body were exhausted. "Keep pushing," she repeated with a smile as I breathed loudly.

In her eyes was a message; my spirit and body were being brought back, and the Lord wished for me to push myself in order to recondition my body which had been deteriorating for so long due to heart failure.

Suddenly, I was back. After a three-hour surge of heat had entered my body and filled it a week or so before, the Lord was bringing me back from the threshold of death, and preparing me to get to work on my next task. "Keep pushing," she repeated with a knowing smile as we both disappeared.
****

Wandering through the grand mansion, I couldn't believe my eyes. Having been taken back in time to the world of Russia right before the Revolution in the early 1900's, I was now being given a guided tour of the home of Arta and Helen Uzebacheff (Maiden name - Sagradeff), the great-great grandparents of my three children; Melissa, Mary and Jacob, by a cordial maid.

Helen had died at the age of forty before the war, but Arta had gone on to face the trying times of the Revolution with his four sons and two daughters. When the Russian Revolution had come, this aristocratic and very wealthy Armenian family was separated, as my children's great-grandfather, Joseph Uzebacheff, would never see his father and several of his siblings again in this life. Losing his eldest brother, Manuk, a doctor, and a sister to the armies of Stalin, the entire family was thrown out of their home and separated by war. Another brother, Ivan (after whom my husband's father was named), would die a little bit later after receiving the wrong prescription from a pharmacy. His two sisters, Ann and Katharine, had been married to two brothers, and Joseph's youngest brother, Jacob, would survive the war, dying in 1972 of natural causes. Joseph and Jacob would be reunited after the war. Arta, their father, died in 1920 of unknown causes.

Joseph, a member of the White Army at the age of eighteen, walked from Tiblisi to Istanbul, Turkey, crossing over the Southern Mountains of Russia into Persia which is currently present-day Iraq, completely separated from every member of his family for the first time in his young life. 5000 men were with him, living off of bugs and rainwater, seventeen of those men arrived alive in Persia; among them, my husband's grandfather and my children's great-grandfather, Joseph Uzebacheff. Crossing the river from Russia to Persia, his good friend was thrown from the boat and immediately sucked into a whirlpool where he would meet his fate, that of death. As Joseph made it to the other side, he fell to his knees in tears, kissed the ground and shouted out to the heavens, "Why me, Lord, why me?!?!?"

Returning to Russia after the Revolution, grandpa's greatest remembrance was of the time he spent at an orphanage, where he spent his time picking up children orphaned by the war off of the streets covered in maggots and bugs, and bringing them to shelter and safety.

Arta had a brother, Joseph's Uncle VaGram, who had immigrated to America as an engineer, doing work for the Russian's on the railroads. Providing Joseph with the means to cross the ocean and come to America, we would only discover later in the century that Uncle VaGram had spent most of his adult life giving anonymous scholarships to children in Russia, hoping to rebuild the country of his origin. When it was discovered by our family what he had done, there was quite a great number of students in Armenia, a province of the Soviet Union, who had received scholarships to Universities. A front page article had been done on his life in the province where this had taken place.

In America, Joseph went from being an aristocrat of his time to becoming a true common man. Meeting (1926) and marrying (1928) Oxana Harkevitch, a governess and immigrant from Italy, who had Russian roots, as well; Ivan, their only son, was born in 1929. Ivan met Anne, the daughter of Czechoslovakian immigrants - Maria (Maiden Name - Vanicek) and Joseph Hornik - and had three children. Their oldest son would eventually become my husband, Andy.

Wandering through the mansion, I was overwhelmed with the opulence of it. Showing me the way it might have looked at the time of the Revolution, an overlapping reality merged with the images which might have reflected the building in later years. After it had been seized by the Communists, it had become a hospital.

Taken to a solitary room, my soul was being shown some of the things that may have existed at the time of Arta and Helen's lives. An old car was in the room, the type which had no roof over the passenger compartment. Many other early-nineteenth century items were scattered around; clothing, furniture, and other household belongings. But the maid led me to a desk.

Rummaging through the desk, I now noticed many servants walking amongst the corridors as if they were continuing at this moment to do what they might have done in the early 1900's. Directing my attention to the maid who had guided my tour and was now assisting me in looking for whatever it was I had been sent here to find, I asked, "What do you know about the people who lived here?" "The man of the house was very kind," she said, "and we were very well taken care of." Immediately, I understood that she was referring to the servants of the house.

Arta wished for me to find something very important to his wife, and I continued to fumble through the drawers until I came upon the objects which I immediately knew to be that for which I had been sent.

Holding in my hands a set of five different books, I was entranced by them. Two of them were written by Helen Uzebacheff, and had appeared to me in the form of a formerly published book which was now out of print. At the moment, it appeared that perhaps this book represented a lifetime that had yet to be documented, the knowledge of which had yet to be contained. Much of the two books contents appeared to contain spiritual wisdom attained during her short life.

Gazing now at the other three books, they were written by other people of whom I didn't yet know. Upon one of the covers was a depiction of something in regards to World War II. Could this be the life knowledge of Uncle Andrew Hornik born in 1913, the man whom my husband had been named after? Anne, Andy's mother, had an older brother who had given his life while fighting on the island of Leyte in 1943 during World War II at around the age of 30.

Taking my hand, the maid was now leading me back into the large corridor which had been the hallway of this grand mansion, guiding me towards another building on the lush and spacious grounds where I was about to meet Arta, my children's great-great grandfather and be given the chance to talk with him face to face. But as we walked towards the gate, I began to disintegrate. Reaching towards this mystical mirage, I shouted, "No, not yet!" But my time for this eve was apparently now over.

My journey into death had taken me into the fascinating world of my ancestry. Because I had been so close to the gateway of death, my deceased friends and relatives from this life had become very present to me, but I had also discovered a whole slew of ancestors nearby of whom I'd not previously known. Moved beyond words at the care and concern of those who resided in the world beyond 'death' for those of us who remain in the world of the 'living,' I was amazed at the overlap and how closely we remain intertwined, despite the lack of awareness of most of humanity at their presence.

Perhaps in this overlapping of worlds, the world of the living and the world of the 'dead,' greater knowledge was to be obtained. Perhaps some of the mysteries of our existence could be found in the histories of our ancestors. Perchance, such matters as individual and religious lineage and planetary evolution . . . could overlap?

Time had come for me to get to work on genealogy. For if we forget the original dream and from whom it came, we lose the destination. In order to remember the dream, we must remember those who have come before. Our triumphs are borne on the backs of those who toiled, suffered and struggled to make them possible. Once upon a time, long, long ago, somebody had a dream . . .

****

Images and mirages penetrated my vision as the Lord filled me with a deeper understanding of my next task. Worried that I may not be able to contain what had been shown to me, I pondered before leaving the mystical realm as to how I would bring it back into the physical world and remember it. Despite my best efforts, I returned with no further memory of the experience beyond the profound knowledge that I'd seen something of magnificence and great import.

Returning to the spirit world, my soul was taken to join the members of a large family. Two parents and six children, I was saddened to learn that one of the older boys who appeared to be in his early twenties was dying of Cardiomyopathy, a disease I shared. Talking with him, he said, "My doctors have told me that there is nothing more we can do, I am close to death."

Having walked that road myself, I was deeply moved by the sorrow of this family. At the dinner table, I sat next to him and his mother, and quietly listened as they spoke of the hardship of this cruel situation. Placing my arm around her shoulder, I spoke to his mother. "Several weeks ago, I was in the same position." I said. "And today, the Lord has brought me back. Do not lose hope." (My condition had improved in part due to a change in medication, but it was my sincere belief that there was also divine intervention [an episode of heat] involved because it had improved so dramatically that the medication change seemed an unlikely source of the entire transformation. My belief was that I'd improved dramatically due to both factors, and that God was bringing me back to some degree, perhaps to make it possible for me to continue working; but to what level or for how long, we didn't yet know. My condition remained terminal but stable for the moment, and hopefully for years to come.)

My words were not that helpful, and I fully understood, because I'd been in their shoes just weeks before. When actually engaged in the battle, you have no idea of how it will end. You cannot expect people engaged in warfare for the life of themselves or a loved one, to focus on hope alone.

A grieving process is underway which is normal and required, in order for the soul to prepare for whatever outcome may cross their doorstep. Because statistically speaking, death is very often a greater probability than a healing of any kind, and death is a journey which is usually taken without the traveler's conscious consent.

****

Sitting on the back porch, my spirit was communicating with my four year old son in the future, when he was grown and ready to marry. Talking with his fiancée,' she asked, "Is it hard to let go?" "Well," I replied, "It's hard to explain, but yes, it is hard to let go, but at the same time, I *know* in my heart that it's something that I must do because it is time." Looking at me with understanding, I continued, "I'm just very glad he chose someone like you, that's what I've wished for him." Smiling at me, she spoke only with her eyes. For a moment, I felt the searing pain that would come with that moment, as a mother, in stepping aside and allowing him to go forward with another person, although at the same time I felt the absolute necessity of doing so.

Realizing suddenly where we were sitting, it was the first home that my husband and I had owned after we had married. Pointing to a rose bush near the fence, I shouted to my son, "I planted that rose bush a few weeks after your oldest sister was born!" Nodding in acknowledgement, I was guided by an unseen hand towards the side of the fence.

Almost breaking out into tears, I shouted, "Oh, my God, Lacey!" Lacey had been my neighbor in that home, an elderly woman who had turned her backyard into a veritable victory garden. During her life, she would harvest seeds from her voluminous array of flowers, and give them to me to plant in my own yard. Next to her was the elderly woman who had lived across the street from her, who had been her best friend. Having died while we lived there, Mary was a sweet, sweet lady who also loved to plant flowers.

Hugging the two of them, I remembered how they had both lived on that street their entire lives. Both were widowed, and had lived on their own for many years after the deaths of their husbands. Lacey had owned her home free and clear, and I remembered what she had told me one day while I was sitting in her living room hearing about her life. "If you handle your finances well during your life," she said, "you should be able to show something for it by the time you're my age." Because she owned her small two bedroom one bath home free and clear, she was sharing with me how she and her husband had never made much money because he had been a blue collar worker, but they had lived simply and paid for what they owned. Because of this, she was able to live comfortably in her later years.

While we had been her neighbor, Lacey had sort of adopted me, and I had very fond memories of these two grand ladies. As I hugged them and felt deep joy in their vision, I reveled in our reunion and the realization that despite how long ago this had been; the two of them were still keeping an eye on our family from the world beyond. How honorable this was to my soul.

Turning again to my momentarily full-grown son, he was wandering into the backyard gathering something from the grass. Noticing a residue on the lawn, I said, "Oh, yeah, that's the pollution that comes from the paper factory down the street. Nothing you can do about it." (Many factories of all sorts surrounded this area we had formerly lived, and pollution was a way of life there.) Nodding and intrigued by this, because he had grown up in the mountains where such things did not occur, he held it in his hands with a look of concern.
****

Going back in time to the period in which I got married, my soul was bade to experience it from a different vantage point. Remembering that there was an element of 'having' to get married, although I was not pregnant. Complications due to my own immaturity and youth would arise, but my spirit was still very much excited because I loved my future husband.

Having been taken into the house to wait for a message which was due to arrive from my husband's family, I was pacing the room, nervous as to how they may feel about me as their future daughter-in-law. As the doorbell rang, I went to the door with expectancy, as a delivery man handed me a pile of about twenty or thirty letters from them. Immediately, one fell to the floor, with an attached gift.

Gazing at the interesting package, it had some new publishing software included, which I immediately felt had symbolic value. Representing support of the path of writing in my life, it was almost as if the gift held within it energies that would bring the publication of my work to fruition. Looking towards the attached note, I immediately recognized the handwriting, although I doubt that I've ever seen it during this lifetime. 'Nina Harkevitch,' it said in English, as I rushed to open the letter. But as I did so, I was pulled away from the scene before I could read her words.

Aunt Nina was Andy's grandmother's sister. Oxana had been married to Joseph Uzebacheff, the son of Arta and Helen. But her side of the family held great interest and intrigue, as well.

Nina was an Italian doctor, teacher, poet and a painter, whose written works had been published Germany and St. Petersburg. Known for her generosity as a physician, many of her patients became her friends. When she passed away, it was this that people remembered about her the most. Having lived a long life, she died at 92 of old age.

Oxana and Nina had a brother named Nikita, an accomplished Pianist at the Conservatory of Munich, who died a tragic death due to pneumonia in 1932, at the age of 22. Adrian Harkevitch, their father, conducted a choir in the Russian Orthodox Church, and had married Anna Levitsky, a very accomplished piano player who had hopes of becoming a concert pianist. Because of the times and the foreordained roles of women, she was unable to pursue that dream during her lifetime. Also a painter, one of Anna's paintings had been given to us by Oxana of a friend of her mother's which hangs in our hallway.

Several other stories within Oxana's family hold intrigue, as well. Joseph Vassilieve (Wife - Sophia), the father of her grandmother, was a priest and spiritual advisor to the Russian Czar, Alexander II, and was sent to Paris to found the Russian Orthodox Church in France in the year 1847. Saint Alexandre Nevsky Church in Paris was founded in 1861 and still stands today as his living legacy. Oxana's grandfather, Archpriest Vladimir Levitsky, founded the Russian Orthodox Church of the Nativity of Christ and of Saint Nicholas the Thaumaturge in Florence. Having given a loan to a young art student so that he might be able to attend school around the year of 1869, the young and very brilliant painter contracted Tuberculosis and died. Because the family had no money to repay the loan, they offered her grandfather an unfinished painting of

St. Peter which had been painted by the decedent. Hanging on our living room wall, this painting appears complete, but if you look closely at the hands, you will see that it was left undone. Beyond this, the painting looks like it could have been painted by one of the great masters, and remains as a living legacy of the amazing talent that was so cruelly torn away from this world by a disease which had yet to be cured; a tragic example of the cost of an individual life.

How many of us forget the legacy of our forebears? Certainly I have, and the most profound revelation of this recent surge of ancestral visits, lies within the realization that though we have forgotten our forebears, they still remember and look over us. Such love, and yet most of us remain so unaware of their watchful eyes and loving embrace. Souls we've never known, never met in this life, and yet we are the fruit of their womb, their great-great grandchildren, and the line of the dream that began with them . . .

As my spirit awoke, the words 'Tomb of Bereavement' were placed within my head, although I was yet unaware of their meaning.

****

Having been taken to a party to honor the recent 'healing' I'd received, about 200 souls were gathered at a church to celebrate. During the party, I was made to know that my 'healing' was a partial one, and that the Lord had granted me renewed vigor and strength, but that I was not cured. Beyond this, it was clear that I would need to remain on medication, because my healing was being accomplished through drugs, and that mine was to be a medical miracle with limited parameters. Apparently, I remained in danger of sudden death, and at this moment, my life had been extended through a grace from God, but it was a temporary extension. Because I'd had a few such extensions already, it became clear that I must use the time given my soul well in the service of God, and that I could continue to ask for repeated extensions as the time came; but at this moment, I was due to die unexpectedly of sudden death sometime in the future, near or far wasn't shared, when I would appear to be doing quite well.

Overwhelmed by this information, I followed the large crowd as they began filing into a large hallway to begin a journey to an unknown destination. Walking quietly through the corridors, they slowly became very grand and ornate caverns, stalagmites majestically hanging from the ceilings and protruding from floors. Very bright, it was unlike an Earthly cavern because it was well lit and spacious.

As we were traveling through the caverns, I ran into many spirits I recognized on a soul level, but did not know in my current Earthly life. It occurred to me that some of these familiar faces could very well be ancestors, and the reunions with these people were so comforting and warm, I cannot properly give it justice. Very many of them were old, old friends, of whom I could not place, but seeing them again was an awesome experience. Immediately, we began talking about old times that I don't remember from this life, but perhaps from many others and from times between them.

An old and very sick woman wearing an oxygen tank was struggling to get through the cavern, and her full-grown son - tall, thin, and red-headed - was attempting to help her. But she would go into breathing fits and something resembling cardiac arrest every few minutes. Annoyed, he was embarrassed by her difficulties and started saying things to her that were unkind. Relating to the predicament of the older woman due to my own condition, I couldn't help but wonder why in the world anybody would have brought her into this place in the first place. Approaching the red-headed man, I didn't immediately recognize him, but would later. "Don't you realize how much you really love your mother?" I shouted at him with anger. "You're not angry at *her*, but rather, you're angry at the situation. You do all of this for her because you *know* that if she wasn't with you, you'd *miss* her a great deal more than she cramps your style now!" Our society can be very unkind to the sick, but those of us who have lost someone who had a burdensome illness realize that the void caused by their absence is often more difficult and painful than living with the disease.

Despite my rude display, the man had listened to my words, and immediately calmed. "You really helped me," he said, as his eyes began searing into my own and recognition began to emerge, "I really need someone like you in my life. I've been acting like a hillbilly to fit in, but I've really needed something and someone deeper." Moved by his words, he finished, "If you could learn to control your anger, you could really help people like me." In that moment, I realized that this was so very true and made an inner resolution to work harder to restrain my own anger when attempting to instruct souls.

Continuing forward, he became very patient with his mother, as we all entered into a grand palace within the cavernous heavenly realm. What had been a corridor, opened up into a huge and well-lit room of great beauty. Amongst the cavernous rock were crystals, amethyst and other natural gems and elements of beauty. A grand setup resonated before me, as hundreds of people were sitting in a group of stands, not unlike the bleachers you might see at a football stadium. Recognizing them as people and souls I had seen in the city of the Palace, a wrenching understanding hit my soul.

Immediately and without doubt, I knew that I had crossed from the world of life, into the world of death.

Without any further adieu, my soul was led to the other side of the cavern where the red-headed man awaited my arrival. Instantly, I recognized him, although I had spoken with him previously without knowing who he had been. I'd been taken to a mountain retreat in the heavens at the bidding of the Master. Having been introduced to this man, my soul immediately underwent a ceremony of 'marriage' to him, despite the fact that I didn't understand what was going on. After accepting my three Earthly children, and a young thirteen-year old guardian angel (Lisao) of whom I had just adopted as my own child in the same ceremony as his own, we parted; the mystery as elusive as it had been when I'd arrived.

Again, I'd seen him in the city of the Palace during my tour of the afterworld sphere. No words had been exchanged, and in fact, he hadn't seemed to notice my presence at that time. On a few other occasions, I'd met him in the afterworld sphere, but hadn't given it much thought.

Coming towards me with great intensity, he shared with me some type of compatibility testing that had been done on the two of us. "You and I score in the two's and three's," he said excitedly, "that's much higher than I've ever scored with anybody else." Apparently, this score was based on a scale from zero to four, and two and above were considered quite good. Ramifications of what he was saying were rather great for me, in that it seemed he was using a subtle approach to tell me that death was approaching. Because it had been my impression that this relationship, whatever it may be, lay beyond the world of form, any reference to the two of us being together seemed to imply that my life was in danger, and that was all I could think about as he spoke. "It has been fore-ordained that we will be spending more time together," he said very joyfully, "and we will be doing that in one and a half days."

Feeling great conflict, the familiarity and joy I felt with these people my soul apparently knew in the after-life made me wish on some level to be with them. But at the same time, I understood the ramifications of this. In no way did I want to die and leave my family, husband and children behind, but my spirit yearned to be in both worlds on some level. Feeling drawn to this red-headed man in an inexplicable way, at the same time, my spirit felt repelled because he represented death to me.

Curious but nervous about the meaning of his words, I immediately understood that I was not out of danger in regards to death, but I didn't feel that death was imminent, either, so their meaning was mysterious. But the Lord had made it excruciatingly clear that my life was not guaranteed, and as I stood amongst the gathering of joyous and friendly dead people, it was abundantly understood that when the appointed time would arrive for me to die, my journey would be taken with those who truly loved me.

****

Standing in front of me, the angelic man listened with patience as I spoke. "I'm really trying hard," I said, "I know that I am not completely healed, but I'm taking full advantage of this unique change in my physical abilities. I'm pushing harder, and really trying to do all that I can to stay as well as possible, and stay alive for my family." Pausing for a moment, he began to speak in a very calm manner which denoted his reference to humanity as a whole. "He doesn't *try* to bring death his way," he said, "It just goes to him." A wave of energy came over me as I understood his words.

Realizing that although there are things we can sometimes do to improve our odds in such a situation, the reality remains that we all must eventually die and it will come to us in its own time, not necessarily our own. Especially important for those who suffer incurable or terminal illnesses to hear, they often feel that death is a personal failure. Some will make it, others will not, and some will make it for a while as others go quickly. Neither outcome denotes a more valiant fight or a more worthy individual; it is all about fate, destiny and God's divine timing, the element which remains unknown and mysterious to each one of us until 'death goes to him.'

****

Wandering through the Italian villas, the streets were narrow and the homes were attached to one another. Water was standing on the road in puddles, as if a rainstorm had just passed through. Having just come from a home along one of these streets, I'd felt so peaceful there. As if symbolic, the large old wooden door had a window in the shape of a heart, and there was peace, contentment and tranquility within its confines. Because it was an older building, there was a lot of large ornate wood used in the decor, but I knew that the homes were attached to one another as if in one long row.

Before having been taken there, I'd undergone a wondrous journey into the life of a young man, who though robust and strong, had taken ill suddenly and died. Not a large man, he was of small build, and somewhat short. Handsome, he had a very playful energy and showed me some of the pranks he had participated in during his short life.

An old woman approached who I didn't recognize, but I said to her immediately, "This guy is a little bit on the nutty side!" Without changing her expression or displaying any sense of my rudeness, she said, "Actually, he was very charming." Intrigued, I still didn't know who these people were or why they were showing me such things.

Now that I was walking through the streets of Italy near a row of villas of some sort, I instinctually entered a door in the side of one of them. Inside, the building was cramped and small, and for no apparent reason, I began to discuss with the manager the possibility of fitting my medical offices within its confines. "Don't you realize this building is much too cramped for a doctor's office?" I said. But as the words came out of my mouth, the rooms transformed into a medical facility, cramped but very functional and quaint. Saying nothing more, I was led into another room to an office across the hall which had a small cafe' attached to it.

Entering the office, the secretary appeared as a very conservative woman, her hair pulled behind her ears. But before I could ascertain what was going on, another woman entered the office who looked just like her, except that she had done different things with her hair, clothes and make-up, and was a bit racier. Apparently, she was having an active affair with her employer, the man in the office behind the secretarial desk. Another identical 'her' entered the office, and had her hair cut very, very short. Having become a postal worker of some kind, she was also a lesbian. Two others entered, and went about their business, completely superfluous and unaware of the presence of other selves. As the overlapping realities played out in front of me, I realized that I was being shown that none of our destinies are set in stone, for we have many optional paths to choose from. For this woman, I was being shown five.

Casually walking over to the cafe', some guy was giving me 'the eye,' and I coyly smiled back. But as I walked towards the back, another gentleman appeared who was very tall and good-looking. Repeating the actions of the other man in the cafe', I smiled back at him also, flattered by his attention. But suddenly his demeanor changed, "You need to stop doing that!" Without any further adieu, I literally straightened up and shifted my energy in a flash to a more appropriate stance, realizing that such vanity was a sin.

"Nina Harkevich is trying to reach out to you," he said, "go find her." Nodding that I would, he added, "I'll even give you an assistant to operate as a liaison between you and your ancestors." A man appeared out of the blue; tall, skinny and with black hair, who smiled in his desire to assist. "Thanks!" I said to them, as I walked off alone to find my husband's great aunt.

Walking back towards the medical office in the same building, it had now become a morgue of some kind. Many people, mostly women for some reason, were dead and dying. Those who had already passed were shrouded in white cloth, while those who were still in the dying throes laid on cots that were stacked three high to the ceiling. Going towards the back of the room, I was instinctually led to a wooden crypt which supposedly contained the remains of Nina Harkevitch.

Opening the crypt, my husband, Andy, was now standing at my side, present during this momentous occasion. Inside, there laid three plastic red roses, a funeral card, and something that was wrapped in white fabric and rolled into a ball. Taking the funeral card, I noticed that on the front cover were the names of about twenty different ancestors, most of whom I did not recognize except for Arta and Helen Uzebacheff. Inside it said, "Ninitchka Harkevitcha," and below it were the dates of her birth and death.

Approaching me from the side was an older woman with darkish hair pulled back in a bun. On her face was a radiant smile, as she reached towards me. Noticing that a small paper was in her hand, I asked, "Do you have the note from Nina for me?" Without saying a word, she gave it to me.

Inside the note was a picture of a little girl holding a lamb in her left hand. Immediately, I thought of the picture I'd seen of Nina as a little girl sitting on the lap of her great grand-father, an Archpriest of the Russian Orthodox Church and founder of the Church in Florence, Italy. Perhaps he was the symbolic lamb?

Suddenly, a great many people entered the room and began changing it from a morgue to a library, which would be particularly appropriate for Nina, because along with being a doctor, she had been a great teacher of anatomy.

Looking to Andy, I said, "You've got to help me with this, please try to remember all these items so you can help me bring this back." "I won't remember," he said, "you'll need to ask somebody else to help you."

"I know what I'll do," I thought, "I need my assistant." Calling out, he instantly appeared in the room and began wandering through it to gather the information which would be vital for me to bring back into the physical realm. Reaching for two decorative dishes, they were a plate and a matching bowl with a white background and a brownish painting on them. Depicting about thirty birds flying in the same direction, I turned to my assistant, "What do you think it means?" I asked him. Pointing to the very bottom where very small words had been inscribed, I read, "E Pluribus Unum Christ."

Now surrounded in a vast library of books, I thanked my assistant for pointing that out to me as the other gentleman from before had entered the room. "You shifted well," he said, "and you are a much more attractive spirit when engaged in the proper energy." Nodding in acknowledgement of this truth, we both chuckled at my previous silliness.

At this moment, all that I had seen began to come together for me. Remembering the heart window in the door of the home, I knew that this was Nina's residence, and the heart represented the warmth and love that had resided there as she welcomed young and old, rich and poor within its confines; to teach them and to assist some who were sick. Nina had become a doctor in great part due to the tragedy which befell her brother, Nikita, who had died of pneumonia and pleurisy at the age of 22. Charming and playful, the young man I had met was my husband's great Uncle Nikita who had died long ago. Obviously, the doctor's office in the building was Nina's office, which was built from scraps into a very functional and helpful place of healing for her many patients.

Finally, I looked up the meaning for "E Pluribus Unum Christ." Although I'd known the first part of it to be a common American phrase, I'd forgotten its origin and meaning. Looking it up, its translation read, "Out of Many, One," which I immediately construed as a reference to the connection between myself, my family and our ancestors. But placing the word, "Christ" after it expanded its meaning beyond such borders. "Out of Many, One Christ." Written in 1776, the symbol of this message was the eagle in flight.
****

In the midst of the night, my body began experiencing a fast heart-rate and excessive nausiousness. Entering into sleep, my spirit had collapsed into another realm. Before me were the doctors and nurses who had come to my aid before. "Are you going to cross over tonight of cardiac arrest?" One asked very casually and with humorous sarcasm, as he held a hypodermic needle in his hand. "Oh," I replied in shock, "I'm at risk of dying again tonight, huh?" Nodding that indeed such was the case, I began concentrating a great deal on going back, as he plunged the needle into my arm just as he had done before, and my spirit immediately awoke back in my body.
****

CHAPTER THIRTEEN

Having recently crossed over, the man who had come to me months before in danger of damnation along with a legion of demons for me to battle; returned with a very different message.

Turning to see his glowing face, I was astonished at the light that surrounded his soul and the bright smile which adorned his face. Could this be the same man who had been working through so much anger? Could this be the man who had never allowed the name of Jesus to touch his lips during his life? Indeed . . . it was.

Smiling with joy in our reunion, he gently took my left hand to his mouth kissing it with kindness, love and respect. In my heart, I knew that this gesture held a thank-you, but it was also a great gesture of unconditional love. Because I had helped to save his soul, he was now watching over me with my ancestors. He'd adopted me, so to speak. Honored beyond words, nothing needed to be said as he gazed into my eyes with love. Wonder filled my soul to see such a transformation within a soul. What had once been filled with darkness, now glowed with the brightest light!

Turning, I noticed a legion of extra-terrestrial spacecraft was now traveling with me, above me in the sky. About thirty silver crafts, spherical in shape though bearing an unusual conical center, hovered silently above my soul as I walked along the pathway of life.

Taking me towards my next destination, I was directed to a very old house which looked somewhat like a haunted mansion. Immediately, a young man and his wife approached me, shaking my hand in greeting; unaware of the information being imparted to me about the status of his soul. An unseen voice explained, "He is in danger of meeting his death in five days; and if he dies at this time his soul will be damned." Acknowledging the tragedy of this man's situation, I silently bid the question of what I might be able to do. "If you accept, you will suffer for a time and offer it up to prevent his untimely death. If you do so, he will not die at this time, and more time will be given him to change his dominion." Nodding that I would accept this cross, it was finished.

Although this man was in a profession which would usually be associated with those who serve the light, he had chosen darkness; abusing power to fulfill his own ends. Remaining completely unaware of the judgment which had befallen him, he breezed through his death date with no regard for the tragic consequence which had barely been avoided. As for me, I got very sick, coughing uncontrollably for weeks. As promised, I offered it up for this soul's salvation.

Breezing towards a beautiful holy church, my son, Jacob, was now in my arms. Entering the building, we were drawn immediately to a large and ornate statue of the Blessed Virgin which sat silently on an altar. Placing my son before the feet of the Virgin, a very holy priest quietly approached us. Filled with the Holy Spirit, the priest placed his hands upon my son and blessed him. As he did so, my body was forced into a sitting position, and my legs were lifted up as if on an ottoman by an unseen force. Knowing instantly that this was being done by the Blessed Virgin, I inherently understood that she was begging my indulgence during this time of illness, so that I might not put myself in danger of death during this auspicious time.

As we prepared to leave the church, all the exits disappeared and I realized that the Lord wished for me to live in His house at all times. Turning to enter a room where a choir began singing heavenly songs, my spirit was whisked back into my body within seconds.

****

Traversing the far caverns, my soul was led deep into the tomb of my ancestors by a single male spirit, draped in white. Amongst the depths were caves, each one holding a set of dry white bones. Walking quietly and methodically by each tomb, I gazed at the bones as a misty image began to emerge and the spirit of each ancestor slowly appeared from the ether, quietly standing and turning to reach a singular hand to my soul. Images of about twenty unknown ancestors rose to meet my soul as I walked by their individual resting places. Gently nodding as I slowly passed, I allowed myself to take in their many faces. Feeling their beckon, I could not inquire further at this time, but acknowledged in silence their need . . . and my calling.

Perhaps one of them was 'Ma' Crane, my grandmother's sister, who had founded and run a maternity hospital in Provo, Utah before the hospitals had been built. Or my grandfather on my mother's side, who was forced to become a German soldier during World War II. What stories he had to tell, but he didn't live long enough for me to hear them. How odd it is to think that my children's ancestors were fighting on opposite sides of the battlefield in that horrific time. What if my other grandfather on my father's side was among them? He had died to save the life of one of my cousins by throwing her out of the way of an oncoming car and taking the impact upon himself. Certainly, such an act shows a soul who held great care and interest in the lives of his grandchildren. Perhaps some of those bones represented my earlier Mormon ancestors who crossed over to Utah from the East with Joseph Smith, or my great-great grandmother who was involved in a polygamous marriage? Others could have been a number of carpenters who had fulfilled a long line of apprenticed descendants of mine in Germany from my mother's family. Hard to tell, but I was being urged forward by my guide so I moved ahead.

Ahead of us was a grand tomb, gilded in gold, pearls and jewels, standing magnificently before us. Having reached the end of the line of caverns, we emerged upon an open vista which sparkled in the color of blue-green. Without speaking, my guide conveyed to me that this golden shrine was the 'Tomb of the Ten Commandments,' as he reached his hand forward in invitation to enter. Amazed and thrilled, I walked towards this magnificently quaffed specimen which emanated holiness beyond my comprehension. Walking inside the small entryway . . . all went black.

****

Emerging from the clouds, the darkness came in a powerful wind towards me and my family. Thrusting ourselves to the ground, we gathered together to protect one another during the attack but were not fast enough. Shouting to Andy, I said, "Throw yourself on top of Jake!" but he didn't respond quickly enough and Jacob was being blown out of our reach. An interior voice spoke within me, and it said that my recent attempts to record the music beyond 'Galactica' were being generated by my ego, rather than God's will. Thus, I had given entry for dark forces to assault me both physically and spiritually. Because I had heart failure, recording vocally was very difficult on my body, and doing so to great lengths was no longer advised.

Acknowledging my mistake, and recognizing from the scenario that I had made a grave misjudgment; it was clear that my children should always be my first priority, and I should do nothing that would put them in danger of losing their mother any sooner than absolutely necessary.

****

Standing in an office that I had worked at as a younger woman, I was remembering the many people with whom I had known and the general dynamic of this long ago place. All of us had lost contact many years before, and in fact, I'd forgotten many of these people who had once been such important friends. Interestingly, I was shown a former boss who had demonstrated certain issues, and was shown that this had continued and expanded during his life. Chuckling to myself, I walked around the office to observe how people were currently doing and most of them were doing quite well.

But when I casually walked over to the cubicle of two older men who had watched over me in my youth, I was greatly surprised to see that it was empty. Although I had not known them that well even when I'd worked in this environment, they had always kept an eye on me in fatherly way, looking out for me because I was young and inexperienced in the world.

Confused by their absence, I turned to inquire about it when I suddenly saw a sight that filled me with joy and glee. Surrounded in light, the two were standing behind me in their glorified bodies as they had passed from this world several years before. In my conscious waking life, I had completely forgotten about them, and so the Lord had given them an opportunity to take me back to this time so that I might remember their watchful care. As they stood before me, they conveyed that they continued to watch over my soul from beyond, and they wished for me to remember the special fatherly interest they had taken in me during my youth. Apparently, it had continued into the next life and I was quite honored.

A cosmic quality enveloped their presence which filled me with joy in seeing them. Despite my previous forgetfulness, seeing them generated an almost ecstatic state. Reaching their hands to me, I thanked them and expressed joy in our reunion as they held my hand for only a moment before disappearing from the scene.

****

Standing before me, Nina Harkevitch was smiling a grand grin as she appeared as she would have looked as a young girl. Beside her was her sister, sub-conscious astral, with a daze upon her face indicating her lack of awareness of this experience. Reaching her hands out to the ether, Nina said, "I want to show you something."

Whisped away, my spirit was now standing on a lush college campus in the 1920's. A large and beautiful building stood in the front and center of a green and verdant valley; beyond the front lawn of the building were several small roads with many small houses standing aside one another. Behind the college was a very beautiful valley surrounded by several small woods and some type of water. Unable to recall whether it was a river or a small lake or pond, I only recall the water.

Nina did not confirm or deny my suspicions, but I wondered if we had known each other earlier in her life?

Walking along a road towards my own home, I ran into an old friend named Brian, who had been gone for some time. "Brian!" I shouted, "How *are* you? Where have you been?" Very quietly, he explained that he had been sick, and although he had been doing better for some time, he was now dying of terminal cancer. So sad to hear such news, we began walking together in the other direction towards the college. As we strolled into the valley and woodlands behind the college, he told me about his plight and what was to happen to him. Despite the seriousness of his condition, he was totally at peace with his impending doom because he'd had plenty of time to accept it. Holding his hand, I said, "Well, there's something you don't know about me, as well." Looking at me with interest, I said, "I'm also dying, and I understand what you're sharing with me." Surprised, but not shocked, he asked what was wrong with me. Apparently, during this time I'd also suffered from heart failure; but because of the time-frame, there was no hope.

Realizing that much time had passed, dusk was now upon us. Offering to walk me home, I was somewhat hesitant because of his condition, but allowed him to do so. As we came closer to my house, he collapsed complaining of pain in his lower leg. Feeling his calf, I could discern a lump, but made no mention of it. "Wait here, I'm going to run and get my mom and dad to help." Shouting out a four-digit phone number, he asked me to phone his parents.

Arriving at my house just a few yards away, I quickly informed my parents of the need, and the two of them ran to Brian's aid while I called his family. Using the four-digit number he had given me, a woman was speaking on the other end of the line in Italian. When arriving on the scene a few minutes later, I noticed anger in my father's eyes as he observed the way Brian looked at me. But he put his anger aside and we all picked him up and got him inside where he could lie down in a warm place.

At that moment, my spirit quickly flashed through several moments in the future which clearly delineated the path that was to come. Brian and I became engaged, spending a great deal of time together, but he passed within a year, and I was gone within a year of that.

Standing before Nina and her sister, she nodded as I felt a close bond. And then she was gone . . .

****

Before my eyes lay a gravel road of rocks which floated effervescently on top of the ocean waters. As it led to a heavenly island, Andy and I rode our car carefully over the etheric pathway. Afraid of sinking during the journey, the weight of my car began to depress into the water several times during the crossing. A guard waited at the dock of the island, and without words, asked me why I had come. "I was invited by a cousin." I said. Joyful to hear this, he said, "Oh, Paul and Jenny! You are welcome; I'll take you to them."

Arriving at their very humble single-wide mobile home planted amidst a very lush and green island rainforest, I walked in quietly. Noticing a sign on the wall, it said, "What are you losing to live in the world that you do?" A very small man approached me very quietly, a woman at his side. Unable to discern who he was, I only knew that he was a 'cousin' in some way to my family. "We gave up everything," he said, "to come to this island which honors spiritual values. What are *you* losing to live in the world that you do?" In unison, Andy and I said, "Ourselves, everything, our dignity, our integrity." Without any further words, he nodded as if he understood, and turned to walk away. In a split second, we were gone.

****

Gently rising from form, my spirit hovered over my body for but a moment as it then moved slowly to the floor, directly in front of the gateway at the door of my bedroom that had been prepared for my exit. A voice began speaking words of great wisdom of which I remembered none. But his words were so eloquently beautiful; I had wished to record each one. "You have no need to fear your final end," he said. Within moments, I was prancing along a woodland pathway, as beautiful music began playing all around me.

Following many bends and curves in the path, I came across a young man dressed in ancient garb. Immediately, I asked, "Do you come on behalf of the darkness or the light?" "Of the light, Madame," he said, as he bowed respectfully before me. "Allow me to introduce myself, Madame," he continued, "as I was St. Thomas Aquinas's scribe." Very honored, I didn't know exactly what he meant. Had he helped the saint write his words during his own life, or had he *copied* his works later? I did not know. "It is my great honor to escort you now, Madame," he said, "to the place that the great writer's of the Lord all gather." Feeling quite unworthy of such a gathering, the music again began to emanate all around me and we continued to walk together.

Suddenly, I felt my soul begin to pull away from this woodland pathway and towards my body, as the scribe said, "Remember, Madame, you have no need to fear your final end."

****

153

PAINTINGS

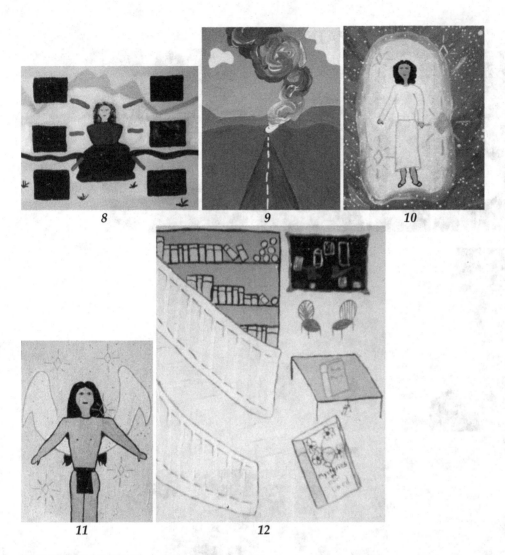

TITLE OF PAINTING - - CHAPTER/PAGE

1. Swirling Stars and Orb, Intro-5
2. Babaji, 2-22
3. Satan, 2-25
4. St. Michael, 2-34
5. Crystal Enclosure, 4-53
6. Sacred Host Comes Alive, 4-55
7. Doorway to Heaven, 5-66
8. Peaceful Purgation, 7-93
9. Ascension Rocket Trail, 8-93
10. Friend in her Resurrected State, 9-103
11. Native American Angel, 9-105
12. The Palace of Ancient Knowledge, 10-126

HYMNS

OPERATOR OF THE SKY
Fast

1. 7. Where in this dream, can new skies take hold
   An illusion of light in your dream
2. Where in my heart, can I find the seed
   A beginning of love taking hold
3. Operator of the sky, here's my question in the night
   No more sorrow, alibis, just dreams
4. Perpetrator of the sun, I see that life has just begun
   The answer lies at one humanity
5. Where in my mind, can I find the Lord
   Just a moment of light in my soul
6. Operator of the sky, teach my soul to see the light
   No illusions of light, just reality
   Operator of my mind, help me to recognize the signs
   Reach to destinies, unfound, in my dreams

MODERN DAY SLAVES
Powerful

1. Peeking between the bar frames
   Seeking to find the light
   Hoping that time will free them
   They live in a world of plight
2. The faces they see don't feel them
   They don't recognize their face
   The soldiers of shade act as masters
   To the modern day slaves
3. 6. When will we free them, who are we to choose
   All life is sacred, not meant to be abused
4. They live in many cities
   In dictatorial states
   No one knows how to save them
   They're modern day slaves
5. Jailed for their uniqueness
   Their lives a whirlwind fate
   No human life is sacred
   They're modern day slaves
7. He's speaking through the bar frames
   Would you look into his eyes
   His pain is just like yours and mine

What Your Eyes Will Never Show

Marilynn Hughes

1. You can wear those dark sunglasses
   And the clothes you just bought
   You can smile at all the people
   And walk big and tall
   You can act all calm and happy
   Live your life on the go
   But nothing can hide
   What your eyes will never show
2. You can walk right by a homeless man
   Just a beggar on the street
   You can drive right thru the poor side of town
   Cause you've got food to eat
   You can tell yourself it's hopeless
   There's nothing you can do
   But no words will ever hide
   What your eyes will never show
3. It's a hateful world we live in
   And it's up to us to change
   We cannot simply give in
   Let's care, enough to change
4. Let's take off our dark sunglasses
   And look at our world
   We war with our neighbors
   And the Earth we call home
   You can pretend it's okay

But your heart will always know
And no words will ever hide
What your eyes will never show
5. It could be a whole new world
   Where love would always reign
   Where tears would never hide
   To disguise, all the pain
6. Let's put down the wall of silence
   That blocks love's flow
   I can see it peeking slowly
   From your eyes, yeah, it shows
7. You can walk right by your neighbor
   But, honey, it still shows

You Could be a Fantasy

Marilynn Hughes

157

YOU COULD BE A FANTASY
Slow
Lyrics

1. You could be a fantasy to me
   You and me could reach for eternity
2. To find a star in you
3. Fly harmony in the sky and you will see
   Soar evermore on the wings of white horses
4. To see a star in you
5. I'm a rider, I am a rider, Assisi rider
   I'm a rider, I am a rider, Assisi rider
6. You could be a reality to me
   You have become as one in imagery
7. We've become reality, in God
8. I'm a rider, I am a rider, Assisi rider
   I'm a rider, I am a rider, Assisi rider
9. Take me home, take me home, Assisi brother
   Take me home, take me home, Assisi brother

I Believe in Love

Marilynn Hughes

1. 3. 4. I believe in love, in love
   I believe in love, in love
2. There's a cold wind in the moonlight
   That chills the heart of me
   I feel so much excitement, my spirit's feeling free
   Cause deep in my heart, I feel so much joy
   That's where the love is, I believe in joy

Dream With Me

Marilynn Hughes

DREAM WITH ME
Fast
Lyrics

1. Where is your dream, that you can become
   A World . . . as one
   Reach to the stars, lighted realms lay
   Fly from the ground, remember the way
   Dreamer live on, in oceans and streams
   Dreamer, dream high, dream with me

COUNTRY ROAD
Vibrant

1. It was an old country road
   That I walked down all my life
   It was the way I'd always go
   When things didn't go quite right
   A river ran on that grassy hill
   I'll always follow, that old country road
2. There was more to that place
   It was to me a sacred ground
   I felt the calming grace
   And dancers came without a sound
   A river ran on that grassy hill
   I'll always follow, that old country road
3. River run, river follow, river take me home
4. That tiny road is far away
   But in my heart I see the hill
   It will always be my place
   To set my restless spirit still
   A river ran on that grassy hill
   I'll always follow, that old country road
5. 6. River run, river follow me, river take me home
   To that old country road

Angel in Waiting

Marilynn Hughes

Breeze in the Willow

Marilynn Hughes

ANGEL IN WAITING
Melancholy
Lyrics

1. 7. Trailing . . . Sailing . . . Wailing . . . in the night
2. I'm falling down a mountain, a victim's disguise
   Urging life within me to fly
3. Trapped between the heavens and the earth below
   I'm an angel in waiting, so slow
4. 9. Flying . . . Sighing . . . Crying . . . Please make it right
5. Between the night and sunrise, you'll hear my bells
   I'll call to you in music, please help
6. I'm circling you in neon, a lighted malaise
   I look into your eyes, they're glazed
8. You'll hear me in the ether, I feel your regret
   No need to sign your sorrow, it's not over yet
   When will you hear me, the call of earth's design
   Return to the master . . . and fly

1. There's a breeze in the willow, the gentle flight
   There's a seed with the fellow, who rides the sky
2. The land here is fertile, but dry from no rain
   The seed must be planted, to flourish in the vein
3. 8. 9. It's a seed of life, a seed of eternity
   It's a seed of love, one more time for humanity
4. There's a man in my window, who calls my name
   His eyes fill with tears, when he sees the pain
5. He told me once it could change, Ohh Oh Oh Oh
   Oh Oh Oh
   He begged me please won't you see, you are my
   only link
6. Who . . . will . . . you . . . be
   Will you care about humanity
7. There's a song in the soul of man, a song of love
   It's hidden from the conscious mind, by
   deception's blood
10. There's a breeze in the willow, there's a breeze in
    the willow

Green Peace

Marilynn Hughes

GREEN PEACE
Moderate
Lyrics

1. To ride a mustang in the night
   A sigh, an eagle in flight
   To swim, aside a dolphin's fin
   Climb a mountain's tip
   Ocean's in the wind
2. A dream, or so it seems
   A tree, dropping heaven's leaves
   A sky, filled with cloudy lies
   No one answers why
   Mother Earth must die
3. 6. 7. You see
   Men can hardly read
   The message of the sea
   The wisdom of a tree
   Oh oh oh, Green peace
   Let's create, Green peace
4. To care, each one of you I dare
   To share, our planet with our heirs
   To find, a part of you inside
   That no longer hides
   Seeks to make things right
5. To be, the message of the sea
   To plea, we need the air to breathe
   To unite, humans with all life
   The air with the sky
   Mother Earth will smile

Near Death

Marilynn Hughes

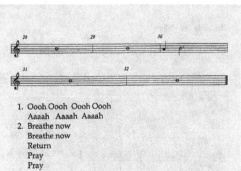

1. Oooh Oooh Oooh Oooh
   Aaaah Aaaah Aaaah
2. Breathe now
   Breathe now
   Return
   Pray
   Pray

Adaleda of God

ADALEDA OF GOD
Lively, Fast
Lyrics

1. There's a face in my memory, I see in my mind sometimes
   A gentle melody, I recall the voice in the night
2. Her image grows ghostly, as her pale white linen blows
   No one else sees her, but I always hear her voice
3. 5. 7. 8. She calls out Adaleda, Adaleda, Adaleda, Adaleda of God
4. Night is for the fleeting glance, the world beyond our senses comes alive
   Angels sing their soft romance, hidden in their song is life
6. They are with us, we need to hear them, angels of God, hear them call

Lift Up Your Hearts

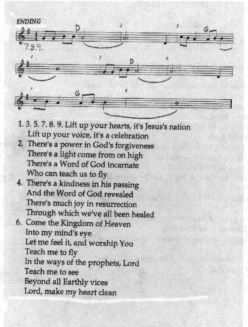

1. 3. 5. 7. 8. 9. Lift up your hearts, it's Jesus's nation
   Lift up your voice, it's a celebration
2. There's a power in God's forgiveness
   There's a light come from on high
   There's a Word of God incarnate
   Who can teach us to fly
4. There's a kindness in his passing
   And the Word of God revealed
   There's much joy in resurrection
   Through which we've all been healed
6. Come the Kingdom of Heaven
   Into my mind's eye
   Let me feel it, and worship You
   Teach me to fly
   In the ways of the prophets, Lord
   Teach me to see
   Beyond all Earthly vices
   Lord, make my heart clean

162

High Road

HIGH ROAD
Fast, Lively
Lyrics

1. She's driving down the road, just following the wind
   She's headed for a mountain, where all her dreams have been
   She's searching for the high road, a place where new lives begin
   She's waiting there for no one, but she . . . may come back again
2. 4. 5. Searching for the high road
   The place where she'll come alive
   Searching for the high road
   Where all her dreams reside, where all her dreams reside
3. She's heading for a valley, but she knows it's on the way
   If she's going to reach that temple, she's going to pass through some mistakes
   She's gonna take the high road and understand the plan
   She's got a ways in front of her, but she . . . may come back again

Life Above Me

LIFE ABOVE ME
Moderate
Lyrics

1. Sometimes I fight the changes, sometimes I hide
   Sometimes I run from danger, sometimes I cry
2. Late at night I reach to old ones, in a mountain hold
   Then I wake and greet a new day, wisdom's lot foretold
3. 6. 7. And I think about life . . . in the valley
   Life . . . in the trees
   Life . . . in the oceans
   And life . . . above me
4. Sometimes I grab the new day, on its breath I glide
   Sometimes I reach to heaven, that's when I fly
5. Early dawn I grasp the essence, my soul takes a ride
   The strands of life melt right into me, that's when I take flight

Visiontown
Marilynn Hughes

1. 3. 5. 7. Welcome to Visiontown, please enter without a sound
2. Night is brewing, spirits moving, vision comes in the night
4. Waitings ample, movement samples, silence in Visiontown
6. Wisdom enters, here in the dark, here in Visiontown
8. Many come here, many forget . . . Visiontown

Born Beneath the Soul
Marilynn Hughes

1. Born beneath the soul
   Born beneath the soul
   Born beneath the soul
   Oh, oh, oh, the soul is waiting

Can You Feel it in Your Soul
Marilynn Hughes

1. The tallest trees guide some of our nighttime stars
A gentle breeze moves the clouds so very far
It's not hard to see how life flows in all things
Can you feel it in your soul
2. The solar rays provide food for all that's green
And every life finds its needs met through the rain
It's not hard to see how life flows in all things
Can you feel it in your soul
3. 5. 6. Beyond natural senses where vibrations hold the key
That's where you'll feel it
That's where you'll know it in your soul
4. Among the mountains, lie shelter for the wild
And in the nighttime we are guided by the stars
It's not hard to see how life flows in all things
Can you feel it in your soul

Dreamquest

Marilynn Hughes

DREAMQUEST
Moderate
Lyrics

1. There's a voice that calls to me in the night
Asking me to see
Beckon sounds from the fiery sky
The spirit quest to be
2. The howling wind requests the rite
Swaying pines retreating
The gateway serves to call the light
A forest face is bleeding
3. 5. A misty face fills the green
The forest image so serene
Magical lace enshrines the thought
The end of the old I saught
4. Tomorrow's vision seeks the day
A dawn of new awakening
Cloudy sunsets, immortal rays
Old illusions shaking
6. A dreamquest filled with colored eyes
Seeking truth beyond me
No more visions of shadowed lies
I know I believe I see
7. I know
I believe
I see

I Remember His Name

Marilynn Hughes

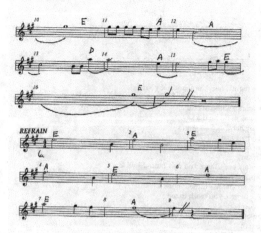

I REMEMBER HIS NAME
Moderate
Lyrics

1. He came to this world as a child
   Before he reached manhood, he died
   The vision and memory still clear
   But yet I don't remember the year
2. 4. 7. But I remember his face, and the laughter
   I remember the grace of his smile
   I remember his way of turning sorrow to gladness
   I remember his name
3. My brother and he were a pair
   Children playing without a care
   They grew, graduated, got a job
   For a time, though, their lives did part
5. In a river once, I nearly died
   He pulled me out and saved my life
   The phone call came, left me in shock
   He had died, it broke my heart
6. Now I see him in my dreams
   He lets me know that he's still okay

HAUNTED BY A MEMORY
Slow, Mysterious

1. Haunted by a memory
   Haunted by what used to be
   Haunted by a hologram
   Of a child, of a child
2. Rainy days and stormy nights
   Haunted scenes fill the twilight
   Your face won't go, it's a mystery
   True love never dies
3. 6. True love never dies
   I'll be haunted all my life
   Fading scenes of the lonely one
   My own image in the sky
4. Haunted by a memory
   Haunted by one who loved me
   Haunted by my own ignorance
   God sent her away
5. Sleepless nights, remembering
   Lonely days, forgetting
   Wishing I could go back in time
   And help her choose another way

166

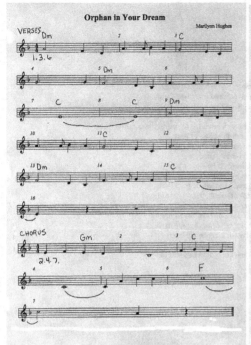

Orphan in Your Dream
Marilynn Hughes

1. Deep in the night, I hear the sounds of your
cries
An ocean apart, another world
You call to me, as if I hold a key
Reach for my hand and it's yours
2. 7. But I'm an orphan
Yes, I'm an orphan
In your dream
3. You look in my eyes, there's no way I can disguise
Feelings inside . . . of me
You are in pain, life has turned into a game
Somewhere in time you reach to me
4. I'm still an orphan
Yes, I'm an orphan
In your dream
5. 8. There's a world that is your own
And a world I know as true
Orphan, orphan
6. You're far away, I know I can't really stay
The ocean blocks me from your view
Stay, hold my hand, remember all that we had
Tomorrow, you'll wake and you'll know

Ancestral Image
Marilynn Hughes

1. 3. 5. All around me's just another world
Men and women, boys and little girls
Running before me are all my dreams
Ancestral image within my reach
Those behind me must be seen
In the light
I go where the movement flows
I see
They're free
And they're me
I go where the sunset rolls
I fly
So high
In the sky

2. Beyond all I had seen
   I'd never known their face
   And their image retains
   Their vibrations through space
   But through silence comes their wisdom
   Let their soul release the dream
   Our hearts be born together
   Through the pain

4. There a fire in my heart
   That can bring me to sight
   In the world of the night
   God leads souls to the light
   But the rain must come to guide us
   And the seeds must fill the rain
   Our hearts be born together
   Through the pain

FACES & SOULS
Bright

1. A scene fills my mind, my soul goes back in time
   Wandering through years, through faces and fears
   Who am I now, will I go home somehow
   Have I learned from the pain, am I still the same
2. 4. Who will I be tomorrow, who will I be in a year
   All that I know, are the faces and the souls
   Of those who'se walked with me
3. Reaching through time, I seek another sign
   Your image so clear, though you're no longer here
   You exist in a space, where the mist hides your face
   You are my guide, take my hand on this night

JOURNEY THROUGH A TEAR
Moderate
Lyrics

1. 7. I once knew a man who would ride the sun
He followed a road I could never see for long
He was a mysterious man, a mystical man, to me
Finally, I see
2. I once held an image of love inside my heart
Then life came and hardened the very core, I'd gone too far
It was a mysterious thing, a mystical thing, to me
Finally, I see
3. 5. 6. Life is an ocean, a journey through a tear
It's love that comes to free us, and tear away the fear
4. I once felt the world was at fault for lives gone wrong
But now I see life as an angry child, begging for love
It's not such a mysterious thing, a mystical thing, at all
Not at all

For the Old Man — Marilynn Hughes

FOR THE OLD MAN
Moderate

1. 4. One more sigh for the ocean, one more sigh for the sky
One more sigh for the old man who cried (died)
2. One more breath for the water, one more breath for the seer
One more breath for the old man . . . who cared
3. One more sigh, one more tear, one more drop of water to bear

Time — Marilynn Hughes

TIME
Moderate

1. Time, immeasurable as time will always be
Time's been good to me
You, a memory flicker past that lives in time
A time you were alive
Ride the wave of time
2. Love, it feels so real when I look in your eyes
A picture of surprise
Truth, I thought I saw it all in
God, we sure loved you
3. 5. Now I see the writing on the pages of all time
What you were and what you are now are different
States of mind
But time holds the memory
In time it will always be . . . Love
6. (Guitar) Nanananananananananana
Time's been good to me
(Guitar) Nanananananananananana
Ride the wave of time

When I Dream
Marilynn Hughes

1. 4. What does it mean when I dream
It's not always what it seems
What does it mean when I dream
About you
2. In a whisper of a moment
Your face goes by my eyes
You're gone in only seconds
But your soul has touched my life
3. 6. Another night, another year
Another space that might be clear
Where are you now
5. My vision fades so slowly
When you phase into my realm
You're gone and yet you're with me
In my dreams, and in heaven

That Time Won't Leave my Mind
Marilynn Hughes

1. 7. A face I remember, down in my dreams
Was it years or forever, so far away it seems
That time won't leave my mind
2. His eyes were the color of cloudy windswept skies
And deep in his aura, a soul as bright as light
The memory of his face fills me with grace
And deep in my heart we'll never part
3. 6. I wonder where he is right now
I wonder if he feels me somehow
Can he hear my thoughts and know what I mean
When I say, you are my dream
4. A child in his essence, hardly knowing how to feel
Reaching for the answers, for fearing them, as well
As hard as he tried, he still died
5. I reached for his spirit, we love him from long ago
Every time he looked at me, I gazed deep in his soul
And whatever you do, we still love you
And deep in our hearts, we'll never part

AND THE DREAM'S STILL ALIVE
Joyous

1. My mother was an immigrant
Saw wars and blood and strife
My father was an army man
Who fell for Mom one night
2. She followed him to America
The land of the free
Dreaming of a brighter place
And children they had three
3. 6. 7. And the dream's still alive . . . in America
The world across the sea
Celebrations of life and a growing dream
A world . . . at peace
4. I was the lonely one
To others it seemed so
When I met him I fell adrift
A sea of vision's glow
5. My girl was born one silent night
Crying confused tears
Sometimes I see so much in her
I wonder what she will be . . .

And the Dream's Still Alive — Marilynn Hughes

I'll Never Wonder — Marilynn Hughes

171

I'LL NEVER WONDER
Lively

1. I've often wondered where you are today
   Memories wander to places far away
2. Nights on oasis where love makes souls fly
   Days filled with sadness 'cause, we never said good-by
3. Whatever you're reaching
   Whatever you're seeking
   You will find it somehow
4. I'll never wonder where you are again
   I know you're following the light that takes you home
5. I trust God's wisdom in taking you when He did
   (No words)
6. I loved you then
   I'll see you again
   I will meet you there . . .
7. Whatever you're reaching
   Whatever you're seeking
   You will find it
   And I'll meet you there

Faerietale Angels

Marilynn Hughes

FAERIETALE ANGELS
Moderate

1. 3. 5. 6. Whatever happened to faerietale angels
   Ponies, dancers and wings
   Whatever happened to heaven and romance
   Whatever happened to me
2. I dreamed of an angel, with white golden wings
   Behind her were stars and mermaids who sing
   Celestial visions of all magnitudes
   Behind me, I thought I felt you
   Behind me, I was sure it was you
4. I seem to recall, a day gone by
   The stories and visions, the midnight flights
   Sweet little girl it came so easy to you
   Remember the world that we knew
   Remember the world that we knew

GALACTICA
Soundtrack
All Songs written, performed and engineered by Marilynn Hughes.

Unlike 'The Mysteries of the Redemption' where the music was placed with the experience wherein it was given to me, these songs were given to me separately from the experiences in the book, and thus, bear no page numbers.

Index of Hymns

1.) Operator of the Sky
2.) Modern Day Slaves
3.) What Your Eyes Will Never Show
4.) You Could Be a Fantasy (For Andy, my husband)
5.) I Believe in Love
6.) Dream With Me
7.) Country Road
8.) Angel in Waiting
9.) Breeze in the Willow
10.) Green Peace
11.) Near Death
12.) Adaleda of God
13.) Life Above Me
14.) High Road
15.) Visiontown
16.) Lift Up Your Hearts
17.) Born Beneath the soul - Chapter 9, Page 153
18.) Can You Feel it in Your Soul - (Given by John Denver)
19.) Dreamquest - (Given by Jim Morrison of the Doors)
20.) I Remember His Name - (For Doug, my friend who died in a car accident at 21)
21.) Haunted by a Memory - (For Karleen, my dear friend who shared her after-death journey in Galactica)
22.) Orphan in Your Dream – (For Karleen)
23.) Ancestral Image - (For Arta and Helen Uzebacheff)
24.) Faces & Souls - (For all my ancestors)
25.) Journey Through a Tear - (For Arta, from great-great granddaughter, Melissa, who recalls his visits in her dreams as a young child)
26.) For the Old Man - (For Joseph Uze[bacheff] a.k.a. grandpa)
27.) Time - (For Uncle Andy Hornik)
28.) When I Dream - (For Nina Harkevitch)
29.) That Time Won't Leave my Mind - (For Nikita Harkevitch)
30.) And the Dream's Still Alive - (For my Mother and Father)
31.) I'll Never Wonder - (For all those who've been lost prematurely, in their youth, before their destiny had a chance to become manifest)
32.) Faerietale Angels - (For Melissa, Mary and Jacob, my sweet children and my greatest gift)

To contact the author or to inquire about the CD containing performances of the 32 songs in this book, please contact:

MarilynnHughes@aol.com

ANCESTORS

Andrew and Marilynn Hughes
(Hughes/Hornik)   (Spicer/Grundig)
(Uze[bacheff]/Harkevitch)   (Spicer/Stevens) (Grundig/Hergl)

When Joseph Uzebacheff came to the United States, his name was too difficult for others to remember, so he shortened it to Uze. Ivan, his son, later made the spelling less complicated by changing it to Hughes.

ANCESTRAL LINES
Andy's Side
Uzebacheff

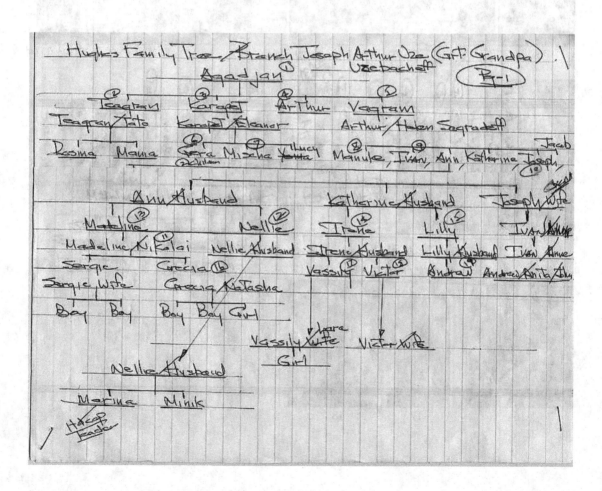

174

Andy's Side
Harkevitch

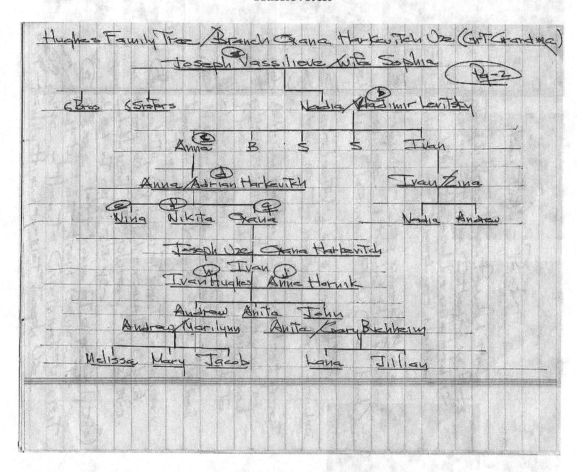

Hughes Family Tree / Branch Oxana Harkevitch Uze (Grt Grandma)

Joseph Vassilieve / wife Sophia   Pg-2

6 Bros   5 Sisters   Nadia / Vladimir Levitsky

        Anna   B   S   S   Ivan

    Anna / Adrian Harkevitch   Ivan / Zina

    Nina   Nikita   Oxana   Nadia   Andrew

        Joseph Uze / Oxana Harkevitch
        Ivan
    Ivan Hughes / Anne Hornik

        Andrew   Anita   John
    Audrey / Marilynn   Anita / Gary Bichheim

    Melissa   Mary   Jacob   Lana   Jillian

19   20   21   22

SAINT-ALEXANDRE-NEVSKY
1861 ~ PARIS ~ 1961

176

Andy's Side
Hornik

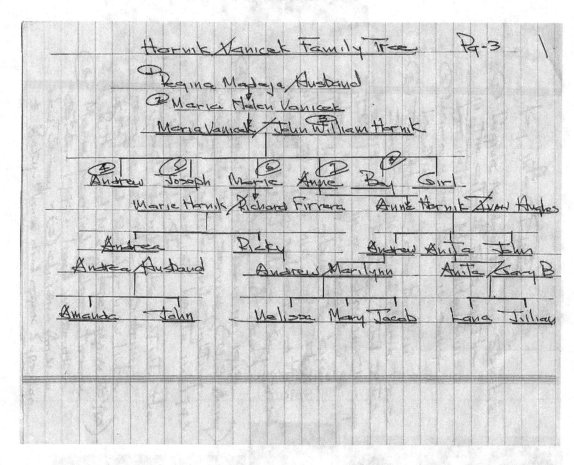

Hornik Vanicek Family Tree   Pg-3

① Regina Madeja / Husband
② Maria Helen Vanicek
Maria Vanicek / John William Hornik ③

① Andrew   ② Joseph   ③ Marie   ④ Anne   ⑤ Boy   Girl

Marie Hornik / Richard Firrera   Anne Hornik / Ivan Hughes

Andrea   Ricky   Andrew Anita John

Andrea / Husband   Andrew Marilynn   Anita / Gary B

Amanda   John   Melissa Mary Jacob   Lana Jillian

39   40   41

42 43 44 45

46

47

**Marilynn's Side
Spicer**

48

49

50

51

52

53

54

55

56

Marilynn's Side
Grundig

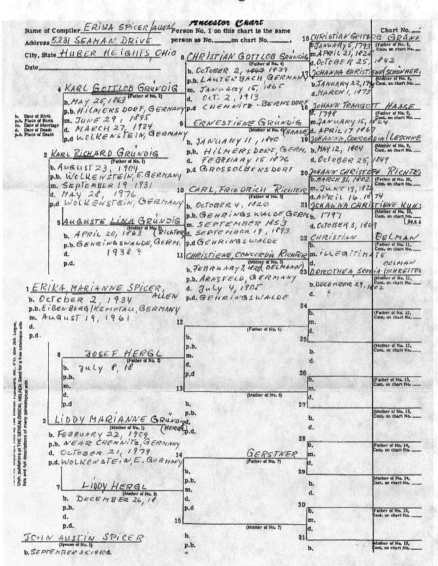

Ancestor Chart

Name of Compiler ERIKA SPICER/ALLEN
Address 5231 SEAMAN DRIVE
City, State HUBER HEIGHTS, OHIO
Date_____

Person No. 1 on this chart is the same person as No.____ on chart No.____.

Chart No.____

b. Date of Birth
p.b. Place of Birth
m. Date of Marriage
d. Date of Death
p.d Place of Death

16 CHRISTIAN GOTTLOB GRUND
b. JANUARY 5, 1793 (Father of No. 8,
m. APRIL 21, 1824 Cont. on chart No.
d. OCTOBER 25, 1842

8 CHRISTIAN GOTTLOB GRUNDIG (Father of No. 4)
b. OCTOBER 2, 1837 1839
p.b. LAUTERBACH GERMANY
m. JANUARY 15, 1865
d. OCT. 2, 1913
p.d CHEMNITZ - BERNSDORF

17 JOHANNA CHRISTIENE SCHONHER
b. JANUARY 22, 1794 (Mother of No. 8,
d. MARCH 1, 1873 Cont. on chart No.

4 KARL GOTTLOB GRUNDIG (Father of No. 2)
b. MAY 25, 1863
p.b. HILMERSDORF, GERMANY
m. JUNE 29, 1895
d. MARCH 27, 1924
p.d WOLKENSTEIN, GERMANY

18 JOHANN TRAUGOTT HAASE
b. 1798 (Father of No. 9,
m. JANUARY 15, 1824 Cont. on chart No.
d. APRIL 17 1867

9 ERNESTIENE GRUNDIG (HAASE) (Mother of No. 4)
b. JANUARY 11, 1840
p.b. HILMERSDORF, GERM.
d. FEBRUARY 15 1876
p.d GROSSOLBERSDORF

19 JOHANNA CONCORDIA (LESCHNE
b. MAY 12, 1804 (Mother of No. 9,
d. OCTOBER 25, 1849 Cont. on chart No.

2 KARL RICHARD GRUNDIG (Father of No. 1)
b. AUGUST 23, 1904
p.b. WOLKENSTEIN, E. GERMANY
m. SEPTEMBER 19, 1931
d. MAY 28, 1976
p.d WOLKENSTEIN, GERMANY

20 JOHANN CHRISTOF# RICHTE
b. MARCH 31, 1802 (Father of No. 10,
m. JUNE 19, 182 Cont. on chart No.
d. APRIL 16. 1874

10 CARL, FRIEDRICH RICHTER (Father of No. 5)
b. OCTOBER 4, 1820
p.b. GEHRINGSWALDE GERM.
m. SEPTEMBER 1853
d. SEPTEMBER 19, 1893
p.d GEHRINGSWALDE

21 JOHANNA CHRISTIENE KUN
b. 1797 (Mother of No. 10,
d. OCTOBER 3, 1869 LMA4

5 AUGUSTE LINA GRUNDIG (RICHTER) (Mother of No. 2)
b. APRIL 20, 1863
p.b. GEHRINGSWALDE, GERM.
d. 1938 ?
p.d.

22 CHRISTIAN OELMAN
(Father of No. 11,
m. ILLEGITIMATE Cont. on chart No.
d.

11 CHRISTIENE, CONCORDIA RICHTER (OELMANN) (Mother of No. 5)
b. FEBRUARY 7, 1825
p.b. ARNSFELD, GERMANY
d. JULY 4, 1905
p.d. GEHRINGSWALDE

23 DOROTHEA SOPHIA (SCHREITER)
b. DECEMBER 29, 1802 (Mother of No. 11,
d. ? Cont. on chart No.

1 ERIKA, MARIANNE SPICER, ALLEN
b. OCTOBER 2, 1934
p.b. EISENBERG/KEMPTAU, GERMANY
m. AUGUST 19, 1961
d.
p.d.

24
b. (Father of No. 12,
m. Cont. on chart No.
d.

12 (Father of No. 6)
b.
p.b.
m.
d.
p.d

25
b. (Mother of No. 12,
d. Cont. on chart No.

6 JOSEF HERGL (Father of No. 3)
b. JULY 8, 18
p.b.
m.
d.
p.d

26
b. (Father of No. 13,
m. Cont. on chart No.
d.

13 (Mother of No. 6)
b.
p.b.
d.

27
b. (Mother of No. 13,
d. Cont. on chart No.

3 LIDDY MARIANNE GRUNDIG (HERGL) (Mother of No. 1)
b. FEBRUARY 22, 1909
p.b. NEAR CHEMNITZ, GERMANY
d. OCTOBER 21, 1979
p.d. WOLKENSTEIN, E. GERMANY

28
b. (Father of No. 14,
m. Cont. on chart No.
d.

14 GERSTNER (Father of No. 7)
b.
p.b.
m.
d.
p.d

29
b. (Mother of No. 14,
d. Cont. on chart No.

7 LIDDY HERGL (Mother of No. 3)
b. DECEMBER 26, 18
p.b.
d.
p.d.

30
b. (Father of No. 15,
m. Cont. on chart No.
d.

15 (Mother of No. 7)
b.
p.b.
d.
p.d

31
b. (Mother of No. 15,
p.b. Cont. on chart No.
b.

JOHN AUSTIN SPICER (Spouse of No. 1)
b. SEPTEMBER 25, 1930 d.

Utah, publishers of THE GENEALOGICAL HELPER. Send for a free catalogue with lists and full descriptions of many genealogical aids.

57

58

59

60

61

62

63

64

65

66

67

68

1. Uzebacheff brothers
2. Arthur Uzebacheff
3. Helen Uzebacheff (Sagradeff)
4. Uzebacheff home in Russia
5. Joseph Uzebacheff (Uze)
6. Joseph Uzebacheff at the orphanage
7. Joseph, Oxana, and Ivan Uze
8. Joseph and Oxana Uze, 50th wedding anniversary
9. Ivan Uze (Hughes)
10. Ivan and Anne Hughes
11. Ivan and Andrew Hughes
12. Anita Hughes (Buccheim)
13. John Hughes
14. Andrew Hughes
15. Gary and Anita Buccheim (Hughes)
16. Hughes family
17. Andrew and Marilynn Hughes (Spicer)
18. Andrew Hughes with Melissa, Mary, Jacob
19. Joseph Vassilieve
20. Russian Orthodox Church, Paris, France
21. Vladimir Levitsky
22. Russian Orthodox Church, Florence, Italy
23. Russian Orthodox Church, Florence, Italy
24. Adrian Harkevitch
25. Nadia Levitsky
26. Oxana, Nikita, and Nina Harkevitch
27. Oxana Harkevitch (Uze)
28. Nikita Harkevitch
29. Nina Harkevitch
30. Oxana Harkevitch arrives in America
31. Joseph and Oxana Uze
32. Oxana Uze with her son, Ivan
33. Andrew is born
34. Painting of Nina Harkevitch
35. Nina Harkevitch in later years
36. Ivan Hughes visits Nina Harkevitch
37. Italy loved her, Nina Harkevitch's memorial
38. Vladimir Levitsky's great-great-great grandson, John Hughes, visits Russian Orthodox Church, Florence, Italy
39. Joseph Hornik
40. Maria Hornik
41. Hornik Family
42. Andrew Hornik
43. Anne Hornik on her wedding day
44. Anne Hornik (Hughes) in choir
45. Hornik family in later years

46. Hughes family
47. Maria and Joseph Hornik with their grandchildren
48. Spicer family (First Generation)
49. 'Ma' Crane, Elizabeth Stevens Crane, sister of Ruth Spicer, Marilynn's Grandmother on Father's Side
50. Crane Maternity Hospital, founded and Run by 'Ma' Crane
51. John and Erika Spicer (Grundig)
52. Spicer family (Second Generation)
53. Spicer family (Second Generation)
54. Marilynn Spicer (Hughes) with her dog, Joy
55. Marilynn Spicer (Hughes) with father, John Spicer, on wedding day
56. Melissa, Jacob, and Mary Hughes
57. Karl and Liddy Grundig
58. Erika Grundig (Spicer)
59. Grundig family, Karl in his German military uniform
60. Grundig family
61. Erika Grundig (Spicer)
62. John and Erika Spicer with their new baby
63. Erika Spicer with Cindy, Mike, and Marilynn
64. Erika Spicer (Allen) with new husband, Vernon Allen
65. Spicer, Allen, and Hughes clans
66. Mike, Catrina, Cameron, and Courtney Spicer
67. Erika Spicer (Allen) with Cindy Spicer
68. Cindy's husband, Rick

PROPHETS, SAINTS, MYSTICS AND SAGES

1   2   3   4   5   6

7   8   9   10   11   12

13   14   15   16   17   18   19

20   21   22   23   24   25

26   27   28   29   30

1.) A.C. Bhaktivedanta Swami Prabhupada
("The Path of Yoga," By A.C. Bhaktivedanta Swami Prabhupada, Bhaktivedanta Book Trust, 1995)
2.) Abdul Baha *(Bahai Distribution Service)*
3.) Abdul Baha in Later Years *("Religions of the World" By Lewis M. Hopfe, From the Baha'i Distribution Service, Prentice Hall, 1994)*
4.) Abraham (Tradition purports him to have written Sepher Yezirah) *("The Book of Life", By Newton Marshall Hall and Irving Francis Wood, Volume 2, Page 34, Edwin John Prittie - Artist, John Rudin & Co., Inc, 1923)*
5.) Avalokiteshwara *(A Monk from Shasta Abbey, Mt. Shasta, California)*
6.) Spinoza *("My Jewish World," Volume 6, Page 3, By Rabbi Dr. Raphael Posner, Encyclopaedica Judaica, 1975)*
7.) Black Elk *("The Sacred Pipe," Recorded by Joseph Epes Brown, Photograph by J.E. Brown, University of Oklahoma Press, 1953)*
8.) The Buddha *("The Teachings of the Compassionate Buddha," Edited by E.A. Burtt,Cover, Mentor Religion, 1955)*
9.) Chief Joseph *("I Will Fight no More Forever," By Merrill D. Beal, Photograph by Historical Society of Montana, Ballantine Walden, 1963)*
10.) Christ *("Christ and the Fine Arts," The Ascension,' Gottlieb Peter Biermann - Artist , Page 469, Gramstorff Brothers, Inc., MA Harper & Row, 1938)*
11.) Confucius *("Religions of the World,"Page 231, The Granger Collection, By St. Martin's Press, 1993)*
12.) Devaki (Mother of Krishna) *("KRSNA," By A.C. Bhaktivedanta Swami Prabhupada, Bhaktivedanta Book Trust, 1970)*
13.) Dogen *("Moon in a Dewdrop," Edited by Kazuaki Tanahashi, Hokyo-Ji, Fukui Prefecture, North Point Press, 1985)*
14.) Earth Store Bodhisattva *("Sutra of the Past Vows of Earth Store Bodhisattva," Written by Same, Institute for the Advanced Studies of World Religions, Buddhist Text Translation Society, 1974)*
15.) Emanuel Swedenborg *(Swedenborg Foundation)*
16.) Nanak - Founder of the Sikh's *("Religions of the World" By Lewis M. Hopfe, Section on Sikhism, Prentice Hall, 1994)*
17.) 'Head of a Patriarch' (Enoch)*("The Law and the Prophets," Giovanni Battista Tiepolo - Artist, Page 355, Art Institute of Chicago, Harry N. Abrams, Inc.)*
18.) Hermes *("The Divine Pymander of Hermes," Translated by Dr. Everard, Cover, Wizard Books, 1978)*
19.) Hildegard Von Bingen *("Book of Divine Works," By Hildegard Von Bingen, Page ii, Angela Werneke - Artist, Bear & Co., 1987)*
20.) Jewish Kabbalist Holding the Ten Sephirot *("My Jewish World," By Rabbi Dr. Raphael Posner, Volume 4, Page 7, Joseph Ben Braham Gikatilla - Artist, Encyclopaedia Judaica, 1975)*
21.) Job *("The Book of Life," By Newton Marshall Hall and Irving Francis Wood, Volume 5, Page 288, Helen Bennett - Artist, John Rudin and Co., 1923)*
22.) Krishna *("The Path of Yoga," By A.C. Bhaktivedanta Swami Prabhupada, Bhaktivedanta Book Trust, 1995)*
23.) Lao Tzu *("Great Religions of the World," By the National Geographic Society, 1971)*

24.) Maharishi Mahesh Yogi *("The Science of Being and Art of Living," By Maharishi Mahesh Yogi, International SRM Publications, 1963)*

25.) Maitreya *("The Changeless Nature," By Arya Maitreya & Acarya Asanga,Sherapalden Beru of Kagyu Samye Ling*
- Artist, Karma Drubgyud Darjay Ling, 1979)

26.) Mary *("Christ and the Fine Arts," 'The Sistine Madonna,' Raphael,Page 38, Harper & Row, 1938)*

27.) Milarepa *("Tibet's Great Yogi, Milarepa" By W.Y. Evans-Wentz, From the book 'The Buddhism of Tibet,' By Dr.*
L.A. Waddell, Oxford University Press, 1951)

28.) Mohammed *(" Religions of the World," Page 431, The Granger Collection, By St. Martin's Press, 1993)*

29.) Mohammed with the Angel *("Great Religions of the World," By the National Geographic Society, 1971)*

30.) 'Moses' *("The Law and the Prophets,"Carlo Dolci - Artist, Pitti Palace, Florence, Page 166, Harry N. Abrams, Inc.)*

31.) Mother Teresa *("A Simple Path," Compiled by Lucinda Vardey,Cover, Ballantine Books, 1995)*

32.) Nefertiti *("Tutankhemen," By E. Wallis Budge, Page ii, Limestone Head in the Museum at Berlin, Bell PublishingCo., 1923)*

33.) Padre Pio *("The Agony of Jesus," By Padre Pio, Cover, Photograph Copyright Owner, Federico Abresch of San Giovanni Rotondu, Italy, TAN Books, 1974)*

34.) Paramahansa Yogananda *("Man's Eternal Quest," By Paramahansa Yogananda, Self-Realization Fellowship, 1975)*

35.) Peter *("The Bible in Art," By Clifton Harby, Il Perugino - Artist, Page 381, Sistine Chapel, Garden City Publishing Co., 1936)*

36.) Pythagoras *("The Pythagorean Sourcebook and Library," Compiled/Translated by Kenneth Sylvan Guthrie, Cover, Phanes Press, 1987)*

37.) Short Bull, Lakota Holy Man (who was the Apostle of the 1890 Ghost Dance Preceding Wounded Knee) *("The Encyclopedia of Native American Religion," By Arlene Hirschfelder and Paulette Molin, Page 264, Photograph from the National Anthropolical Archives, Smithsonian Institute, MJF Books, 1992)*

38.) Sri Ramakrishna *("The Gospel of Sri Ramakrishna," By M., Ramakrishna Vivekananda Center, 1942)*

39.) Sri Sarada Devi (Wife of Sri Ramakrishna) *("The Gospel of Sri Ramakrishna," By M., Ramakrishna Vivekananda Center, 1942)*

40.) St. Alphonsus Liguori *("The Great Means of Salvation and of Perfection," By St. Alphonsus Liguori, Cover, Redemptorist Fathers, 1927)*

41.) St. Catherine of Siena *("Mysteries, Marvels and Miracles in the Lives of the Saints," Page 42, By Joan Carroll Cruz, From the Book 'The Life of Catherine of Siena, By Blessed Raymond of Capua, TAN Books, 1997)*

42.) St. Francis of Assisi *("The Francis Book,"Compiled by Roy M. Gasnick, Page 129, Ludovico Dardi da Cigoli - Artist, MacMillan Publishers, 1980)*

43.) St. John the Baptist *("The Bible in Art," Edited by Clifton Harby, Page 171, Titian - Artist,16th Century, Garden City Publishing Co., 1936)*

44.) St. John of the Cross *("Mysteries, Marvels and Miracles in the Lives of the Saints," Page 47, By Joan Carroll Cruz, TAN Books, 1997)*

45.) St. Paul *("The Book of Life," By Newton Marshall and Irving Francis Wood, Volume 7, Page 1, Raphael Sanzio - Artist, Vatican Gallery, John Rudin & Co. Inc., 1923)*

46.) St. Teresa of Avila (*"Mysteries, Marvels and Miracles in the Lives of the Saints,"* Page 46, By Joan Carroll Cruz, TAN Books, 1997)

47.) Therese of Lisieux (*"Story of a Soul, Autobiography of St. Therese of Lisieux,"* Translated by John Clarke, ICS Publications, 1975)

48.) St. Thomas Aquinas (*" Religions of the World,"* Page 383, The Granger Collection, Giovanni Da Fiesole - Artist, St. Martin's Press,1993)

49.) Sufi Crossing the Water on a Prayer Mat (Rumi) (*"Religions of the World,",* Page 476, The Granger Collection, From a Moghul book of 1629, St. Martin's Press,1993)

50.) The 14th Dalai Lama (*"The Path to Enlightenment,"* By the 14th Dalai Lama, Cover, Snow Lion Publications, 1982)

51.) 'The Jewish Rabbi' (*"The Law and the Prophets,"* Rembrandt - Artist,, Page 218, The National Gallery in London, Harry N. Abrams, Inc.)

52.) Thoth (*"Lexicon Universal Encyclopedia, From the Tomb of Ramses I, Volume 7,* Page 84, Lexicon Publications 1987)

53.) Ven. Anne Catherine Emmerich (*"The Life of Christ and Biblical Revelations,"* By Ven. Anne Catherine Emmerich, TAN Books, 1986)

54.) Venerable Mary of Agreda (*"A Popular Abridgement of 'The Mystical City of God,'"* By Venerable Mary of Agreda, Cover, TAN Books, 1978)

55.) Vimalakirti (*"The Holy Teaching of Vimalakirti,"* Translated by Robert Thurman, Cover, Pennsylvania State University Press, 1976)

56.) Zarathustra (*"Religions of the World,"* Reconstruction by D.F. Karaka, Page 59, From the Bettman Archives, St. Martin's Press, 1993)

BIBLIOGRAPHY

Having made a shortened list of some of the more important texts of the world religions, I've made careful note to include texts which have been drawn to me in sacred vision and have been an integral part of energizing my spiritual path. Most of the texts in the bibliography have been brought to me through eternal guidance.

World Scripture is an excellent starting point, as it contains scripture from all world religions on various subjects, as well as, a detailed listing in back of the prescribed texts from all major and minor world religions.

Scriptural texts are the foundation or the root of knowledge. Visionary texts are the branches of the tree. Lives of prophets, saints, mystics and sages are the leaves.

Words in italics are actual book titles, while the unitalicized words are not title names, but rather authors and saints to glean from.

Hinduism: *The Bhagavad Gita As It Is, Srimad Bhagavatam, Upanishads,* KRSNA, *Autobiography of a Yogi, The Divine Romance, Man's Eternal Quest, The Gospel of Sri Ramakrishna*

Judaism: *New Jerusalem Bible, The Talmudic Anthology, The Zohar (Kaballah), The Apocrypha, The Lost Books of the Bible and the Forgotten Books of Eden, The Book of Enoch, Sefer haHinnuch,* Josephus, Philo, *The Way of God, The Path of the Just, The Gates of Repentance*

Zoroastrianism: *The Avesta, The Desatir, A Guide to Zoroastrian Religion*

Buddhism: *A Buddhist Bible, Dialogues of the Buddha, Dhammapada, Threefold Lotus Sutra, Path to Deliverance, The Flower Ornament Scripture, The Holy Teaching of Vimalakirti, Sutra of the Past Vows of Earth Store Bodhisattva, A Guide to the Bodhisattva's Way of Life, Training the Mind in the Great Way, The Life of the Buddha, Moon in a Dewdrop, The Shobogenzo, Tao Te Ching, Chuang Tsu,*

Analects of Confucius, Wen Tzu

Christianity: *Holy Bible, Apocrypha, Lost Books of the Bible and the Forgotten Books of Eden, Dead Sea Scriptures, Gospel of Thomas, Essene Gospel of Peace 1-4, Book of Enoch, Nag Hammadi Library, Pistis Sophia, Gnosis on the Silk Road, The Dialogue of St. Catherine of Siena, The Mystical City of God, Heaven & Hell, The Life of Jesus Christ and Biblical Revelations, The Imitation of Christ,* and the writings of the saints with an emphasis on the following: St. Augustine, Mother Teresa, Padre Pio, St. Alphonsus Liguori, Cure' of Ars, St. Teresa of Avila, St. Thomas Aquinas, St. Francis de Sales, St. John Bosco, St. Ignatius, St. John of the Cross, Emanuel Swedenborg, Martin Luther, John Calvin

Islam: *Holy Qur'an, Sahih Muslim* (The Hadith), *Nahjul Balagha, Imam Gazzali's Ihya Ulum Ud Din, The Life of Mohammad (Translation of Sirat Rasul Allah), Signs of the Unseen, The Doctrine of the Sufi's*

Baha'i: *Tablets of Baha'u'llah, Seven Valleys and the Four Valleys, The Kitab-I-Iqan, The Hidden Words, Prayers and Meditations, Selections from the Writings of the Bab, Tablets of the Divine Plan, Promulgation of Universal Peace*

Mystery Religions: *The Divine Pymander of Hermes, The Emerald Tablets of Thoth, An Interpretation of the Emerald Tablets, The Ancient Mysteries, The Secret Doctrine of the Rosicrucians, Secret Teachings of All Ages, Plotinus: The Enneads,*

Tribal: *Book of the Hopi, Secrets of Mayan Science/Religion, Navajo Religion, Encyclopedia of Native American Religions, African Religions & Philosophy*

To find any of these texts you may call the publishers directly, or go to any book store. The Tattered Cover in Denver, Colorado, is especially helpful, and you may reach them at 1-800-833-9326; ask for the religion section on the second floor. Below is a list of some of the publishers, bookstores, and other companies I have used the most. Many cassette's, videotapes and other religious items are also available from some of the following sources:

HINDUISM

Self-Realization Fellowship (Hinduism, with a Focus on the Works of Paramahansa Yogananda), 213-342-0247

The Bhaktivedanta Book Trust (Hinduism, with a Focus on the Works of A.C. Bhaktivedanta Swami Prabhupada), 3764 Watseka Ave., Los Angeles, CA 90034, 1-800-927-4152

Vedanta Society (Hinduism, with a Focus on the Works of Sri Ramakrishna), 1-800-816-2242

JUDAISM

Feldheim Publishers (Judaism), 200 Airport Executive Park, Nanuet, NY 10954, 1-800-237-7149

Random House, (Judaism, publisher of the Talmud), 400 Hahn, West Minster, MD 21157, 800-733-3000

ZOROASTRIANISM

Ernestine G. Busch (Zoroastrianism with a Focus on the Avesta), El Paso, TX (Call the Tattered Cover.)

BUDDHISM

Wisdom Publications (Buddhism, Sole North American Distributor for the Pali Text Society), 361 Newbury St., Boston, MA 02115, 1-617-536-3358

Snow Lion (Buddhism), P.O. Box 6483, Ithaca, NY 14851, 1-607-273-8519
Parallax Press (Buddhism, with a Focus on the Works of Thich Naht Hahn), P.O. Box 7355, Berkeley, CA 94707, 1-510-525-0101
Shasta Abbey Buddhist Supplies (Buddhism, Zen), P.O. Box 199, Mt. Shasta, CA 96067-0199, 1-800-653-3315
The Buddhist Bookstore (Buddhism), 1710 Octavia St. San Francisco, CA 94109, 1-415-774-7877

CHRISTIANITY
Christian Book Distributors (Christianity, Denominational), P.O. Box 7000, Peabody, MA 01961-7000, 1-508-977-5000
Tan Books (Christianity, Catholic), P.O. Box 424, Rockford, IL 61105, 1-800-437-5876
Focus on the Family (Christianity, Denominational), P.O. Box 35500, Colorado Springs, CO 80935-3550, 1-800-A FAMILY
New City Press (Christianity, Catholic with a Focus on the Works of St. Augustine), 202 Cardinal Rd., Hyde Park, NY 12538, 1-800-462-5980
Swedenborg Foundation (Christianity, with a Focus on the Works of Emanuel Swedenborg), P.O. Box 549, West Chester, PA 19381-0549, 1-800-355-3222
Edgar Cayce Mail Order Bookstore (Christianity, Metaphysical), Sixty Eighth and Atlantic Avenue, P.O. Box 656, Virginia Beach, VA 23451-0656, 1-800-723-1112
Ignatius Press (Christianity, Catholic), P.O. Box 1339, Fort Collins, CO 80522-1339, 1-800-651-1531

ISLAM
Tahrike Tarsile Qur'an, Inc. (Islam), P.O. Box 1115, Elmhurst, NY 11373, 718-446-4370
KAZI Publications (Islam), 3023 West Belmont Ave., Chicago, IL 60618, 773-267-7001
Library of Islam, P.O. Box 1923, Des Plaines, IL 60017-1923
AMS Publishers (Islam, with a focus on Sufi material), 212-777-4700

BAHA'I
Baha'i Distribution Service (Baha'i), 5397 Wilbanks Dr., Hixson, TN 37343, 1-800-999-9019

TRIBAL
Your local bookstore or call the Tattered Cover.

MYSTERY RELIGIONS AND VARIOUS

Barnes & Noble Catalogue (Various), 1 Pond Road, Rockleigh, NJ 07647, 1-800-THE BOOK
Theosophical University Press (Mystery Religions, Theosophy, but Carries Texts of Various Religions), P.O. Box C, Pasadena, CA 91109-7107, 1-818-798-3378
The Urantia Foundation (The Urantia Book), 533 Diversey Parkway, Chicago, IL 60614, 1-312-525-3319

SOURCE LISTING

African Religions and Philosophy, by John S. Mbiti, Heinerman, 1969
Agony, of Jesus, The, by Padre Pio, Tan Books, 1967
Ahaveth Chesed, by the Chafetz Chaim, Feldheim Publishers, 1967

An Interpretation of the Emerald Tablets, by Doral, Brotherhood of the White Temple, 1992
An Introduction to the Devout Life, by St. Francis De Sales, Tan Books, 1923
Analects of Confucius, The, by Confucius, Translator Arthur Waley, Vintage Books, 1938
Ancient Mysteries, The, Editor Marvin W. Meyer, Harper Collins, 1987
Anguttara Nikaya 1-3, Translator Nyanaponika Thera, Buddhist Publication Society, 1981
Anugita, The, Translator Kashinath Trimbak Telang, Wizards Bookshelf, 1981
Apocrypha, The Editor Manuel Kromroff, Dorset Press, 1992
Apologia Pro Vita Sua, by John Henry Cardinal Newman, Doubleday Image Books, 1956
Aryasura's Aspiration/Meditation on Compassion, by Tenzin Gyatso, H.H. the 14th Dalai Lama, Library of Tibetan Works, 1975
Autobiography of a Yogi, by Paramahansa Yogananda, Self-Realization Fellowship, 1946
Autobiography of St. Margaret Mary, The, by Saint Margaret Mary, Tan Books, 1930
Avesta, The, Translator Rev. Ernestine Busch, Ernestine G. Busch, 1985
Baha'u'llah and the New Era, by J.E. Esslemont, Baha'i Publishing Trust, 1923
Being and Vibration, by Joseph Raphael and Mary Elizabeth Marlow, Council Oak Books, 1993
Bhagavad Gita, The, Translator Eknath Easwaran, Nilgri Press, 1985
Bhagavad-Gita As It Is, Translator A.C. Bhaktivedanta Swami, Bhaktivedanta Book Trust, 1986
Bible in Art, The, Editor Clifton Harby, Garden City Publishing Co., 1936
Birth of Purgatory, The, by Jacques Le Goff, Translator Arthur Goldhammer, The University of Chicago Press, 1981
Black Elk Speaks, by John G. Neihardt, University of Nebraska Press, 1932
Blessed Eucharist, The, by Fr. Michael Muller C.S.S.R., Tan Books, 1868
Book of Discipline, The, Translator I.B. Horner, Pali Text Society, 1938
Book of Analysis, The, Translator Pathamakyaw Ashin Thittila, Pali Text Society, 1969
Book of Enoch the Prophet, The, Translator Richard Laurence, Wizards Bookshelf, 1883
Book of the Hopi, by Frank Waters, Penguin Books, 1963
Buddhist Bible, A, Editor Dwight Goddard, Beacon Press, 1938
Call to Remembrance, by Baha'u'llah, Baha'i Publishing Trust, 1992
Candragomin's Twenty Verses on the Bodhisattva Vow, by Sakya Dragpa Gyaltsen, Library of Tibetan Works and Archives, 1982
Catechism of the Catholic Church, by The Holy See, Doubleday Image Books, 1994
Changeless Nature, The, by Arya Maitreya and Acarya Asanga, Translators Ken and Katia Holmes, Karma Drubgyud Darjay Ling, 1985
Chofetz Chaim Looks at: Eternity, The, by The Chofetz Chaim, Bais Yechiel Publications, 1989
Chuang Tsu, by Lao Tsu, Translators Gia-Fu Feng and Jane English, Random House, Vintage Books, 1974
City of God, by Saint Augustine, Translators Walsh, Zema, Monahan, Honan, Doubleday Image Books, 1950
Classic Midrah, The, Translator Reuven Hammer, Paulist Press, 1995
Collected Works of Saint John of the Cross, The, by Saint John of the Cross, Translators Kieran Kavanaugh and Otilio Rodriquez, ICS Publications, 1979
Complete Artscroll Siddur, The, Translator Rabbi Nosson Scherman, Mesorah Publications, Ltd., 1985
Complete Works of Josephus, The, by Flavius Josephus, Translator William Whiston A.M., Krege, 1960
Concise Book of Mitzvoth, The, Editor The Chafetz Chayim, The Feldheim Publishers, 1990

Confessions of Saint Augustine, The, by Saint Augustine, Translator Rex Warner, Penguin
    Books, Mentor, 1963
Contemplative Prayer, by Thomas Merton, Doubleday, 1969
Course in Miracles, The, by The Foundation for Inner Peace, Foundation for Inner Peace, 1975
Dead Sea Scriptures, The, Translator Theodore H. Gaster, Doubleday, Anchor Books, 1956
Denkoroku, The, by Keizan Zenji, Translator Rev. Hubert Nearman, Shasta Abbey Press, 1993
Desatir, The, Translator Mulla Firuz Bin Kaus, Wizards Bookshelf, 1888
Devotion for the Dying, by Mother Mary Potter, Tan Books, 1880
Dhammapada, Translator Harischandra Kaviratna, Theosophical University Press, 1980
Dialogue of Saint Catherine of Siena, Translator Algar Thorold, Tan Books, 1907
Dialogues of the Buddha, Translators T.W. and C.A.F. Rhys Davids and Scholars, Pali Text
    Society, 1921
Diamond Sutra and The Sutra of Hui-Neng, The, Translator A.F. Price and Wong Mou-lam,
    Shambhala Publications, Inc. 1990
Discourse on the Fruits of Recluseship, The, Translator Bhikku Bodhi, Buddhist Publication
    Society, 1989
Divine Crucible of Purgatory, The, by Mother Mary of Saint Austin, Helper of Holy Souls,
    Unknown Publisher and Date
Divine Love and Wisdom, by Emanuel Swedenborg, Translator George F. Dole, Swedenborg
    Foundation, 1985
Divine Mercy In My Soul, by Sister M. Faustina, Translators Drabik, Pearce, Maguire, Marina
    Helpers, 1987
Divine Providence, by Emanuel Swedenborg, Swedenborg Foundation, 1764
Divine Pymander of Hermes, The, by Hermes Mercurius Trismegistus, Translator Dr. Everard,
    Wizards Bookshelf, 1978
Divine Romance, The, by Paramahansa Yogananda, Self-Realization Fellowship, 1986
Doctrine of the Sufi's, The, by Al-Kalabadhi, AMS Press, 1935
Druids, The, by Peter Berresford Ellis, William B. Eerfdmans Publishing Co., 1994
Echoes in the Heavenly Court, Editor Dean of Machon, Feldheim Publishers, 1994
Edgar Cayce, Modern Prophet, by Carter, Hartzell, Reed, Langley, Gramercy Books, 1967
Egyptian Heaven and Hell, The, by E.A. Budge, Open Court, 1905
Emerald Tablets of the Thoth the Atlantean, The, by Thoth the Atlantean, Translator Doreal,
    Brotherhood of the White Temple, 1939
Encyclopedia of Native American Religions, The, by Hirschfelder, Arlene and Molin, Paulette,
    MJF Books, 1992
Epistle to the Son of Wolf, by Baha'u'llah, Baha'i Publishing Trust, 1941
Essence of Self-Realization, The, by Kriyananda (J. Donald Walters), Crystal Clarity Publishers,
    1990
Essene Book of Creation, The, by Edmond Bordeaux Szekely, International Biogenic Society,
    1989
Essene Communications with the Infinite, by Edmond Bordeaux Szekely, International Biogenic
    Society, 1979
Essene Gospel of Peace, The, Vol. 1-4, Translator Edmond Bordeaux Szekely, International
    Biogenic Society, 1981
Essential Rumi, The, by Rumi, Translator Coleman Barks, HarperSanFrancisco, 1995
Ethics of Spinoza, The, by Baruch Spinoza, Carol Publishing Group, 1957

Fathers of the Church, The, Vol. 2, 4, 11, 16, 60, by Saint Augustine, Catholic University of
America Press, 1947-1968

Five Books of Moses, The, Translator Everett Fox, Schocken, 1983

Flower Ornament Scripture, The, Translator Thomas Cleary, Shambhala Publications, 1984

Forgotten Secret of Fatima, The, by Msgr. Joseph A. Cirrincione and Thomas A. Nelson, Tan
Books, 1988

Forty Dreams of Saint John Bosco, by Saint John Bosco, Tan, 1969

Four Doctrines, The, by Emanuel Swedenborg, Swedenborg Foundation, 1763

Fox's Book of Martyrs, by John Fox, Whitaker House, 1981

Gates of Repentance, The, by Rabbeinu Yonah Ben Avaham of Gerona, Feldheim Publishers,
1967

General Principles of Kabbalah, Rabbi Moses C. Luzzatto, Translator Dr. Philip S. Berg,
Research Centre of Kabbalah, 1970

Glories of Mary, The, by Saint Alphonsus Liguori, Redemptorist Fathers, 1931

Gnosis on the Silk Road, Translator Hans-Joachim Klimkeit, HarperSanFransisco, 1993

Gospel of Sri Ramakrishna, The, by M., a disciple of the holy Master, Translator Swami
Nikhilananda, Ramakrishna-Vivekananda Center, 1942

Gospel of the Holy Twelve, The, Translator Rev. Gideon Jasper Richard Ousley, Teofil de la
Torre, N.D., O.D., 1954

Gospel of Thomas, The, Translator Marvin Meyer, HarperSanFransisco, 1992

Grace Abounding, by John Bunyan, Whitaker House, 1993

Great Means of Salvation and of Perfection, The, by Saint Alphonsus Liguori, Redemptorist
Fathers, 1927

Great Ocean-An Authorized Biography of the Dali Lama, by Roger Hicks and Ngakpa
Chogyam, Penguin Books, 1984

Group of Discourses, The, Translator K.R. Norman, Pali Text Society, 1992

Guide to the Bodhisattva's Way of Life, A, by Shantideva, Translator Steven Batchelor, Library
of Tibetan works and Archives, 1979

Guide to the Zoroastrian Religion, A, Translators Firoze M. Kotwal and James W. Boyd,
Scholars Press, 1982

Heaven and Hell, by Emanuel Swedenborg, Translator George G. Dole, Swedenborg Foundation,
1976

Hell and How to Avoid Hell, by Fr. F.X. Schouppe S.J. and Thomas A. Nelson, Tan Books, 1989

Hidden Words and Selected Holy Writings, The, by Baha'u'llah, Baha'i Publishing Trust, 1985

Hildegard of Bingen's Book of Divine Works, Editor Matthew Fox, Bear & Co., 1987

History of Witchcraft, The, by Fr. Montague Summers, Barnes & Noble, 1993

Holy Bible, The (King James Version), World Bible Publishers, 1989

Holy Qur'an, by Muhammed, Translator Maulana Muhammed Ali, Ahmadiyyah Anjuman
Isha'at Islam, 1917

Holy Teaching of Vimalakirti, The, Translator Robert A.F. Thurman, Pennsylvania State
University, 1976

Hymns of Hermes, The, by G.R.S. Mead, Phanes Press, 1991

Hymns of the RGVEDA, Translator Ralph T.H. Griffith, Motilal Banarsidass, Date Unknown

Ihya 'Ulim-Ud-Din, by Imam Gazzali, Translator Al-Haj Maulana Fazal-Ul-Karim, Kazi
Publications, Date Unknown

Imitation of Christ, The, by Thomas A. Kempis, Barbour & Co., 1984

Interior Castle, by Saint Teresa of Avila, Translator E. Allison Peers, Doubleday Dell, Image Books, 1961

Introduction to Saint Thomas Aquinas, Editor Anton C. Pegis, Random House, 1945

Itivuttaka, The, Translator John D. Ireland, Buddhist Publication Society, 1991

Jesus Christ 1 and 2, by Ferdinand Prat S.J., Translator John J. Heenan, S.J., Bruce Publishing Co., 1950

Kabbalah, by Gershom Scholem, Penguin Books, Meridian, 1974

Khutubat-I-Jumu'ah, Editor Maulana H. Ashraf Ali, Sh. Muhammad Ashraf, Date Unknown

KITAB-I-AQUDAS, The, by Baha'u'llah, Baha'i Publications, 1993

KITAB-I-IQAN, The, by Baha'u'llah, Baha'i Publishing Trust, 1931

KRSNA, Translator A.C. Bhaktivedanta Swami Prabhupada, Bhaktivedanta Book Trust, 1996

Kybalion, The, by Three Initiates, Yogi Publication Society, 1912

Large Sutra on Perfect Wisdom, The, Translator Edward Conze, University of California Press, 1975

Legends and Lore of the American Indians, Editor Terri Hardin, Barnes & Noble, 1993

Letters, Volume I, Padre Pio of Pietrelcina, Editor Melchiorre of Pobladura and Alessandro of Ripabottoni, Our Lady of Grace Capuchin Friary, San Giovanno Rotodondo, Italy, 1984

Life and Glories of Saint Joseph, by Edward Healy Thompson M.A., Tan Books, 1888

Life and Holiness, by Thomas Merton, Doubleday, 1962

Life and Teaching of the Masters of the Far East, by Baird T. Spalding, DeVorss &Co., 1948

Life of Jesus Christ and Biblical Revelations, The, by Ven. Anne Catherine Emmerich, Tan Books, 1914

Life of Muhammad, The, Editor A. Guillaume, Oxford University Press, 1995

Life of the Blessed Virgin Mary, The, by Ven. Anne Catherine Emmerich, Translator Sir Michael Palairet, Tan Books, 1954

Life of the Buddha, The, Translator Bhikku Nanamoli, Buddhist Publication Society, 1972

Little Flowers of Saint Francis, The, by Brother Ugolino di Monte Santa Maria, Translator Raphael Brown, Doubleday Image, 1958

Living Buddha, Living Christ, by Thich Naht Hahn, Parallax Press, 1995

Lost Books of the Bible/Forgotten Books of Eden, Translator World Bible Publishers/Alpha House, World Bible Publishers, 1926

Love of Christ, The, by Mother Teresa, Translator John A. Otto, Harper & Row, 1982

Maggid of Dubno and his Parables, The, by Benno Heinemann, Feldheim Publishers, 1967

Mahabharata, The, Editor C. Narasimhan, Columbia University Press, 1965

Man and God, by Voctor Gollancz, Houghton Mifflin, 1950

Man's Eternal Quest, by Paramahansa Yogananda, Self-Realization Fellowship, 1975

Mansions of the Soul, by H. Spencer Lewis, SupremeGrand Lodge of AMORC, 1930

Marital Love, by Emanuel Swedenborg, Swedenborg Foundation, 1768

Masters of the Path, by Dr. Javad Nurbakhsh, Khaniqanhi-Nimatullahi Publications, 1980

Meaning of Life, The, by Tenzin Gyasto H.H. the 14th Dalai Lama, Wisdom Publications, 1992

Mediaeval Legends of Christ, by A.S. Rapport Ph.D., Nicholson, Ivor, & Watson, 1934

Meditation Prayer on Mary Immaculate, by Padre Pio, Translator Laura Chanler White, Tan Books, 1974

Moments Divine Before the Blessed Sacrament, by Fr. Frederick A. Reuter K.C.B.S., Tan Books, 1922

Moon in a Dewdrop, Editor Kazuaki Tanahashi, North Point Press, 1985

My Utmost for His Highest, by Oswald Chambers, Barbour and Co., 1935

Mystical City of God, by Ven. Mary of Agreda, Translator Fiscar Marison, Blue Army of Our Lady of Fatima, 1949

Mystical City of God, The, Abridged, by Ven. Mary of Agreda, Tan Books, 1978

Mystical Life of Jesus, The, by H. Spencer Lewis, Supreme Grand Lodge of AMORC, 1929

Mystical Visions, by Hildegard Von Bingen, Bear & Co., 1986

Nag Hammadi Library, The, Translator Coptic Gnostic Library Project, Harper Collins, 1978

Nahjul Balagha, by Imam Ali Ibn Abu Talib, Translator Sayed Ali Reza, Tahrike Tarsile Qur'an, Unknown

Native Religions of North America, by Ake Hultkrantz, HarperSanFransisco, 1987

Navajo Religion, by Gladys A. Reichard, Princeton University Press, 1950

Nectar of Devotion, The, by A.C. Bhaktivedanta Swami Prabhupada, Bhaktivedanta Book Trust, 1970

Nectar of Instruction, The, Translator A.C. Bhaktivedanta Swami Prabhupada, Bhaktivedanta Book Trust, 1975

New American Bible, The, World Bible Publishers, 1970

New Jerusalem Bible, The, Doubleday, 1985

New Oxford Annotated Bible, The, Oxford University Press, 1946

On Christian Doctrine, by Saint Augustine, Translator D.W. Robertson Jr., Macmillan, 1958

On Evil, by Saint Thomas Aquinas, Translator Jean Oesterle, University of Notre Dame Press, 1995

On Free Choice of Will, by Saint Augustine, Translators Anna Benjamin and L.H. Hackstaff, Library of Liberal Arts, 1964

On the Kabbalah and its Symbolism, by Gershom Scholem, Translator Ralph Manheim, Shocken Books, 1965

Orations of Muhammad, The, by M. Muhammad Abaidul Akbar, Sh. Muhammad Ashraf, 1954

Our Lady of Fatima's Peace Plan From Heaven, Tan Books, 1950

Padre Pio: The True Story, by C. Bernard Ruffin, Our Sunday Visitor, 1982

Path of Discrimination, The, Translator Bhikku Nanamoli, Pali Text Society, 1991

Path of Purification, The, by Bhadantacariya Buddhagosa, Translator Bhikku Nanamoli, Buddhist Publication Society, 1975

Path of the Just, The, by Rabbi Moshe Chaim Luzzatto, Feldheim Publishers, 1966

Path of the Righteous Gentile, The, by Chaim Clorfene and Yakov Rogalsky, Feldheim Publishers, 1987

Path of Yoga, The, by A.C. Bhaktivedanta Swami Parbhupada, Bhaktivedanta Book Trust, 1971, 1979

Path to Deliverance, by Nyanatiloka Mahathera, Buddhist Publication Society, 1952

Path to Enlightenment, The, by Tenzin Gyatso, H.H. the 14th Dalai Lama, Snow Lion Publications, 1995

Philosophies and Religions of India, The, by Yogi Ramacharaka, Yogi Publication Society, 1930

Pilgrim's Progress, The, by John Bunyan, Barbor & Co., 1993

Pistis Sophia, Translator G.R.S. Mead, Kessinger Publishing Co., Date Unknown

Plotinus: The Enneads, by Plotinus, Translator Stephen MacKenna, Larson Publications, 1992

Prayers and Heavenly Promises, by Joan Carroll Cruz, Tan Books, 1990

Prayers and Meditations, by Baha'u'llah, Translator Shoghi Effendi, Baha'i Publishing Trust, 1938

Prayers of Saint Francis, The, Editor W. Bader, New City Press, 1988

196

Prayertimes with Mother Teresa, by Eileen and Kathleen Egan, Doubleday, 1989

Preparation for Death, by Saint Alphonsus Liguori, Translator Robert A. Coffin, Tan Books, 1857

Promulgation of Universal Peace, The, by Abdul-Baha, Baha'i Publishing Trust, 1982

Prophet, The, by Kahlil Gibran, Walker & Co., 1923

Purgatory, by Fr. F.X. Schouppe S.J., Tan Books, 1926

Pyramidology (Three Volumes), by Adam Rutherford, Institute of Pyramidology, 1957

Pythagorean Sourcebook and Library, The, Translators Guthrie, Taylor, Fairbanks, Phanes Press, 1987

Rama Story, The, by Bhagavan Sri Sathya Sai Baba, Translator N. Kasturi, Sri Sathya Sai Books and Publications, 1981

Red Record, The, Translator David McCutchen, Pavery Publishing Group, Inc., 1993

Reincarnation, An East-West Anthology, Editors Head and Cranston, Theosophical Publishing House, 1961

Revelations of Divine Love, by Juliana of Norwich, Translator M.L. del Mastro, Image Doubleday, 1977

Revelations of Saint Bridget, by Saint Bridget, Tan Books, 1965

Rosary Novenas to Our Lady, by Charles V. Lacey, Benziger, 1926

Sacred Pipe, The, by Joseph Epes Brown, Norman & London, University of Oklahoma Press, 1953

Saddharma-Pundarika or the Lotus of the True Law, Translator H. Kern, Dover Publications, 1963

Sahih Muslim (The Hadith, Volumes 1-4), by Imam Muslim, Translator Abdul Hamid Siddiqi, Nusrat Ali Nasri for Kitab Bhavan, Date Unknown

Samyutta Nikaya 1-3, Translator John D. Ireland, Buddhist Publication Society, 1981

Sayings of Paramahansa Yogananda, by Paramahansa Yogananda, Self- Realization Fellowship, 1952

Science of Being and Art of Living, The, by Mahrishi Manhesh Yogi, International SRM Publications, 1966

Secret Doctrine of the Rosicrucians, The, by Magus Incognito, Yoga Publication Society, 1949

Secret Doctrines of Jesus, The, by H. Spencer Lewis, AMORC, 1937

Secret of Divine Civilization, The, by Abdul-Baha, Baha'i Publishing Trust, 1957

Secret of the Rosary, The, by Saint Louis Mary De Montfort, Translator Mary Barbour, Montfort Publications, 1965

Secret Teachings of All Ages, The, by Manly P. Hall, Philosophical Research Society, 1977

Secrets of Mayan Science/Religion, by Hunbatz Men, Translators Diana Ayala and James II Dunlap, Bear & Co., 1990

Sefer haHinnuch, Ascribed to: Rabbi Aaron of Barcelona haLevi, Feldheim Publishers, 1523

Selections from the Writings of the BA'B, by The BA'B, Translator Habib Taherzadeh, Baha'i World Centre, 1976

Sepher Yezirah, Translator Dr. Isidor Kalish, L.H. Frank & Co., 1877

Sermon on the Mount According to Vedanta, The, by Swami Prabhavananda, New American Library, 1963

Seven Valleys and the Four Valleys, The, by Baha'u'llah, Baha'i Publishing Trust, 1945

Shobogenzo-Zuimonki, Translator Shohaku Okumura, Kyoto Soto-Zen Center, Date Unknown

Sign of Contradiction, by Karol Wojytla (Pope John Paul II), Seabury Press, 1979

Signs of the Unseen, by Rumi, Translator W.M. Thackston Jr., Threshold Books, 1994

Sinner's Guide, The. by Ven. Louis of Granada, O.P., Tan Books, 1883

Some Answered Questions, by Abdul-Baha', Baha'i Publishing Trust, 1930

Son of the Sun, by Savitri Devi, Supreme Grand Lodge of A.M.O.R.C., 1946

Songs of the Soul, by Paramahansa Yogananda, Self-Realization Fellowship, 1983

Soul Sanctified, The, Tan Books, 1873

Speaking in Tongues, by Felicitias D. Goodman, University of Chicago Press, 1972

Spiritual Combat, The, by Dom Lorenzo Scupoli, Translators William Lester and Robert Mohan, Tan Books, 1945

Spiritual Doctrine of Saint Catherine of Genoa, The, by Saint Catherine of Genoa, Tan Books, 1874

Spiritual Exercises of Saint Ignatius, The, by Saint Ignatius, Translator Anthony Mottola Ph.d, Image Books, 1964

Sri Guru Granth Sahib, (4 Volumes), Translator Gurbachan Singh Talib, Publication Bureau, Punjabi University, 1995

Srimad Bhagavatam (Volumes 1-3), Translator A.C. Bhaktivedanta Swami Prabhupada, Bhaktivedanta Book Trust, 1972

Srimad Bhagavatam (Part One), Translator A.C. Bhadtivedanta Swami Prabhupada, Bhaktivedanta Book Trust 1975

Srimad Bhagavatam (An Abridgement), Translator Swami Prabhavananda, Sri Ramakrishna Math, Date Unknown

Saint Antony of the Dessert, by Saint Athanasius, Translator Dom J.B. McLaughlin, Tan Books, 1924

Saint Athanasius On the Incarnation, by Saint Athanasuis, Translators Religious of C.S.M.V.A., Saint Vladimirs, 1944

Saint Francis of Assisi, by Saint Francis of Assisi, Thomas Nelson Publishers, 1989

Saint Michael and the Angels, Compiled from approved sources, Tan Books, 1977

Story of A Soul, by Saint Therese of Lisieux, Translator John Clark .C.D., ICS, 1975

Strive for Truth, Volumes 1-3, by Rabbi Eliyahu E. Dessler, Feldheim Publishers, 1978

Sutra of the Past Vows of Earth Store Bodhisattva, Translator Heng Ching, Buddhist Text Translation Society, 1974

Tablets of Baha'u'llah, by Baha'u'llah, Translator Habib Taherzadeh, Baha'i Publishing Trust, 1978

Tablets of the Divine Plan, by Abdul-Baha', Baha'i Publishing Trust, 1977

Taharas Halashon, Translator David Landesman, Feldheim Publishers, 1994

Talmud, The, Classics of Western Spirituality Series, Paulist Press, 1989

Talmudic Anthology, The, Editor Spitz Newman, Behrman House, Inc., 1945

Tao Te Ching, by Lao Tsu, Translators Gia-Fu Feng and Jane English, Random House, Vintage Books, 1972

Tao Te Ching, by Lao Tsu, Translator Victor H. Mair (from the Ma-Wang-Tui Manuscripts), Bantam, 1990

Teachings of Lord Caitanya, Translator A.C. Bhativedanta Swami Parabhupada, Bhakivedanta Book Trust, 1985

Teachings of Lord Kapila, Translator A.C. Bhativedanta Swami Parabhupada, Bhakivedanta Book Trust, 1977

Teachings of Queen Kunti, by A.C. Bhativedanta Swami Parabhupada, Bhativedanta Book Trust, 1978

Teachings of Sri Ramakrishna, by Advaita Ashrama, Swami Mumukshananda, 1994

Teachings of Sri Sarada Devi ,the Holy Mother, Editor Sri Ramakrishna Math, Sri Ramakrishna Math, Date Unknown

Teachings of Swami Vivekananda, Editor Advaita Ashrama, Advaita Ashrama, 1994

Theology of Saint Paul, The, by Fernand Prat S.J., The Newman Bookshop, 1926

Therese Neumann, by Adalbert Albert Vogl, Tan Books, 1987

Third Secret of Fatima, The, by Brother Michael of the Holy Trinity, Translator Anne Barbeau Gardiner, Tan Books, 1991

Thoughts and Sayings of Saint Margaret Mary, by Saint Margaret Mary, Tan Books, 1935

Three Pure Land Sutras, The, by Hisao Inagaki, by Nagata Bunshodo, 1994

Three Ways of the Spiritual Life, The, by Rev. R. Garrigou-Lagrange O.P., Tan Books, 1938

Threefold Lotus Sutra, The, Translators Kato, Tamura, Miyasaka, Kosei Publishing Co., 1971

Tibetan Book of the Dead, The, Editor W.Y. Evans-Wentz, Oxford University Press, 1960

Tibetan Book of the Great Liberation, The, Editor W.Y. Evans- Wentz, Oxford University Press, 1954

Torah, The, Translator Jewish Publication Society of America, Jewish Publication Society of America, 1962

Training the Mind in the Great Way, by Gyalwa Gendun Druppa (The First Dalai Lama), Translator Glenn H. Mullin, Snow Lion Publications, 1993

Travelers Narrative, A, by Abdul-Baha', Translator Edward G.Browne, Baha'i Publishing Trust, 1980

Treasury of Judaism, A, Editor Philip Birnbaum, Hebrew Publishing, 1957

Trinity, The, by Saint Augustine, Translator Edmund Hill O.P., New City Press, 1991

True Christian Religion, The, by Emanuel Swedenborg, Swedenborg Foundation, 1771

True Devotion to Mary, by Saint Louis De Montfort, Translator Fr. Federick Faber, Tan Books, 1941

Twleve Steps to Holiness and Salvation, The, by Saint Alphonsus Liguori, Translators Rev. Paul Leik and Rev. Cornelius Warren, Tan Books, 1986

Udana, The, Translator John D. Ireland, Buddhist Publication Society, 1990

Unknown Life of Jesus Christ, The, by Nicolas Notovitch, Translator Alexina Loranger, Tree of Life Publications, 1894

Upanishands, The, Translator Eknath Easwaran, Nilgiri Press, 1987

Urantia Book, The, by Urantia, Urantia Foundation, 1955

Vedanta-Sutras, by Vyasadeva, Translator George Thibaut, Motial Banarsidass Publishers, 1904

Voice of the Saints, The, Editor Francis Johnston, Tan Books, 1965

Walking in the Sacred Manner, by Mark St. Pierre and Tilda Long Soldier, Simon & Schuster, 1995

Way of Divine Love, The, by Sister Josefa Menendez, Tan Books, 1972

Way of Perfection, The, by Saint Teresa of Avila, Translator E. Allison Peers, Doubleday Dell, Image Books, 1964

Way of the Sufi, The, by Idries Shah, Arkana Penguin Books, 1968

Ways of Reason, The, by Rabbi Moshe Chaim Luzzatto, Feldheim Publishers, 1989

Wen-Tzu, by Lao-tzu, Translator Thomas Cleary, Shambhala Publications, 1991

Whispers From Eternity, Paramahansa Yogananda, Self-Realization Fellowship, 1949

Wisdom of the Elders, by David Suzuki and Peter Knudtson, Bantam Books, 1992

Wisdom of the Idiots, by Idries Shah, Octagon Press, 1969

Wonders of the Holy Name, The, by Fr. Paul O'Sullivan O.P. (E.D.M.), Tan Books, 1946

Word of the Buddha, The, Translator Nyanatiloka, Buddhist Publication Society, Date Unknown

Works of Philo, The, by Philo, Translator C.D. Yonge, Hendrickson, 1995

World Scripture, by the International Religious Foundation, International Religious Foundation, 1991

Zohar, The, Translators Harry Sperling and Maurice Simon, Sonicio Press Ltd., 1984

Printed in the United States
by Baker & Taylor Publisher Services

Printed in the United States
by Baker & Taylor Publisher Services